T0360974

Cross-Border Mergers and Acquisitions

Cross-border mergers and acquisitions (CBM&A) activity has become an important vehicle for firms' internationalization and corporate restructuring over the past three decades. Despite the huge volume of global CBM&A activity, however, there are few books that carefully explore the strategies, motives and consequences of global mergers and acquisitions.

This book discusses and synthesizes the theoretical literature on the motivation and performance of international merger activities. Focusing on the UK as a top acquiring country in the European Union, the authors examine the recent trends in cross-border mergers and acquisitions, motives for cross-border mergers and acquisitions, the mergers integration process, home and host countries' macroeconomic consequences on mergers and acquisitions and shareholders' wealth effects on CBM&A.

This book explores and sheds much-needed light on the UK CBM&A market, what drives it and what lessons can be learned for other regions around the globe.

Moshfique Uddin is Senior Teaching Fellow in Accounting and Finance at Leeds University Business School, UK. Before joining Leeds University Business School, he was Lecturer in accounting and finance at University of York and Leeds Metropolitan University, UK. He completed his PhD in the area of cross-border mergers and acquisitions, has published in the area of mergers and acquisitions and is currently doing research in the area of empirical finance.

Agyenim Boateng is a Professor of Finance & Banking at Glasgow Caledonian University, UK. He received his PhD in Economics Studies from the University of Leeds. His current research interests include mergers and acquisitions, excess reserves and bank risk taking in emerging markets. He has published in a number of international journals including *Journal of International Financial Markets, Institutions and Money, International Journal of Accounting, International Business Review, Management International Review* and the *Journal of International Financial Management and Accounting.*

Routledge Advances in Management and Business Studies

For a full list of titles in this series, please visit www.routledge.com

Cross-Border Mergers and Acquisitions

UK Dimensions

**Moshfique Uddin and
Agyenim Boateng**

Routledge
Taylor & Francis Group

NEW YORK AND LONDON

First published 2014
by Routledge
711 Third Avenue, New York, NY 10017

and by Routledge
2 Park Square, Milton Park, Abingdon, Oxon OX14 4RN

Routledge is an imprint of the Taylor & Francis Group, an informa business

© 2014 Taylor & Francis

The right of Moshfique Uddin and Agyenim Boateng to be identified as authors of this work has been asserted by them in accordance with sections 77 and 78 of the Copyright, Designs and Patents Act 1988.

Library of Congress Cataloging-in-Publication Data

Uddin, Moshfique.
Cross-border mergers and acquisitions : UK dimensions / by Moshfique
    Uddin and Agyenim Boateng.
        pages cm.— (Routledge advances in management and business
studies ; 59)
        Includes bibliographical references and index.
    1. Consolidation and merger of corporations—Great Britain.
2. International business enterprises—Finance.   I. Boateng, Agyenim.
II. Title.
    HD2746.55.G7U33 2014
    338.8′3—dc23
    2014002185

ISBN: 978-0-415-83660-9 (hbk)
ISBN: 978-0-203-45823-5 (ebk)

Typeset in Adobe Caslon Pro
by Apex CoVantage, LLC

To our parents and families

Contents

PART II
Trends, Patterns, Motives and Determinants of
UK Cross-Border Mergers and Acquisitions

PART III
Integration and Performance of Cross-Border Mergers
and Acquisitions

Tables

Figures

Abbreviations

AR	Abnormal Return
AIM	Alternative Investment Market
ANOVA	Analysis of Variance
APEC	Asia Pacific Economic Cooperation
BHAR	Buy and Hold Abnormal Return
CAPM	Capital Asset Pricing Model
CIS	Commonwealth of Independent States
CPI	Consumer Price Index
CBM&A	Cross-Border Mergers & Acquisitions
CAR	Cumulative Abnormal Return
DTI	Department of Trade and Industry
DMM	Domestic Market Model
EIU	Economist Intelligence Unit
EU	European Union
FTSE	Financial Times Stock Exchange
FDI	Foreign Direct Investment
GDP	Gross Domestic Product
IMM	International Market Model
IMF	International Monetary Fund
LSE	London Stock Exchange
M&A	Mergers & Acquisitions
MNC	Multinational Company
MNE	Multinational Enterprise
ONS	Office of National Statistics
OLS	Ordinary Least Squares
OECD	Organisation for Economic Co-operation and Development
OLI	Ownership, Location and Internalization
R&D	Research & Development
SEM	Single European Market
SIC	Standard Industry Classification
UK	United Kingdom
UNCTAD	United Nations Conference on Trade and Development
US	United States of America

Preface

Cross-border mergers and acquisitions (CBM&A) activity continues to excite interest among academics and practising managers and has become an important vehicle for firm's internationalization and corporate restructuring tool over the past three decades. Companies from different geographic origins are merging with each other or one company acquiring another for various financial and strategic reasons to enhance shareholders' wealth. UNCTAD (2010) has reported that in the year 2007, total value of completed cross-border deals reached a staggering US$1,000 billion. However, it is surprising that despite the large volume of global CBM&A activities, few available books carefully explore the trends and patterns, motives that inspire CBM&A and consequences of the huge investments in global mergers and acquisitions activities. Using the UK as a top acquiring country in the European Union, we explore the recent trends in CBM&A, review and synthesize the literature on CBM&A over the past 30 years and examine motives for CBM&A, home and host countries' macroeconomic consequences on mergers and acquisitions, shareholder's wealth effects on M&As.

THE SPECIFIC THEMES OF THE BOOK

This volume considers three main themes.

1. Overview and Literature Review

Under this section, we provide an overview of the CBM&A and review the various competing theories in respect of the literature explaining motivation and performance of international merger activities. We go on to identify, examine and synthesize the firm level factors that underpin the managers' decisions to undertake CBM&A activities. This theme is covered in Chapters 1 through 3.

2. Trends, Patterns and Determinants of CBM&A

In Chapters 4 through 6 we present a number of new empirical contributions in regard to the trends, patterns, macroeconomic determinants of CBM&A and firm-level motivation for CBM&A. Chapter 4 traces the wave behaviour, recent trends, patterns and distribution of CBM&A in the UK. Using the data from both the Office of National Statistics and the United Nations Conference for Trade and Development (UNCTAD), this chapter provides a succinct analysis of trends and patterns of the CBM&A in the UK including, geographical and sectoral distribution of CBM&A from 1987 to 2010. An empirical work on macroeconomic influences in the UK CBM&A is presented in Chapter 5. The thrust of Chapter 6 is what motivates UK firms to make CBM&A. Specifically, this chapter aims to discern firm-specific motives commonly cited by acquisition managers at the time of acquisition decision. The chapter develops hypotheses and uses primary data from acquisition managers of selected bidding firms to rank the relative importance of motives and a parsimonious set of motives for the sample studied by means of factor analysis for CBM&A.

3. Integration and Performance of CBM&A

The third theme of this volume deals with the mergers and acquisitions integration process (a piece of work funded by CIMA and with contribution from Dr Roberta Bampton) and the performance of CBM&A from the financial standpoint.

Using multiple case studies, Chapter 7 examines the post-acquisition integration process. In Chapter 8, short-run performance of the UK CBM&A is investigated. Using accounting and stock market data, Chapter 9 examines whether the UK acquirers create value in the long run.

One of the interesting features of this book is that it has been written in the context of the UK which is significant in that the UK is outside the European Single Currency Zone and yet has been the top acquiring and target nation in the world. We believe that this monograph offers a rich piece of scholarly studies which touch on the patterns and trends, determinants, integration process and performance of CBM&A.

The book will be useful for academics/researchers, practising managers, postgraduate level students in corporate finance, strategic management, marketing and international business and libraries

AUTHORS' ACKNOWLEDGEMENTS

At Routledge/Taylor and Francis, we want to thank Laura D.H. Stearns for her encouragement. Lauren M. Verity and Mae Lum provided consistent support and understanding when we missed our deadlines. We wish to acknowledge the helpful comments of the reviewers—Professors Keith Glaister and Isaac Otchere— on the initial proposal. We also want express our sincere thanks to Dr. Roberta Bampton who carried out the interviews for empirical analysis in Chapter 7. We gratefully acknowledge the support of Chartered Institute of Management

Accountants for the funding support of the initial investigation of the role of management accountants in M&A integration study which has been further extended in Chapter 7.

Dr. Moshfique Uddin
Senior Teaching Fellow in Accounting and Finance
Leeds University Business School
University of Leeds

Professor Agyenim Boateng
Professor of Finance and Banking
Glasgow School of Business and Society
Glasgow Caledonian University, Glasgow, UK

Part I

Overview and Review of Literature of Cross-Border Mergers and Acquisitions

1 An Overview of Cross-Border Mergers and Acquisitions

1.1 BACKGROUND

Almost everywhere in the world the story of economic development involves FDI, from the Persian Gulf's oil fields to Ghana's gold mining fields, Malaysian's rubber plantations and Spain's telecommunications (Boateng, 2001). One dominant way by which a firm engages in business outside its national borders is through cross-border mergers and acquisitions (CBM&A). The United Nations Conference on Trade and Development (UNCTAD, 2000) reported that CBM&A account for the majority of FDI outflows. A number of reasons have been given to explain the rising proportion of CBM&A of FDI. First, CBM&A activities are seen as the most rapid and radical means of expanding and changing the economic organization of the firm, leading to swift changes in shareholder wealth (Morck et al., 1990). Parvinen and Tikkanen (2007) argue that M&A process is one of the most extensive initiatives aimed at the economic and organizational transformation of the firm. Second, UNCTAD (2000) attributes the reasons behind the surge in CBM&A in recent times to the economic reforms and liberalization around the world during the past two decades. Moreover, the creation of the regional economic and political union such as European Union (EU) has also led to a huge surge in the CBM&A activities (see Danbolt, 1995; Gugler et al., 2003).

Traditionally, the fundamental motives behind mergers and acquisitions (M&A) revolve around financial and strategic considerations. These encompass economies of scale and scope and synergy (Eun et al., 1996), quicker access to international markets (UNCTAD, 2000), risk diversification and accessing valuable intangible assets (Morck and Yeung, 1992). Synergy, diversification, undervaluation, tax arbitrage and strategic acquisition theories lend support to the justification of corporate M&A. Nevertheless, a number of empirical studies have challenged these justifications by suggesting that CBM&A are not always a value enhancing activity of the corporate concern, rather in many cases they actually destroy shareholders' value. The debate regarding CBM&A also comes from purely economic and political grounds. For example, it has been argued that cross-border acquisitions do not increase the productive capacity within an economy rather CBM&A transfers the ownership and control of the firm to the foreign owners (UNCTAD, 2000). This transfer may lead to a reduction in employment and foreign exchange loss. Moreover, foreign oligopolistic acquirers may create an imbalance in the local market by enhancing their control thereby reducing the competition. At the extreme end, large multinational acquirers may even pose a threat to the national interest and security by exerting pressure on the host government. However, facts and figures of worldwide CBM&A flows clearly show that neither the negative empirical evidence on performance of CBM&A nor the economic and political fears deter their growth.

1.2   DEFINITIONS AND TYPES OF MERGERS AND ACQUISITIONS

Mergers and acquisitions occur when two separate firms come together in which only one company ceases to exist. Following the merger and acquisition, the acquired company is subject to managerial, economic and legal control of the acquiring company. In a takeover or an acquisition, one company takes over the control of assets and liabilities of another company. Acquisitions may range from partial to complete acquisitions. With complete acquisition (100% control), the acquired firm ceases to exist. In terms of merger, two companies combine, but few companies really merged. UNCTAD (2000) suggests that mergers and acquisitions basically mean acquisitions.

Mergers and acquisitions are classified into three types:

- Horizontal M&A occurs when two companies in the same industry come together to combine.
- Vertical M&A occurs between two companies in different stages of production; for example manufacturing and marketing combine.
- Conglomerate M&A involves two unrelated businesses.

CBM&A is defined as the purchase of the trade name and assets of one company (an acquiree) by another company (an acquirer), headquartered outside the country where the acquired company is located as the combination of two companies of different nationalities. In a cross-border acquisition, the control of assets and operations are transferred from a local to a foreign company, with the former becoming an affiliate of the later (UNCTAD, 2000).

1.3   MOTIVATION FOR THE BOOK

CBM&A activity has become an important vehicle for firm's internationalization and corporate restructuring over the past three decades. Companies from different geographic origins are merging with each other as never before. UNCTAD (2010) reported that in the year 2007, total value of completed cross-border deals reached a staggering US$1,000 billion. Gregory and McCorriston (2005) pointed out that CBM&A constitute the main form of FDI in the UK. For example, in 1999, the outward CBM&A account for 76% of total UK FDI (UNCTAD, 2000). Between 1991 and 2005, the UK was the largest acquiring nation in the world. In terms of inward CBM&A activities, the UK has been the second-largest destination in the world during the same period and the top acquiring and target nation in Europe since 1991. The spectacular growth of the UK CBM&A activities needs special attention from the researchers in order to understand the underlying causes and consequences of this huge flow of international acquisition activities. Although the volume of CBM&A literature are considerable, the findings are diverse, encompassing finance, corporate strategy and international business, and, more important, lacks sufficient integration. The theoretical explanation, development and the empirical findings of CBM&A activities from the UK remain fragmented. In this book, we provide the timely synthesis and consolidation of extant literature and examine the consequences of the UK CBM&A.

1.4 OUTLINE OF THE BOOK

The aims and objectives of this study set out in this chapter are addressed through separate but interrelated analyses.

In Chapter 2 we review and synthesize the theoretical and empirical literature relating to the motivation behind CBM&A.

Chapter 3 reviews the literature focusing on the question: Do CBM&A add or destroy value for acquirer and target firms? This chapter reviews and provides a synthesis of the relevant literature of CBM&A performance over the last 30 years.

In Chapter 4 we trace the wave behaviour, recent trends, patterns and distribution of CBM&A in the UK. Using the data from both the Office of National Statistics and UNCTAD, this chapter provides a succinct analysis of trends and patterns of the CBM&A in the UK including geographical and sectoral distribution of CBM&A from 1987 to 2010.

Chapter 5 uses a number of theoretical frameworks including eclectic paradigm of John Dunning, an empirical work on macroeconomic influences in the UK CBM&A is presented. Prior literature has extensively covered the ownership and location advantages accruing to US multinationals thanks to their geopolitical clout and the relative strength of the US dollar. More recently, we have seen the single currency in Europe, and this chapter analyzes the influences of the UK outside the European single-currency zone on CBM&A activities.

The primary question of Chapter 6 is: What motivates the UK firms to make CBM&A? Specifically, this chapter's aim is to discern firm-specific motives commonly cited by acquisition managers at the time of the acquisition decision. The chapter develops hypotheses and uses primary data from acquisition managers of selected bidding firms to rank the relative importance of motives and a parsimonious set of motives for the sample studied by means of factor analysis for CBM&A.

Chapter 7, "Managing the Post-Acquisition Integration Process: An Examination of Accounting Task Integration," uses interviews with senior managers to examine the post-acquisition integration process. The issues examined include human integration and task integration, and how the sub-processes of human and task integration interact to foster value creation is discussed

Chapter 8 uses share-price data to investigate the short-run performance of CBM&A.

Chapter 9, "A Study of the Changes in Operating Performance of the UK Cross-Border Mergers and Acquisitions," uses accounting and stock market data to examine whether the UK acquirers create value in the long run.

In the final chapter (Chapter 10) we provide a useful summary of the empirical research findings and their implications for policy and further extensions in the future.

1.5 SUMMARY

This chapter has established the context of the study, has set out the aims and scope of the book and has described the importance of the study and the basic structure of the book. It is evident from the preceding discussion that the focus of the book is about examining the trends, the motivations and the determinants of UK CBM&A and to evaluate their short- and long-run performance.

REFERENCES

Boateng, A. (2001). *Dimensions of International Joint Ventures in Ghana and Nigeria*, Unpublished PhD Dissertation, University of Leeds, UK.

Danbolt, J. (1995). An Analysis of Gains and Losses to Shareholders of Foreign Bidding Companies Engaged in Cross-Border Acquisitions into the United Kingdom: 1986–1991, *European Journal of Finance*, Vol. 1(3), pp. 279–309.

Eun, C.S., Kolodny, R. and Scheraga, C. (1996). Cross-Border Acquisitions and Shareholder Wealth: Tests of the Synergy and Internalization Hypotheses, *Journal of Banking and Finance*, Vol. 20, pp. 1559–1582.

Gregory, A. and McCorriston, S. (2005). Foreign Acquisitions by UK Limited Companies: Short- and Long-Run Performance, *Journal of Empirical Finance*, Vol. 12(1), pp. 99–125.

Gugler, K., Mueller, D.C., Yurtoglu, B.B. and Zulehner, C. (2003). The effects of merger: An international comparison, *International Journal of Industrial Organization*, Vol. 21(5), pp. 625–653.

Morck, R., Shleifer, A. and Vishny, R. (1990). Do managerial objectives drive bad acquisitions? *Journal of Finance*, 45, pp. 31–48.

Morck, R. and Yeung, B. (1992). Internalization: An Event Study Test, *Journal of International Economics*, Vol. 33(1/2), pp. 41–56.

Parvinen, P. and Tikkanen, H. (2007). Incentive Asymmetries in the Mergers and Acquisitions Process, *Journal of Management Studies*, 44(5), pp. 759–787.

United Nations Conference on Trade and Development (UNCTAD) (2000). *World Investment Report 2000: Cross-Border Mergers and Acquisitions and Development*, New York: United Nations.

United Nations Conference on Trade and Development (UNCTAD) (2010). *World Investment Report 2010: Investing in Low Carbon Economy*, New York: United Nations.

2 Theoretical and Empirical Literature
Cross-Border Mergers and Acquisitions

2.1 INTRODUCTION

M&A activity is a popular corporate development, yet complex and has attracted significant interest from both the popular press and academic literature over the past three decades. The complex phenomenon which acquisitions represents has generated the research interests from a broad range of management disciplines, including finance, corporate strategy and economics (Cartwright and Schoenberg, 2006). As a result, over the course of time, M&A research has been approached from a myriad of theoretical perspectives. The purpose of this chapter is to review the distinct strand of thoughts in respect of why CBM&A take place. Drawing heavily on FDI and finance literature, the chapter proceeds as follows: The next section traces the theoretical development of CBM&A. This encompasses the industrial organization theory, the eclectic paradigm, the resource-based view and the internalization theory. We then focus our attention specifically on the literature which has been used to explain the reasons behind CBM&A, mostly in finance literature, over the past three decades. The final section summarizes this chapter.

2.2 THEORETICAL DEVELOPMENT OF CBM&A

The theoretical literature in respect of CBM&A are largely derived from the theories of FDI as CBM&A is one important entry mode of FDI by multinational corporations (Chen and Findlay, 2003). The United Nations Conference on Trade and Development (UNCTAD, 2000, 2012) reports that over the past three decades, most of the world FDI has been carried out via CBM&A. Although the theories discussed in the following sections have been used predominantly to explain why FDI takes place, researchers in the international market for corporate control have found them to be equally applicable to CBM&A (see Sudarsanam, 2003; Kiymaz, 2004). This is because an announcement of CBM&A represents two distinct decisions. One is the selection of entry mode, and the other one is the foreign expansion of the local firm. Studies therefore discuss the motives behind CBM&A as an entry-mode choice of FDI. Consequently, several theoretical frameworks used to explain the FDI can be borrowed to explain the CBM&A transactions. These encompass the industrial organization theory, the internalization theory, the resource-based theory and the eclectic paradigm.

2.2.1   The Industrial Organization Theory

The industrial organization hypothesis introduced by Hymer (1976) and supported by Kindleberger (1969), Caves (1971, 1982) and Dunning (1988) focuses on a firm's behaviour vis-à-vis its competitors. Drawing heavily on the work of Bain (1956), Hymer (1976) challenged the assumption of the model of perfect competition and concentrated on a firm's ability to deter competition in a market. His views then formed the basis of Kindleberger's (1969) 'market imperfections model', which posits that for direct investment to flourish, firms must fulfil two conditions; namely (1) the MNE must possess monopolistic advantages or firm specific advantages that outweigh the disadvantages of being a foreign firm, and (2) the market for these advantages must be imperfect. Some of these market imperfections that always lead to the development of MNEs include knowledge advantages (such as patent-protected technology, managerial skills), distribution networks, economies of scale and product differentiation. Industrial organization theory is seen as one of the strategic theories of merger waves and as accounting for the mechanism through which one merger is related to the other. For example, the industrial organization literature has focused (almost exclusively) on strategic interaction through the product market (Toxvaerd, 2008). Using the industrial organization theory to explain CBM&A as an entry mode of FDI, Datta et al. (2003) contend that the existence of the firm specific assets leads the local firms to pursue high-control entry modes such as greenfield investments or CBM&A.

2.2.2   The Eclectic Paradigm

The most popular theory of FDI by far is the eclectic paradigm (also known as OLI), developed by Dunning (1977, 1988, 2003). The eclectic paradigm is an attempt to consolidate a number of ideas into an integrated approach of explaining international production engaged in by transnational corporations (Dunning, 1977, 2000). The eclectic paradigm posits that, at any given moment, international production will be determined by the configuration of OLI. Ownership refers to the firm-level specific factors which enable firms to gain competitive ownership advantages which other firms do not have, such as trademark, production technique and entrepreneurial skills, to engage in FDI. Such advantages may result from the firm's privileged ownership of a set of profitable resources and capabilities and the firm's capability to coordinate and organize these strategic assets in the foreign markets. These strategic assets include intangible assets such as technological know-how, managerial skills, famous brand name and firm-level-specific factors such as access to raw materials, management, capital, economies of scale and political power. According to Dunning (1977, 1988), having the ownership of strategic assets is significant but not sufficient for making FDI decisions.

Location is another leg of the OLI paradigm tripod for explaining the extent and the pattern of global production. Location refers to advantages that the firms may enjoy if they locate the value creating transactions across their national boundaries rather than conduct domestic transaction when they have ownership advantages. The location theory posits that locational advantages in a host country are significant determinants of the choice of outward investment (Horst, 1972). As pointed out by a number of researchers, location based advantages include various factors such as natural resources, attractive government policies, tariff and non-tariff barriers, infrastructure and labour force, income and growth, demand for the product, capital and financial services, availability of cheap raw materials, wage differential and labour productivity (see Dunning, 1988; Billington, 1999).

The third variable (internalization) is the organizational forms by which firms combine their ownership advantages with location advantages to maintain and improve their competitive positions. Internalization advantages determine whether foreign production will be organized through markets (licensing) or hierarchies (FDI). Internalization posits that firms can extract abnormal returns from outward investments by internalizing market imperfections of the host country when their firm-specific resources and capabilities cannot find comparable value elsewhere (Caves, 1971; Williamson, 1975; Buckley and Casson, 1976; Morck and Yeung, 1991). Overall, the eclectic paradigm indicates that the firm which has the intangible assets (who), with the ability to internalize those assets (why) should go for foreign investment if the firm can materialize some benefits specific to a particular location abroad (where). Dunning (1993, p. 76), however, stresses that the eclectic paradigm is not a theory of MNE or FDI per se, but rather an organizational framework for examining the activities of enterprises engaging in cross-border activities.

Prior studies such as those conducted by Kish and Vasconcellos (1993), Vasconcellos and Kish (1998), McCann (2001), Kiymaz (2009) and Uddin and Boateng (2011) have used the OLI theory to explain CBM&A inflows and outflows. Authors such as Datta et al. (2003), Chen and Findlay (2003) and Sudarsanam (2003) stated that the eclectic paradigm also provides a better explanation of the selection of entry mode. Sudarsanam (2003) argues that if the firm has ownership advantages and internalization advantages and if the host country has location advantages, then the firm should go for foreign production by acquisition investments. For example, Brouthers and Brouthers (2000) and Hennart and Reddy (1997) state that high market growth as well as low market growth in the host economy make acquisitions a desirable way to enter into the foreign market compared to greenfield investments.

2.2.3 The Resource-Based View

The resource-based view posits that the possession of critical resources by a company enables it to gain a competitive advantage (Bain, 1968; Wernerfelt, 1984). Amit and Schoemaker (1993, p. 36) refer to strategic assets as the set of difficult to trade and imitate, scare appropriable and specialized resources and capabilities that underpin the firm's competitive advantages. Amit and Schoemaker interpret the resources deeper, dividing the resources into two categories: resources and capabilities. From the point of view of Amit and Schoemaker, resources are merchantable and not firm specific whereas capabilities are firm specific. Heeley et al. (2006) point out that resources and capabilities are the principal sources of a firm's profitability and are the underlying foundation of a firm's competitive advantage. With respect to the resource-based view, knowledge, especially tacit knowledge, is the most significant strategic assets (Kogut and Zander, 1992). Although a firm's knowledge base can be developed by a number of knowledge-increasing investments over time, acquiring the external knowledge base is an important way for enterprises to grow knowledge.

With the increasing significance of knowledge for the existence of multinationals, the access to strategic assets has been considered as one of the main motives behind outward investment and CBM&A in particular (Deng, 2004; Luo and Tung, 2007; Nadolska and Barkema, 2007; Boateng et al., 2008). Heeley et al. (2006) suggest that the main work a firm needs to do is to employ strategies such as M&A to obtain, manage and deploy the resources and capabilities which allow the firm to obtain positive economic benefits. A number of studies have examined the motivation for CBM&A from the resource-based perspective (Hennart, 1991; Eisenhardt and Schoonhoven, 1996; Madhok, 1997; Deng, 2004; Heeley et al., 2006; Luo and Tung, 2007; Boateng et al., 2008) and organizational learning perspective (Barkema and Vermeulen, 1998; Vermeulen and Barkema, 2001). These studies suggest that CBM&A are motivated by the opportunity to acquire new capabilities and to learn new knowledge. Thus, as Ohmae (1989, p. 145) argues, "today's products rely on so many different critical technologies that most companies can no longer maintain cutting edge sophistication in all of them". Therefore, tapping external sources of know-how becomes an imperative. Acquisition of existing foreign business allows the acquirer to obtain resources such as patent protected technology, superior managerial and marketing skills, and overcome special government regulation that create a barrier to entry for other firms (Errunza and Senbet, 1981). Shimizu et al. (2004) endorse this view by suggesting that firms may engage in M&A in order to exploit intangible assets. This line of reasoning is consistent with the resource-based view which suggests that firms can generate economic rents by implementing strategies such as M&A to exploit rare, costly to imitate and non-substitutable resources (Caves, 1990; Barney, 1991; Amit and Schoemaker, 1993).

2.2.4   The Internalization Theory

The internalization theory is mainly based on the idea of transaction cost first developed by Coase (1937). This idea was later extended and put the forefront of international business research by Buckley and Casson (1976), Caves (1982), Rugman (1982), Hennart (1982) and Teece (1983). The theory suggests that firms will engage in FDI because they want to replace the costly market transaction by internal cost-saving transactions. In other words, firms expand across the borders because the transaction costs incurred in international intermediate product markets can be reduced by internalizing these markets within the firm (McManus, 1972; Buckley and Casson, 1976; Hennart, 1982). If a firm has a subsidiary in the foreign location, then it can transfer knowledge, information and other necessary products for production without being dependent on the market. This will increase the independence of the firm and be helpful in reducing the cost of market dependence. Based on the internalization theory, it has been argued that the firms will select the mode of entry of FDI that will minimize total transaction and production costs (Williamson, 1975; Hennart, 1991). As such, assets with higher transaction cost and higher uncertainty would be internalized through high-control entry modes with a view towards reducing the transaction cost (Klein et al., 1990). Madhok (1997) further contends that firms with unique skills should try to internalize transactions with high-control entry strategies to avoid the greater risk of losing its specific knowledge to the competitors.

Internalization theory has been used to explain why CBM&A occur. Shimizu et al. (2004) suggest that CBM&A may also be initiated to internalize an acquirer's intangible assets to reduce or avoid transaction costs. This view is consistent with the internalization theory which suggests that firms with intangible assets should invest abroad in order to avoid the costly market mechanism of transferring those assets (Buckley and Casson, 1976). In short, CBM&A may be motivated by the internalization of the acquirer's various intangible assets. Conversely, the acquirer can also use the target's intangible assets by the way of reverse internalization. Internalization and reverse internalization can help acquirers to avoid any misappropriation of intangible assets and reduce transaction costs. The studies of Seth et al. (2000, 2002), Cheng and Chan (1995), Eun et al. (1996), Morck and Yeung (1992) and Markides and Ittner (1994) have rendered support for internalization and reverse internalization as motives for CBM&A.

2.3 MOTIVES FOR CBM&A

M&A involve the purchase and sale of assets worth billions of dollars, and as a result, the economic importance of M&A is hard to ignore. Accordingly, a vast theoretical and empirical body of literature has sought to uncover the motives behind the mergers. Chen and Su (1997) have identified several hypotheses to explain why CBM&A take place. These are the technology transfer hypothesis, the undervalued target hypothesis, the co-insurance hypothesis, the enhanced liquidity hypothesis, the size hypothesis, the redeployment of corporate capital hypothesis, the inefficient management hypothesis and the tax advantage hypothesis. Harris and Ravenscraft (1991) have also put forward several explanations of CBM&A, such as an argument based on imperfections and costs in product and factor market, an argument based on biases in government and regulatory policies and an argument based on imperfections and asymmetries in capital markets. Gonzalez et al. (1998) used the undervaluation hypothesis of domestic mergers and acquisition to explain the CBM&A. Moreover, Seth et al. (2000) suggested that the synergy, hubris or managerialism hypotheses may better explain the CBM&A. In addition to these, Danbolt (2004) promoted the concept of international risk diversification, market access, exchange rate effects and managerial factors as determinants of CBM&A. After careful review of the available literature on the conceptual explanations of CBM&A, several hypotheses have been identified that can better explain the causes and development of CBM&A. These hypotheses have their roots in the FDI and M&A theories and, in some cases, by nature, overlap. For a better understanding of these hypotheses, a brief discussion is provided in the following sub-sections.

2.3.1　Synergy

M&A are primarily undertaken to benefit from the synergy in combining the physical operations of the two merging firms (Bradley et al., 1988). In other words, acquisitions take place when the value of the combined firm is greater than the sum of the value of individual firms (Seth et al., 2000). The sources of synergy in domestic mergers and acquisitions include operational synergy such as economies of scale and scope (Copeland et al., 2005) and managerial synergy (Trautwein, 1990; Sudarsanam et al., 1996). However, the presence of different types and degrees of frictions across international markets compared with the domestic market implies that different sources of synergy underlie cross-border acquisitions relative to domestic acquisitions (Seth et al., 2000, 2002). Seth et al. (2000, 2002) contend that internalization and reverse internalization are two dominant sources of synergy from the CBM&A. Based on the monopolistic advantage theory and the internalization theory of FDI, Seth et al. (2000, 2002), Cheng and Chan (1995) and Eun et al. (1996) argue that if a firm has firm-specific assets with public goods property that are difficult to share because of the danger of misappropriation, then the firm should penetrate the foreign market by acquiring an existing asset. Thus, acquisition in the international market helps the firm to avoid the danger of misappropriation of valuable intangible assets and thereby promotes the possibility of generating monopoly profit which may constitute part of the synergistic gain from international acquisitions. Reverse internalization also provides a source of synergy by allowing the bidding firm to acquire skills from the target firm. The concept of internalization and reverse internalization are almost same except viewed from opposite direction. In case of internalization, the bidding firm acquires the target to exploit its valuable intangible assets in the international market without losing control of the asset or letting others to manoeuvre the benefits, but in case of reverse internalization, the bidding firm acquires skills or valuable intangible assets from the target firm (Seth et al., 2002). The possibility of internalization and reverse internalization through cross-border acquisitions has been supported by a number of authors, such as Magee (1977) and Caves (1982). Moreover, Harris and Ravenscraft (1991), Morck and Yeung (1992), Marr et al. (1993), Markides and Ittner (1994), Eun et al. (1996), Vasconcellos and Kish (1996) and Chen and Su (1997) extended their support for the internalization and reverse internalization as possible causes of international mergers and acquisitions. Recently, Ghauri and Buckley (2003), Chen and Findlay (2003) and Goergen and Renneboog (2004) also pointed out the role of internalization and reverse internalization in explaining CBM&A. International mergers and acquisitions can also create synergy by ensuring economies of scale and scope for the merging companies. Doukas and Travlos (1988) recognize the fact that international acquisitions provide firms with opportunities to capitalize production economies on a global scale that may occur in both the marketing and manufacturing spheres. Kish and Vasconcellos (1993), Datta and Puia (1995), Ghauri and Buckley (2003), Chen and Findlay (2003) and Goergen and Renneboog (2004) also accept the role of international M&A in capturing the benefits of economies of scale and scope for the participating firms. CBM&A can create synergy by providing a firm with the quickest way of entering the foreign market. The faster market-access rationale of CBM&A has been supported by Marr et al. (1993), UNCTAD (2000), Seth et al. (2000) and Chen and Findlay (2003). Marr et al. (1993) stated that takeovers are generally quick and can affect a foreign firm's revenue and market share immediately. Seth et al. (2000) state that acquiring an existing foreign facility provides a means for the rapid exploitation of the potential synergistic gains compared with de novo entry. In a similar way, Chen and Findlay (2003) contend that by acquiring an existing company, the acquiring firm can immediately have access to a local network of suppliers and customers. The quick entry to the foreign market through acquisition can become a potential source of synergy because it is a strategic move for beating the rivals in taking over a commanding position in the foreign market or in limiting the rivals' activities in the foreign markets or in increasing the market share of the firm. Another potential source of synergy in international M&A is its disciplinary role in the international market for corporate control. Seth et al. (2000, 2002) stated that a possible source of gain in foreign acquisitions arises if agency costs vary systematically across countries and foreign acquirers have specialized expertise, relative to domestic acquirers, in reducing agency costs in domestic targets. Generally, takeovers motivated by disciplinary reasons aim to eliminate the inefficient management in the target firms and to replace them with an efficient set of management from the acquiring firm. In the case of CBM&A, because the management skills are intangible assets, the disciplinary motive is consistent with the synergistic motive if the foreign bidder possesses superior management skills and uses that to an inefficient international target (Marr et al., 1993). The disciplinary role of CBM&A has also been supported by Kish and Vasconcellos (1993), Corhay and Rad (2000), Rossi and Volpin (2004) and Goergen and Renneboog (2004). The discussion of synergy of CBM&A makes clearer the point that multiple sources of synergies are available in international M&A and that these potential sources of synergy leads a firm to make an international acquisition rather than keeping itself within the national boundary.

2.3.2 Diversification

Diversification—a well-documented strategy for expansion of firms—has been suggested as one of the dominant reasons for CBM&A (Seth, 1990; Trautwein, 1990; Shleifer and Vishny, 1992; Markides and Ittner, 1994; Denis et al., 2002).

It is argued that international acquisitions do not only provide access to important resources but also allow firms an opportunity to reduce the costs and risks of entering into new foreign markets (Porter and Fuller, 1986; Boateng and Glaister, 2003). Seth (1990) reported that the desire to reduce both operational and financial risks through geographical market diversification is a source of value to cross-border acquisitions but not domestic acquisitions. For example, the sources of value such as those associated with exchange rate differences, market power conferred by international scope and the ability to arbitrage tax regimes are unique to international mergers (Manzon et al., 1994; Morck and Yeung, 1992; Seth et al., 2000, 2002). Moreover, because economic activities in different countries are less than perfectly correlated, portfolio diversification across boundaries should reduce earnings volatility and improve investors' risk–return opportunities. Simply put, corporate diversification through mergers and acquisitions helps the participating firms to get the benefit of co-insurance (Lewellen, 1971; Kim and McConnell, 1977; Asquith and Kim, 1982), the reduction of risk (Hughes et al., 1980; Reed and Luffman, 1986), the reduction of the firm's default risk and increasing the debt capacity (Halpern, 1983; Shleifer and Vishny, 1992) and creation of an internal capital market (Stulz, 1990). A number of studies, including Errunza (1977), Lessard (1973), Logue (1982) and Davis (1991), have rendered support for the risk-reduction argument through portfolio diversification. It therefore follows that firms may engage in CBM&A primarily to reduce risk through diversification.

However, the effectiveness of corporate diversification has been criticized on the grounds that in a perfect capital market, investors can get the diversification benefit by personally holding a well-diversified portfolio with lower costs (Kiymaz and Mukherjee, 2000). Amihud and Lev (1981) stated that diversification can be used by the management as a protection of the value of their human capital. Ahmed et al. (2003) have pointed out that corporate diversification increases the information asymmetry between managers and shareholders. Harris et al. (1982) stated that increased diversification makes it more difficult to get information about the firm. Therefore, information asymmetry costs are higher in conglomerates than in more focused firms. Despite the criticism of industrial diversification, researchers favour international or global diversification on the grounds that there are imperfections in the product and factor markets at international levels and in international capital markets and that, indeed, these markets are fragmented. The imperfections in the international product and factor markets are identified by Hymer (1976) and are supported by Buckley and Casson (1976), Dunning (1977) and Harris and Ravenscraft (1991). Conn and Connell (1990) stated that capital markets across nations may be segmented because of capital controls, information asymmetries and exchange risk. Harris and Ravenscraft (1991) also recognized the imperfections in the capital markets. Recently, Bailey and Choi (2003) also concluded that although the world capital markets are integrating, it is still far from complete integration. The authors contend that though there are positive forces such as international stock listing, technology and information sharing, coordinated macroeconomic policies and liberalization as well as regional economic union and a common currency regime that enhances international market integration, factors such as operational and currency risk, political risk, corruption, imperfect corporate governance and accounting and information asymmetry may inhibit market integration. Hisley and Caves (1985) and Doukas and Travlos (1988) pointed out that different national markets exhibit different levels of integration to international financial markets and that the degree of integration varies over time. Given the evidence of market imperfections and disintegration at the international levels, several authors have suggested global diversification as a tool for minimizing these discrepancies. Caves (1982) therefore argues that international diversification through acquisitions has the effect of stabilizing overall firm returns because economic conditions, market returns and major political climates tend to be uncorrelated across different international market areas. Global diversification as a motive for CBM&A has also been recognized by several other authors such as Shaked et al. (1991), Kish and Vasconcellos (1993), Markides and Ittner (1994), Datta and Puia (1995), Vasconcellos and Kish (1996) and, more recently, Kiymaz and Mukherjee (2000), Corhay and Rad (2000), and Chen and Findlay (2003).

2.3.3 The Valuation Hypothesis

The valuation hypothesis of mergers and acquisitions states that the overall mergers and acquisitions activities should be an outcome of difference in valuation of assets by different economic agents. In general, the overvalued firms should become an acquirer, and the relatively undervalued firms should become the target (Rhoades-Kropf et al., 2005). The valuation difference may be due to information asymmetry (Halpern, 1983) or the economic shocks (Gort, 1969; Mitchell and Mulherin, 1996) at a particular point of time. Based on the literature on the valuation explanation of mergers and acquisitions, it may be argued that if for any reason, such as information asymmetry or economic shock, a firm is undervalued, then the firm may be acquired by other firms to capture synergy out of this valuation difference (Trautwein, 1990). On the other hand, if the firm is overvalued, then the firm may acquire other relatively undervalued firms to take advantage of overvalued shares. Harford (2005) has indicated the possibility of less overvalued firms being acquired by more overvalued firms. Shleifer and Vishny (2003) posited that target management sometimes acts to maximize its own benefit and therefore accepts the offer from overvalued stock to cash up its position. It should be mentioned here that the economic shocks incorporate changes in the economic environment, technological changes or regulatory changes (Mitchell and Mulherin, 1996). The possibility of an information gap as suggested by Steiner (1975), Halpern (1983) and Ravenscraft and Scherer (1987) and the economic disturbance and shocks suggested by Gort (1969) and Mitchell and Mulherin (1996) are even higher in the international market for corporate control because of the existence of market friction and an information gap at the international level. Harris and Ravenscraft (1991), based on imperfections in product and factor markets, concluded that certain domestic assets may be worth more to a foreign buyer than to a domestic purchaser. Considering the possibility of greater value difference in the case of target valuation at international level, Gonzalez et al.

(1998) have developed the undervaluation hypothesis of international M&A. The authors postulated that the existence of service and product market imperfections that cause frictions in the global markets, such as transaction costs or costs associated with barriers to entry, contributes to favouring the acquisition of an existing company. As a result, foreign firms will be encouraged to acquire an existing firm if the firm is undervalued. Gonzalez et al. (1998) also pointed out that the possibility of the foreign firm being an acquirer is greater if the firm is overvalued. Chen and Su (1997) also pointed out the possibility of a firm being a target of a foreign firm if the firm is undervalued.

2.3.4   The Hubris Hypothesis

The basic proposition of the hubris hypothesis (Roll, 1986) is that the managers of the bidding firm will overvalue the target firm and become over confident about their estimation. This overvaluation will eventually lead them to paying too much for the target. The motivation for mergers and acquisition comes from the overvaluation by the bidder's management; that is, the managers become confident that they will be able to create value by acquiring the target firm. Roll (1986) states that takeover reflects an individual decision and that individuals are not rational all the time. Moreover, managers who make the acquisition decision may not be sufficiently experienced to make an accurate valuation of the target firm. These two factors together may lead the managers to make a wrong valuation decision. The prediction of the hubris hypothesis, as described by Roll (1986) for the target firm, is that the return for the target shareholders should increase at the announcement of the merger and decrease if the bid is cancelled. Regarding the total gain of M&A formation, the hubris hypothesis predicts that the total combined takeover gain to target and bidding firm shareholders is non-positive. The prediction of the hubris hypothesis about the bidding firm is that the value of the bidding firm will decrease after the M&A formation. Roll (1986) found support for this prediction based on the work of Dodd (1980), Eger (1983) and Malatesta (1983). Berkovitch and Narayanan (1993) also found strong evidence of hubris in their study. The hubris hypothesis, which is essentially a dominant explanation of domestic M&A, is equally applicable to CBM&A too. The essence of the hubris hypothesis is the asymmetric beliefs by the bidder and target about the wealth gains associated with acquisitions (Seth et al., 2000, 2002). If this is the case, then this gap of valuation belief should be higher in the case of CBM&A due to the greater information asymmetry between the bidder and the target because of their geographical distance. Based on this logic, Seth et al. (2000, 2002) concluded that the hubris hypothesis may be even more relevant in the context of cross-border acquisitions.

2.3.5   The Managerialism Hypothesis

Several authors, such as Jensen (1986), Amihud and Lev (1981), Roades (1983), Seth et al. (2000, 2002), suggest that some mergers and acquisitions are primarily motivated by managerial self-interest, which is at the expense of the firms' shareholders, and for this purpose, managers will knowingly overpay in takeovers. Investors in the capital market have ample scope for diversifying their investment risk by investing in a portfolio of assets. However, the managers of a company do not have any way of diversifying the risk of being displaced (Sudarsanam, 2003). The inability of managers to personally diversify risk makes them feel insecure and motivates them to pursue M&A so that they can diversify the firm's risk and, by proxy, their own, even if it is at the cost of overpayment (Morck et al., 1990). The managerialism hypothesis is also applicable to international mergers and acquisitions. Seth et al. (2000, 2002) contend that managers may pursue foreign acquisitions rather than domestic ones in order to satisfy the risk-reduction objective, because international diversification is perceived to be more beneficial than is domestic diversification. Using the concept of free cash flow, Jensen (1986) and Mathur et al. (1994) also stated that the managerialism hypothesis is applicable to international mergers and acquisitions. It is contended that managers with excess cash flow from a slow growth economy may invest in foreign countries simply to increase the firm's size and resources under their control. Defining the international acquisition as a way of spending excess cash instead of paying it out to the shareholders, Doukas (1995) also endorses the idea of managerialism in the presence of free cash flow.

2.3.6   The Exchange Rate Hypothesis

The exchange rate theory of FDI provides an explanation of how foreign exchange rates and its fluctuations can affect the FDI flow. Aliber (1970, 1971), Froot and Stein (1991) and Caves (1988) advocated the idea that the foreign exchange rate can explain, at least, part of the FDI flows. Aliber (1970, 1971) states that countries with a strong currency tend to invest in foreign countries and that countries with a weak currency tend to be the recipient of the foreign direct investments. Froot and Stein have further developed the area of knowledge regarding the relationship between FDI and exchange rates. Froot and Stein argued that if there is a relationship between wealth position and investments, then there should be an obvious relationship between FDI and exchange rates. When the foreigners hold the non-dollar-denominated wealth, then a depreciation of dollar will increase the relative wealth of the foreigners and reduce the relative cost of capital. This advantage motivates the foreigners to bid more aggressively for the foreign assets which indicate an increase in the FDI outflows for the countries holding non-dollar-denominated assets. As a popular mode of FDI entry, CBM&A is also affected by the changes in the foreign exchange rates. Harris and Ravenscraft (1991) stated that given information asymmetries about an asset's payoffs, entrepreneurs find it very costly to purchase the asset solely with externally generated fund. As a result, entrepreneurs will fund part of the asset cost from their net wealth, which is a function of the exchange rate between the home and the host country. The exchange rate model predicts that foreign buyers will have a purchasing advantage when their currency is strong against the host currency. Scholes and Wolfson (1990) have found support in favour of the exchange rate hypothesis based on the US CBM&A data for the period before and after 1986. It should be noted here that the US dollar was strong before 1986 and that the situation in the CBM&A market was rather stable. But after 1986, a period marked by the weak position of dollar, the US economy hosted a growing number of foreign takeovers. Another strong support of the proposition that exchange rate difference may affect CBM&A comes from the studies of Weston et al. (1990). The authors contend that the exchange rate differential affects the foreign flow of capital by affecting the effective price of the transaction, the financing of the transaction, the cost of managing the acquired firm and repatriating profit to the acquiring firm. The effect of foreign exchange rate on overall level of CBM&A activities has also been supported by Wansley et al. (1983), Kish and Vasconcellos (1993), Kang (1993), Mathur et al. (1994), Corhay and Rad (2000), and Goergen and Renneboog (2004). The overall conclusion of these studies is that the firm from the appreciating currency country should act as an acquirer, whereas the firm from the depreciating currency country should be a target. It should be mentioned here that the actual effect of the foreign exchange rate differential on the magnitude of the CBM&A is not beyond question. For example, Vasconcellos and Kish (1996) have pointed out that the relative weakening of the host currency may have a positive impact on attracting the CBM&A flow. However, inflows of CBM&A may be negatively affected because the strong currency of the home country may depress the repatriated profit and other remittances.

2.3.7   The Tax Arbitrage Hypothesis

The tax arbitrage hypothesis postulates that international acquisitions will occur to capture the benefit arising from the possibility of differential tax rates in different countries. McCann (2001) states that changes in the pattern of home and host countries' corporate taxes may have an influence on both inward and outward acquisitions. The author concludes that a lower tax rate will attract inward acquisitions and a higher tax rate in a country will inspire outward acquisitions to avoid the damage of domestic higher tax rate. Senbet (1979) contends that under a differential tax environment, the value of the firm would be affected positively if the foreign tax rate is lower than the domestic rate. The author concludes that since the corporate tax rate varies from country to country, CBM&A set the possibility of generating profit by arbitraging on tax differences. A tax benefit from international mergers and acquisitions can also arise due to the possibility of differences in accounting treatment. Froot and Stein (1991) argue that the tax benefit from international M&A would be greater in the presence of depreciation and investment tax credit. In support of the tax arbitrage hypothesis of international M&A, Scholes and Wolfson (1990) stated that tax law changes in the U.S. produce global tax clientele effects and that in response to these changes, the U.S. has attracted a substantial number of foreign bidders. Dunne and Ndubizu (1995) have studied the effect of tax on international merger and acquisition activities. They conclude that an international tax differential and differential accounting treatment for goodwill amortization affect the level of international acquisitions at a given point of time or during a period. Based on the work of Lessard (1995), Lessard and Shapiro (1983) and Rutenberg (1985), Manzon et al. (1994) state that in the presence of transfer pricing and borrowing facility from tax-favorable countries, MNCs can arbitrage the national tax system which allows MNCs to pay lower taxes and gives them an advantage over domestic firms. The authors also point out the possibility of tax arbitrage as a possible source of positive announcement period return in case of CBM&A. In addition to these generalized statements regarding tax benefits of CBM&A, Manzon et al. (1994) make some interesting observations regarding the tax benefits of acquiring firms making acquisitions abroad. The authors formulated the hypothesis with empirical support that firms making foreign acquisitions in high-tax countries rather than lower-tax countries can benefit themselves from international operations. Based on the work of Scholes and Wolfson (1992) which states that, in equilibrium, the after-tax profit in different countries (low tax or high tax) should be equal, and using the concept of foreign tax credit advantage of US acquiring firms, the authors hypothesized that firms with no excess foreign tax credits that acquire firms in low-tax countries will earn lower, abnormal returns than will firms with no excess foreign tax credits that acquire firms in high-tax countries. The authors identify the benefit of investing in a higher-tax country by indicating that the tax-related benefit of an investment in a high-tax country to a firm without unused foreign tax credit is that it earns normal after-local-tax returns locally and generates valuable foreign tax credits. The preceding discussion, therefore, points to the fact that foreign acquisitions in both low-tax and high-tax countries can benefit the acquiring firm, as long as there is a difference in tax rates between the countries and supportive tax regulations exist. The role of tax differential in inspiring CBM&A decisions has also been supported by several other authors, such as Cakici et al. (1991), Kang (1993), Servaes and Zenner (1994), Markides and Ittner (1994) and Goergen and Renneboog (2004).

2.3.8 The Strategic Acquisition Hypothesis

The origination and development of CBM&A can also be explained from strategic perspective. Using the maxim in-regret framework, Schenk (2000) suggests that international acquisitions may be undertaken for a purely strategic rather than a value-creation purpose. Caves (1990) proposed the strategic rationale for CBM&A and stated that new transaction opportunities emerge due to constant changes in industries at the international level. Firms possessing different characteristics and a different bundle of commodities can only penetrate a market if they can provide the right set of assets. If an opportunity is seized by a competitor, its profitability improves while profits are reduced for rival firms. By acquiring foreign competitors, a firm brings a more diverse stock of specific assets under its control and can therefore seize more opportunities. In this way, it enhances its own position while pre-empting a competitor from improving its position. Therefore, international M&A can be undertaken to gain strategic advantage which means gaining access to new opportunities and limiting the opportunities of the competitors. The strategic motives for making foreign acquisition have also been identified by Wilson

(1980) who identified aggressive models and defensive models to explain international M&A. Based on the work of Vernon (1971), Wilson postulates that firms should aggressively seek international acquisitions in order to gain competitive advantage over rivals. Using the defensive models such as the follow-the-leader approach and the exchange-of-threat model, Wilson (1980) suggested that firms should make foreign acquisitions to avoid a competitive imbalance that might be created in the market by the acquisition activities of rival firms. Circumventing trade barriers or taking advantage of regulatory changes may be other causes of strategic international acquisitions. The creation of the SEM is an example of a major regulatory change in the European market for corporate control. McCann (2001) has stated that the creation of the SEM will increase acquisitions within the EU area because of the objective of cost reduction and maintaining the competitive position of the participating firms. Moreover, firms outside the EU will acquire EU firms to ensure the possibility of access to the large and developed market. Shaked et al. (1991), Datta and Puia (1995) and Corhay and Rad (2000) stated that international M&A can be formed to circumvent the imposed trade barriers between countries. The strategic explanation of international M&A has also been supported by Hill et al. (1990).

2.3.9   To Facilitate Faster Entry into Foreign Markets

Martin et al. (1998) have suggested that CBM&A can be used to access new and lucrative markets as well as expanding the market for a firm's current goods. Similar conclusions have been drawn by Datta and Puia (1995), who noted that CBM&A activity provides the opportunity for instant access to a market with established sales volume. UNCTAD (2000) also indicated that cross-border mergers provide the fastest means for international expansion. Kogut and Singh (1988), Barkema and Vermeulen (1998) and Boateng and Glaister (2003) argued that it is expensive, difficult and time-consuming to build a global organization and a competitive presence due to issues such as differences in culture, liability of "foreignness", different business practices and institutional constraints. CBM&A offer significant time saving in this respect. For example, CBM&A allow an immediate access to a local network of suppliers, marketing channels, clients and other skills.

2.4   SUMMARY

This chapter has reviewed the theoretical development and the empirical literature of CBM&A. Several theories of FDI have been used to explain CBM&A including the eclectic paradigm, the internalization theory, the resource-based view and the industrial organization theory. Regarding the other motives, the synergy theory stands out as the one which embraces most of the explanation as to why M&A occur. Previous research, in addition to the anecdotal evidence on acquisitions, suggests that synergy is the primary motive for many acquisitions (see Chatterjee, 1992; Ravenscraft and Scherer, 1987; Hitt et al., 2001) For example synergy can be created with acquisitions in several ways. Acquisitions are carried out for efficiency; that is, economies of scale or scope are achieved through consolidation, elimination of redundancies and inefficiencies and improvements in value-chain activities. In similar vein, synergy can also be achieved through integration of complementary resources from the two firms. Chatterjee (1992) and Ravenscraft and Scherer (1987) argue that complementarity is based on different but mutually supportive resources that when integrated can help produce more valuable products. Moreover, synergy can be derived from market power achieved when the combined entity has greater bargaining power in the market place. In short, synergy captures most of the theories discussed and seen as separate theories behind CBM&A.

REFERENCES

Ahmed, M.U., Rahim, N. and Uddin, M.M. (2003). The Market Impact of Changes in Corporate Diversification (Focus): Some New Evidence, *Journal of Academy of Business and Economics*, Vol. 1(1), pp. 137–147.

Aliber, R.Z. (1970). A Theory of Direct Foreign Investments, in C.P. Kindleberger (ed.), *The International Corporation: A Symposium*, Cambridge, MA: MIT Press, pp. 17–34.

Aliber, R.Z. (1971). The Multinational Enterprise in Multiple Currency World, in J.H. Dunning (ed.), *The Multinational Enterprise*, London: Allen & Unwin.

Amihud, Y. and Lev, B. (1981). Risk Reduction as Managerial Motive for Conglomerate Mergers, *Bell Journal of Economics*, Vol. 12(2), pp. 823–837.

Amit, R. and Schoemaker, P. (1993). Strategic Assets and Organisation Rents, *Strategic Management Journal*, Vol. 14, pp. 33–46.

Asquith, P. and Kim, E.H. (1982), The Impact of Merger Bids on the Participating Firm's Security Holders, *Journal of Finance*, Vol. 37, pp. 1209–1228.

Bailey, W. and Choi, J.J. (2003). International Market Linkage, *Journal of Economics & Business*, Vol. 55(5&6), pp. 399–404.

Bain, J.S. (1956). *Barriers to New Competition*, Cambridge, MA: Harvard University Press.

Bain, J.S. (1968). *Industrial Organization*, New York: John Wiley.

Barkema, H.G. and Vermeulen, G.A.M. (1998). International Expansion through start up or through Acquisitions: An Organisation Learning Perspective, *Academy of Management Journal*, 41(1), pp. 7–26.

Barney, J. (1991). Firm Capabilities and Sustained Competitive Advantage, *Journal of Management*, 17(1), pp. 99–120.

Berkovitch, E. and Narayanan, M.P. (1993). Motives for Takeovers: An Empirical Investigation, *Journal of Financial Quantitative Analysis*, Vol. 28(3), pp. 347–362.

Billington, N. (1999). The Location of Foreign Direct Investment: An Empirical Analysis, *Applied Economics*, Vol. 31, pp. 65–76.

Boateng, A., and Glaister, K.W. (2003). Strategic Motives for International Joint Venture Formation in Ghana. *Management International Review*, Vol. 43(2), pp. 107–128.

Boateng, A., Wang, Q. and Yang, T.L. (2008). Cross-Border M&As by Chinese Firms: An Analysis of Strategic Motives and Performance, *Thunderbird International Business Review*, Vol. 50(4), pp. 259–270.

Bradley, M., Desai, A. and Kim, E.H. (1988). Synergistic Gains from Corporate Acquisitions and their Division between the Stockholders of Target and Acquiring Firms, *Journal of Financial Economics*, Vol. 21(1), pp. 3–40.

Brouthers, K.D. and Brouthers, L.E. (2000). Acquisition or Greenfield Start-Up? Institutional, Cultural and Transaction Cost Influences, *Strategic Management Journal*, Vol. 21, pp. 89–97.

Buckley, P.J. and Casson, M. (1976). *The Future of the Multinational Enterprise*, London: Macmillan.

Cakici, N., Hessel, C.A. and Tandon, T. (1991). Foreign Acquisitions in the United States and the Effect on Shareholder Wealth, *Journal of International Financial Management and Accounting*, Vol. 3(1), pp. 39–60.

Cartwright, S. and Schoenberg, R. (2006). 30 Years of Mergers and Acquisitions Research: Recent Advances and Future Opportunities, *British Journal of Management*, Vol. 17(S1), pp. S1–S5.

Caves, R.E. (1971). International Corporations: The Industrial Economics of Foreign Investments, *Economica*, Vol. 38, pp. 1–27.

Caves, R.E. (1982). *Multinational Enterprise and Economic Analysis*, Cambridge: Cambridge University Press.

Caves, R.E. (1988). *Exchange Rate Movements and Foreign Direct Investment in United States*, Discussion Chapter Series, No. 1383, Harvard Institute of Economic Research.

Caves, R.E. (1990). *Corporate Mergers in International Economic Integration*, Working Paper, Center for Economic Policy Research, Harvard University, Cambridge, MA.

Chatterjee, S. (1992). Sources of Value in Takeovers: Synergy or Restructuring—Implications for Target and Bidder Firms, *Strategic Management Journal*, Vol. 13, pp. 267–286.

Chen, C. and Findlay, C. (2003). A Review of Cross-Border Mergers and Acquisitions in APEC, *Asian-Pacific Economic Literature*, 17(2), pp. 14–38.

Chen, C. and Su, R. (1997). Do Cross-border Acquisitions of US Targets Differ from US Domestic Takeover Targets? *Global Finance Journal*, Vol. 8(1), pp. 71–82.

Cheng, L.T.W. and Chan, K.C. (1995). A Comparative Analysis of the Characteristics of International Takeovers, *Journal of Business Finance & Accounting*, Vol. 22(5), pp. 637–657.

Coase, R.H. (1937). The Nature of the Firm, *Economica*, Vol. 4, pp. 386–405.

Conn, R.L. and Connell, F. (1990). International Mergers: Returns to US and British Firms, *Journal of Business Finance & Accounting*, Vol. 17(5), pp. 689–711.

Copeland, T.E., Weston, J.F. and Shastry, K. (2005), *Financial Theory and Corporate Policy*, 4th Edition, New York: Pearson Addison Wesley.

Corhay, A. and Rad, A.T. (2000). International Acquisitions and Shareholder Wealth: Evidence from the Netherlands, *International Review of Financial Analysis*, Vol. 9(2), pp. 163–174.

Danbolt, J. (2004). Target Company Cross-Border Effects in Acquisitions into the UK, *European Financial Management*, Vol. 10(1), pp. 83–108.

Datta, D.K., Herrmann, P. and Rasheed, A.A. (2003). Choice of Foreign Market Entry Modes: Critical Review and Future Directions, *Advances in International Management*, Vol. 14, pp. 85–153.

Datta, D.K. and Puia, G. (1995) Cross-Border Acquisitions: An Examination of the Influence of Relatedness and Cultural Fit on Shareholder Value Creation in US Acquiring Firms, *Management International Review*, Vol. 35(4), pp. 337–359.

Davis, G. (1991). Agents without Principle? The Spread of Poison Pill through Inter-Corporate Network, *Administrative Science Quarterly*, Vol. 36, pp. 583–613.

Deng, P. (2004). Outward Investment by Chinese MNCs: Motivations and Implications, *Business Horizons*, Vol. 47(3), pp. 8–16.

Denis, D.J., Denis, D.K. and Yost, K. (2002). Global Diversification, Industrial Diversification and Firm Value, *Journal of Finance*, Vol. 57, pp. 1951–1979.

Dodd, P. (1980). Merger Proposal, Management Discretion and Stockholder Wealth, *Journal of Financial Economics*, Vol. 8, pp. 105–138.

Doukas, J. (1995). Overinvestment, Tobin's q and Gains from Foreign Acquisitions, *Journal of Banking and Finance*, Vol. 19, pp. 1285–1303.

Doukas, J. and Travlos, N.G. (1988). The Effect of Corporate Multinationalism on Shareholders' Wealth: Evidence from International Acquisitions, *Journal of Finance*, Vol. 43, pp. 1161–1175.

Dunne, K.K. and Ndubizu, G.A. (1995). International Acquisitions Accounting Methods and Corporate Multinationalism: Evidence from Foreign Acquisitions, *Journal of International Business Studies*, Vol. 26, pp. 361–377.

Dunning, J.H. (1977). Trade, Location of Economic Activity and the MNE: A Search for an Eclectic Approach, in B.Ohlin, P.O. Hesselborn and P.M. Wijkman (eds.), *The International Allocation of Economic Activity*, London: Macmillan, pp. 395–418.

Dunning, J.H. (1988). The Eclectic Paradigm of International Production: A Restatement and Some Possible Extensions, *Journal of International Business Studies*, Vol. 19, pp. 1–31.

Dunning, J.H. (1993). *Multinational Enterprises and the Global Economy*, Reading, MA: Addison-Wesley Publishers.

Dunning, J.H. (2000). The Eclectic Paradigm as an Envelope for Economic and Business Theories, *International Business Review*, Vol. 9, pp. 163–190.

Dunning, J.H. (2003). Some Antecedents of Internalization Theory, *Journal of International Business Studies*, Vol. 34, pp. 108–115.

Eger, C.E. (1983). An Empirical Test of the Redistribution Effect in Pure Exchange Mergers, *Journal of Financial and Quantitative Analysis*, Vol. 18, pp. 547–572.

Eisenhardt, K.M., and Schoonhoven, C.B. (1996). Resources Based View of Strategic Alliance Formation: Strategic and Social Effects in Entrepreneurial Firms. *Organisational Science*, Vol. 7(2), pp. 136–150.

Errunza, V. (1977). Gains from Portfolio Diversification into Developed Countries Securities, *Journal of International Business Studies*, Vol. 8(2), pp. 83–99.

Errunza, V. and Senbet, L.W. (1981). The Effects of International Operations on the Market Value of the Firm: Theory and Evidence, *Journal of Finance*, Vol. 36, pp. 401–418.

Eun, C.S., Kolodny, R. and Scheraga, C. (1996). Cross-Border Acquisitions and Shareholder Wealth: Tests of the Synergy and Internalization Hypotheses, *Journal of Banking and Finance*, Vol. 20, pp. 1559–1582.

Froot, K.A. and Stein, J.C. (1991). Exchange Rates and Foreign Direct Investment: An Imperfect Capital Markets Approach, *Quarterly Journal of Economics*, Vol. 106, pp. 1191–1217.

Ghauri, P.N. and Buckley, P.J. (2003). International Mergers and Acquisitions: Past, Present and Future. *Advances in Mergers and Acquisitions*, Vol. 2, pp. 207–229.

Goergen, M. and Renneboog, L. (2004). Shareholder Wealth Effects of European Domestic and Cross-border Takeover Bids, *European Financial Management*, Vol. 10(1), pp. 9–45.

Gonzalez, P., Vasconcellos, G.M. and Kish, R.J. (1998). Cross-Border Mergers and Acquisitions: The Undervaluation Hypothesis, *The Quarterly Review of Economics and Finance*, Vol. 38(1), pp. 25–45.

Gort, M. (1969). An Economic Disturbance Theory of Merger, *Quarterly Journal of Economics*, Vol. 83, pp. 624–642.

Halpern, P. (1983). Corporate Acquisitions: A Theory of Special Cases? A Review of Event Studies Applied to Acquisitions, *Journal of Finance*, Vol. 38(2), pp. 297–317.

Harford, J. (2005). What Drives Merger Waves? *Journal of Financial Economics*, Vol. 77, pp. 529–560.

Harris, R.S. and Ravenscraft, D.J. (1991). The Role of Acquisitions in Foreign Direct Investment: Evidence from the US Stock Market, *Journal of Finance*, Vol. 46(3), pp. 401–417.

Harris, M., Kriebel, C. and Raviv, A. (1982). Asymmetric Information, Incentives and Intrafirm Resource Allocation, *Management Science*, Vol. 28(6), pp. 604–620.

Heeley, M.B, King, D.R. & Covin, J.G. (2006). Effects of Firm R&D Investment and Environment on Acquisition Likelihood, *Journal of Management Studies*, Vol. 43(7), pp. 1513–1535.

Hennart, J.F. (1982). *A Theory of Multinational Enterprise*, Ann Arbor: University of Michigan Press.

Hennart, J.F. (1991). The Transaction Cost Theory of Joint Ventures: An Empirical Study of Japanese Subsidiaries in the United States, *Management Science*, Vol. 37, pp. 483–497.

Hennart, J.F. and Reddy, S. (1997). The Choice Between Mergers/Acquisitions and Joint Venture: The Case of Japanese Investors in the United States, *Strategic Management Journal*, Vol. 18(1), pp. 1–12.

Hill, C.W., Hwang, P. and Kim, C. (1990). An Eclectic Theory of the Choice of International Entry Mode, *Strategic Management Journal*, Vol. 11, pp. 117–128.

Hisley, K.B. and Caves, R.E. (1985). Diversification and Choice of Country, *Journal of International Business Studies*, Vol. 16, pp. 51–65.

Hitt, M.A., Harrison, J.S. and Ireland, R.D. (2001). *Mergers and Acquisitions: A Guide to Creating Value for Stakeholders*, Oxford: Oxford University Press.

Horst, T. (1972). The Industrial Composition of US Exports and Subsidiary Sales to the Canadian Markets, *American Economic Review*, Vol. 62, pp. 37–45.

Hughes, A., Mueller, D.C. and Singh, A. (1980). Hypotheses about Mergers, in D.C. Mueller (ed.), *The Determinants and Effects of Merger*, Cambridge, MA: Oelgeschlager, Gunn & Hain, pp. 27–66.

Hymer, S.H. (1976). *The International Operation of National Firms: A Study of Direct Foreign Investments*, Cambridge MA: MIT Press.

Jensen, M.C. (1986). Agency Costs of Free Cash-Flow, Corporate Finance and Takeovers, *American Economic Review*, Vol. 76, pp. 323–329.

Kang, J.-K. (1993). The International Market for Corporate Control: Mergers and Acquisitions of US Firms by Japanese Firms, *Journal of Financial Economics*, Vol. 34, pp. 345–371.

Kim, E.H. and McConnell, J.J. (1977). Corporate Mergers and the Co-Insurance of Corporate Debt, *Journal of Finance*, Vol. 32, pp. 349–365.

Kindleberger, C.P. (1969). *American Business Abroad: Six Lecturers on Direct Investment*, New Haven, CT: Yale University Press.

Kish, R.J. and Vasconcellos, G.M. (1993). An Empirical Analysis of Factors Affecting Cross-border Acquisitions: US-Japan, *Management International Review*, Vol. 33(3), pp. 227–245.

Kiymaz, H. (2004). Cross-Border Acquisitions of US Financial Institutions: Impact of Macroeconomic Factors, *Journal of Banking & Finance*, Vol. 28, pp. 1413–1439.

Kiymaz, H. (2009). The Impact of Country Risk Ratings on U.S. Firms in Large Cross-Border Acquisitions, *Global Finance Journal*, Vol. 20(3), pp. 235–247.

Kiymaz, H. and Mukherjee, T.K. (2000). Impact of Country Diversification on Shareholders' Wealth in Cross-border Mergers, *Financial Review*, Vol. 35(2), pp. 37–58.

Klein, S., Frazier, G.L. and Roth, V.J. (1990). A Transaction Cost Analysis Model of Channel Integration in International Markets, *Journal of Marketing Research*, Vol. 27, pp. 196–208.

Kogut, B. and Singh, H. (1988). The Effect of National Culture on the Choice of Entry Mode, *Journal of International Business Studies*, Vol. 19, pp. 411–432.

Kogut, B. and Zander, U. (1992). Knowledge of the Firm, Combinative Capabilities, and the Replication of Technology, *Organization Science*, Vol. 3, pp. 383–397.

Lessard, D.R. (1973). International Portfolio Diversification: A Multivariate Analysis for a Group of Latin American Countries, *Journal of Finance*, Vol. 28, pp. 610–633.

Lessard, D. and Shapiro, A. (1983). Guidelines for Global Financing Choices, *Midland Corporate Finance Journal*, Winter, pp. 68–80.

Lessard, J.P. (1995). International Acquisition of US Based Firms: Shareholder Wealth Implications, *American Business Review*, Vol. 13(1), pp. 50–57.

Lewellen, W.G. (1971). A Pure Financial Rationale for a Conglomerate Merger, *Journal of Finance*, Vol. 26, pp. 521–537.

Logue, D.E. (1982). An Experiment in International Diversification, *Journal of Portfolio Management*, Vol. 9(1), pp. 22–27.

Luo, Y. and Tung, R. (2007). International Expansions of Emerging Market Enterprises: A Springboard Perspective, *Journal of International Business Studies*, Vol. 38(4), pp. 481–498.

Madhok, A. (1997). Cost, Value and Foreign Market Entry: The Transaction and the Firm, *Strategic Management Journal*, Vol. 18(1), pp. 39–63.

Magee, S.P. (1977). Multinational Corporations, Industry Technology Cycle and Development, *Journal of World Trade Law*, Vol. 11, pp. 297–321.

Malatesta, P.H. (1983). The Wealth Effects of Merger Activity and the Objective Functions of Merging Firms, *Journal of Financial Economics*, Vol. 11, pp. 155–182.

Manzon, G.B., Sharp, D.J. and Travlos, N.G. (1994). An Empirical Study of the Consequences of US Tax Rules for International Acquisitions by US Firms, *Journal of Finance*, Vol. 49, pp. 1893–1904.

Markides, C. and Ittner, C.D. (1994). Shareholders Benefit from Corporate International Diversification: Evidence from US International Acquisitions, *Journal of International Business Studies*, Vol. 25(2), pp. 343–366.

Marr, M.W., Mohta, S. and Spivey, M.F. (1993). An Analysis of Foreign Takeovers in the United States, *Managerial and Decision Economics*, Vol. 14(4), pp. 285–294.

Martin, X., Swaminathan, A. and Mitchell, W. (1998). Organisational Evolution in the Interorganisational Environment: Incentives and Constraints on International Expansion Strategy, *Administrative Science Quarterly*, Vol. 43, pp. 566–601.

Mathur, I., Rangan, N., Chhachhi, I. and Sundaram, S. (1994). International Acquisitions in the United States: Evidence from Returns to Foreign Bidders, *Managerial and Decision Economics*, Vol. 15(2), pp. 107–118.

McCann, M. (2001). Cross-Border Acquisitions: The UK Experience, *Applied Economics*, Vol. 33, pp. 457–461.

McManus, J.C. (1972). The Theory of International Firm, in G. Pacquet (ed.), *The Multinational Firm and the Nation State*, Galt, Ontario, Canada: Collier-Macmillan, pp. 66–93.

Mitchell, M.L. and Mulherin, J.H. (1996). The Impact of Industry Shocks on Takeover and Restructuring Activity, *Journal of Financial Economics*, Vol. 41, pp. 193–229.

Morck, R. and Yeung, B. (1991). Why Investors Value Multinationality, *Journal of Business*, Vol. 64(2), pp. 165–186.

Morck, R. and Yeung, B. (1992). Internalization: An Event Study Test, *Journal of International Economics*, Vol. 33, pp. 41–56.

Morck, R., Shleifer, A. and Vishny, R.W. (1990). Do Managerial Objectives Drive Bad Acquisitions?, *Journal of Finance*, Vol. 45, pp. 31–48.

Nadolska, A. and Barkema, H. (2007). Learning to Internationalize: The Pace and Success of Foreign Acquisitions, *Journal of International Business Studies*, Vol. 38, pp. 1170–1186.

Ohmae, K. (1989). The Global Logic of Strategic Alliances, *Harvard Business Review*, March–April, pp. 143–154.

Porter, M.E. and Fuller, M.B. (1986). Coalitions and Global Strategy, in M.E. Porter (ed.), *Competition in Global Industries*, Boston, MA: Harvard Business School, pp. 315–344.

Ravenscraft, D.J. and Scherer, F.M. (1987). *Mergers, Sell-Offs and Economic Efficiency*, Washington, DC: The Brookings Institution.

Reed, R. and Luffman, G.A. (1986). Diversification: The Growing Confusion, *Strategic Management Journal*, Vol. 7(1), pp. 29–35.

Rhoades-Kropf, M., Robinson, D.T. and Viswanathan, S. (2005). Valuation Waves and Merger Activity: The Empirical Evidence, *Journal of Financial Economics*, Vol. 77, pp. 561–603.

Roades, S.A. (1983). *Power, Empire Building and Mergers*, Lexington, MA: D.C. Health &Co.

Roll, R. (1986). The Hubris Hypothesis of Corporate Takeover, *Journal of Business*, Vol. 59, pp. 197–216.

Rossi, S. and Volpin, P. (2004). Cross-Country Determinants of Mergers and Acquisitions, *Journal of Financial Economics*, Vol. 74, pp. 277–304.

Rugman, A.M. (1982). *New Theories of the Multinational Enterprise*, London: Croom Helm.

Rutenberg, D. (1985). Manuevering Liquid Assets, in D. Lesserd (ed.), *International Financial Management*, New York: J. Wiley & Sons, pp. 457–471.

Schenk, H. (2000). Are International Acquisitions a Matter of Strategy Rather Than Wealth Creation? *International Review of Applied Economics*, Vol. 14(2), pp. 193–211.

Scholes, M.S. and Wolfson, M.A. (1990). The Effects of Changes in Tax Laws on Corporate Reorganization Activity, *Journal of Business*, Vol. 63, pp. S141–S164.

Scholes, M.S. and Wolfson, M.A. (1992). *Taxes and Business Strategy: A Planning Approach*, Englewood Cliffs, NJ: Prentice Hall.

Senbet, L. (1979). International Capital Market Equilibrium and the Multinational Firm Financing and Investment Policies, *Journal of Financial and Quantitative Analysis*, Vol. 14, pp. 455–480.

Servaes, H. and Zenner, M. (1994). Taxes and Returns to Foreign Acquisitions in the United States, *Financial Management*, Vol. 23(4), pp. 42–56.

Seth, A. (1990). Sources of Value Creation in Acquisitions: An Empirical Investigation, *Strategic Management Journal*, Vol. 11, pp. 431–446.

Seth, A., Song, K.P. and Pettit, R. (2000). Synergy, Managerialism or Hubris? An Empirical Examination of Motives for Foreign Acquisitions of US Firms, *Journal of International Business Studies*, Vol. 31(3), pp. 387–405.

Seth, A., Song, K.P. and Pettit, R. (2002). Value Creation and Destruction in Cross-Border Acquisitions: An Empirical Analysis of Foreign Acquisitions of US Firms, *Strategic Management Journal*, Vol. 23, pp. 921–940.

Shaked, I., Michel, A. and McClain, D. (1991). The Foreign Acquirer Bonanza: Myth or Reality?, *Journal of Business Finance & Accounting*, Vol. 18(3), pp. 431–447.

Shimizu, K., Hitt, M.A., Vaidyanath, D. and Pisano, V. (2004). Theoretical Foundations of Cross-border Mergers and Acquisitions: A Review of Current Research and Recommendations for the Future, *Journal of International Management*, Vol. 10, pp. 307–353.

Shleifer, A. and Vishny, R.W. (1992). Asset Liquidity and Debt Capacity, *Journal of Finance*, Vol. 47, pp. 1343–1366.

Shleifer, A. and Vishny, R. (2003). Stock Market Driven Acquisitions, *Journal of Financial Economics*, Vol. 70, pp. 295–311.

Steiner, P.O. (1975). *Mergers, Motives, Effects, Policies*, Ann Arbor: University of Michigan Press.

Stulz, R.M. (1990). Managerial Discretion and Optimal Financial Policies, *Journal of Financial Economics*, Vol. 26, pp. 3–28.

Sudarsanam, S. (2003). *Creating Value from Mergers and Acquisitions: The Challenges*, London: Pearson Education Limited.

Sudersanam, S., Holl, P. and Salami, A. (1996). Shareholder Wealth Gains in Mergers: Effect of Synergy and Ownership Structure, *Journal of Business Finance & Accounting*, Vol. 23, pp. 673–698.

Teece, D.J. (1983). Technological and Organizational Factors in the Theory of the Multinational Enterprise, in M. Casson (ed.), *The Growth of International Business*, London: Allen & Unwin, pp. 51–62.

Toxvaerd, F.M.O (2008). Strategic Merger Waves: A Theory of Musical Chairs (2008); *Journal of Economic Theory*, Vol. 140(1), pp. 1–26.

Trautwein, F. (1990). Merger Motives and Merger Prescriptions, *Strategic Management Journal*, Vol. 11(4), pp. 283–295.

Uddin, M. & Boateng, A. (2011). Explaining the Trends in Cross-Border Mergers and Acquisitions in the UK: An Analysis of Macro-Economic Factors, *International Business Review*, Vol. 20(5), pp. 547–556.

United Nations Conference on Trade and Development (UNCTAD) (2000). *World Investment Report 2000: Cross-Border Mergers and Acquisitions and Development*, New York and Geneva: United Nations.

United Nations Conference on Trade and Development (UNCTAD) (2012). *World Investment Report: Towards a New Generation of Investment Policies*, New York and Geneva: United Nations.

Vasconcellos, G.M. and Kish, R.J. (1996). Factors Affecting Cross-Border Mergers and Acquisitions: The Canada-US Experience, *Global Finance Journal*, Vol. 7(2), pp. 223–238.

Vasconcellos, G.M. and Kish, R.J. (1998). Cross-Border Mergers and Acquisitions: The European-US Experience, *Journal of Multinational Financial Management*, Vol. 8(4), pp. 431–450.

Vermeulen, F. and Barkema, H.G. (2001). Learning through acquisitions, *Academy of Management Journal*, Vol. 44, pp. 457–476.

Vernon, R. (1971). *Sovereignty at Bay: The Multinational Spread of US Enterprise*, London: Pelican.

Wansley, J.W., Lane, W.R. and Yang, H.C. (1983). Shareholder Returns to USA Acquired Firms in Foreign and Domestic Acquisitions, *Journal of Business Finance & Accounting*, Vol. 10(4), pp. 647–656.

Wernerfelt, B. (1984). A Resource-Based View of the Firm. *Strategic Management Journal*, Vol. 5(2), pp. 171–180.

Weston, J.F., Chung, K.S. and Hoag, S.E. (1990). *Mergers, Restructuring and Corporate Control*, Englewood Cliffs, NJ: Prentice Hall.

Williamson, O.E. (1975). *Markets and Hierarchies*, New York: The Free Press.

Wilson, B.D. (1980). The Propensity of Multinational Companies to Expand through Acquisitions, *Journal of International Business Studies*, Vol. 11(1), pp. 59–65.

3 Thirty Years of Cross-Border Mergers and Acquisitions and Value Creation

A Review and Future Directions

3.1 INTRODUCTION

Whether CBM&A constitute a value creation event has been an overarching theme of research over the past three decades. A number of studies have examined the value creating performance of acquisitions with the bulk of these studies concentrating on advanced market economies such as the US, UK and continental European countries. More recently, we have also seen an increasing number of studies from the emerging-market-economy context because these countries are no longer recipients of these investments but are actively engaged in outward acquisition activities. During the period from 1987 to 2003, the average share of CBM&A purchases in the FDI outflows for developed and developing countries were around 60% and 40%, respectively. These figures suggest that both the developed and developing countries have used CBM&A as a principal mode of FDI entry in the foreign countries. Our content analysis suggests that notable review studies on performance and factors influencing acquisition performance such as Jensen and Ruback (1983); Jarrel et al. (1988), Datta et al. (1992), Andrade et al. (2001) and Bruner (2002) tend to focus on domestic mergers, with only few studies in context of CBM&A. Perhaps, the only review studies on CBM&A are Shimizu et al. (2004) and Chen and Findley (2003). In this book, we attempt to fill this gap by reviewing the performance of CBM&A to improve our current understanding of acquisition performance in the context of both advanced countries and emerging market economies. Specifically, we address the following important research questions:

1. What is performance of target and bidding firms engaged in CBM&A activities?
2. What is the performance of combined firm after announcement of CBM&A?
3. What are the determinants of target and bidding firms' performance?

The chapter examines the target and acquiring firms' performance in both the short and long term. Combined firm performance and factors affecting performance in both developed and emerging countries are reviewed. The final section of the chapter provides a summary and suggestions for future research.

3.2   PERFORMANCE OF CBM&A

The literature of CBM&A performance has been approached and examined from three perspectives: (1) target performance, (2) acquirer performance and (3) factors influencing CBM&A performance.

3.2.1   Target Firm Performance of Developed Country Firms in the Short Term

A number of studies have attempted to find out the target firms' return in the case of CBM&A. The overwhelming conclusion drawn from these studies of more than 25 studies between the period of 1983 and 2004 is that target firms earn significant and positive abnormal returns in CBM&A. The sample coverage of these studies ranges from 1970 to 2000 and with respect to both developed and developing countries. The predominant methodology used in these studies is event study methodology with the majority of the studies using the standard market model, followed by the international market model, the CAPM and mean adjusted return method. The event time ranges from several days surrounding the acquisition announcement to several months surrounding the acquisition announcement. The abnormal return for the target firms ranges from 4% to more than 40% around the acquisition announcement time which are statistically significant in majority of the studies. Table 3.1 provides the summary of the results of studies in respect target firms.

3.2.2   Acquiring Firm Performance of Developed Country Firms in the Short Term

Whereas prior research provides conclusive evidence that the formation of CBM&A leads to massive value creation for target firms, the same is not the case for acquiring firms. Systematic evidence indicates that the results are mixed with a number of studies reporting positive performance while others indicating negative or insignificant performance. In those studies, the performance of bidding firms has been evaluated mostly for short term using standard event study methodology as suggested by Fama et al. (1969). The benchmark return has been calculated by using various models such as the standard market model, the international market model, the index model, the mean adjusted return model and the CAPM; however, the majority of the studies have used the standard market model.

Table 3.2 shows the studies that have reported positive performance for the bidding firms' shareholders for short run include Morck and Yeung (1992), Markides and Ittner (1994), Manzon et al. (1994), Doukas (1995), Cakici et al. (1996), Markides and Oyon (1998), Black et al. (2001), Kiymaz and Mukherjee (2001), Gleason et al. (2002), Kiymaz (2003), Block (2005), Pettway et al. (1993), Kang (1993) and Guo et al. (1995).

Table 3.1 Target Firm Performance (short run) in CBM&A

Authors	Sample Year	Sample Country	Model Used	Event Window	Return
Wansley et al. (1983)	1970–1978 39 acquisitions	US targets	Market Model	–10 to +40 days	38.6% on day 0
Mathur et al. (1989)	1986–1988 18 acquisitions	US targets. Bidders from UK, Europe, Canada, Japan and Australia	Market Model	Various. Maximum from –15 to +15 days	CAR 26% for –1 to +1 day CAR 27% for –15 to +15 days
Conn and Connell (1990)	1971–1980 73 acquisitions	US targets UK targets	DMM IMM DMM IMM	–12 to +12 months	40% on month 0 43% on month 0 18% on month 0 20% on month 0
Harris and Ravenscraft (1991)	1970 –1987 159 acquisitions	US targets. Bidders from UK, Europe, Canada and others	Market Model	From –20 to +4 days and –3 to +1 day	CAR 39.77% (sig.)
Lessard and Robin (1991)	1986–1988 89 acquisitions	US targets	Market Model	–49 to 20 days	14.38% for –1 to 0 days
Cakici et al. (1991)	1982–1987 245 acquisitions	US targets. Bidders from UK, Canada, Germany, France and Japan	Market Model	Various. Maximum from –20 to +5 days	16% for 0 to +1 day (sig.) 22% for –10 to +1 day (sig.)
Shaked et al. (1991)	1975–1983 29 acquisitions	US targets	Market Model	–35 to +35 days	AR 32.64% on day 0 CAR 40.24% for –35 to +35 days (sig.)
Cebenoyan et al. (1992)	1978–1987 73 acquisitions	US targets. Bidders from UK, Europe, Canada, Asia and others	Market Model	–1 to 0 days	6.63% for –1 to 0 days (sig.)
Swenson (1993)	1974–1990 226 acquisitions	US targets. Bidders from UK, Europe, Canada and others	Market Model	Various. Maximum from –20 to +10 days	26.1% CAR for –1 to +1 day (sig.)

Study	Sample	Target/Bidders	Model	Event window	Results
Marr et al. (1993)	1975–1987 96 acquisitions	US targets. Bidders from UK, Europe, Canada, Japan and others	Market Model	Various. Maximum from −60 to +20 days	12% for −1 to 0 days 45% for −60 to +20 days
Pettway et al. (1993)	1981–1991 53 acquisitions	US targets. Japanese bidders	Market Model	Various. Maximum from −21 to +20 days	37% for −1 to 0 days 58% for −21 to +20 days
Kang (1993)	1975–1988 119 acquisitions	US targets. Japanese bidders	Market Model	Various. Maximum from −20 to +20 days	9% for −1 to 0 days 9.4% for −1 to +1 day 9.6% for −2 to +1 day
Dunne and Ndubizu (1995)	1983–1988 95 acquisitions	US targets	Market Model	From −20 to +20 days	Positive and significant
Lessard (1995)	1979–1989 331 acquisitions	US targets. Bidders from UK, Europe, Canada, Australia, Asia and Africa	Market Model	Various. Maximum from −49 to +20 days	CAR 11.04% for −1 to 0 days (sig.)
Dewenter (1995a)	1975–1989 601 acquisitions	US targets	Market Model		22.8% for −20 to +10 days
Dewenter (1995b)	1978–1989 90 acquisitions	US targets	Market Model	From −20 to +10 days	More than 20% for −20 to +10 days window
Cheng and Chan (1995)	1985–1990 70 acquisitions	US targets. Bidders from UK, Europe, Australia, Canada, Japan and others	Market Model	Various. Maximum from −40 to +3 days	21.8% for −1 to +1 day
Parhizgari and Boyrie (1995)	1979–1990 122 acquisitions	US targets. Bidders from UK, Europe, Canada and Japan	Simple OLS SUR Pooling Technique		Negative target return

(Continued)

Table 3.1 (Continued)

Authors	Sample Year	Sample Country	Model Used	Event Window	Return
Eun et al. (1996)	1979–1990 213 acquisitions	US targets. Bidders from UK, Europe, Canada, Australia, New Zealand, Japan and others	Mean-adjusted Return method	–5 to +5 days	37% for –5 to +5 days
Kiymaz and Mukherjee (2000)	1982–1991 141 acquisitions	US targets. Bidders from UK, Europe and others	IMM	Various. Maximum from –10 to +10 days	5% for –1 to 0 days 4.77% for –1 to +1 day
Seth et al. (2000)	1981–1990 100 acquisitions	Non-US targets	Market Model	–10 to +10 days	38.3% for –10 to +10 days
Goergen and Renneboog (2003, 2004)	1993–2000 185 acquisitions	EU targets (UK and Continental Europe)	CAPM	Various. Maximum from –60 to +60 days	9% for –1 to 0 days 13% for –2 to +2 days
Danbolt (2004)	1986–1991 116 acquisitions	UK targets. Bidders from US, Canada, Europe, Australia, New Zealand, Japan and others	Size Deciles and Small Companies Model, Index and Market Model and CAPM	Various. Maximum from –8 to +5 months	19.6% in month zero with size-deciles model 21% in month zero with market model
Chari et al. (2004)	1988–2002 1629 acquisitions	Targets from developing countries	Market Model	–2 to +2 weeks	6.68% for –1 to +1 week 5.51% for –2 to +2 weeks
Campa and Hernando (2004)	1998–2000 80 acquisitions	EU targets	Market Model	Various. Maximum from –30 to +30 days	4.08% for –1 to +1 day 9.66% for –30 to +30 days
Servaes and Zenner (1994)	1980–1989 112 acquisitions	US targets. Bidders from UK, Canada, Europe, Asia and Australia	Market Model	Various. Maximum from –20 to 0 days	13.48 for –1 to 0 days (sig.)
Guo et al. (1995)	1981–1989 82 acquisitions	US targets Bidders from Japan	Market Model	Various. Maximum from –5 to +5 days	8.99% on day 0 (sig.)

SUR = seemingly unrelated regression; sig. = significant.

Table 3.2 Acquiring Firm Performance (short run) in CBM&A

Authors	Sample Year and Sample size	Sample Country	Benchmark Return Model Used	Event Window	Main Findings
Doukas and Travlos (1988)	1975–1983 301 acquisitions	US bidders. Targets from developed and less developed countries	Market Model	Various. Maximum from –10 to +10 days	0.08% on day 0 but insignificant; 0.54% for –10 to +10 days but insignificant
Mathur et al. (1989)	1986–1988 18 acquisitions	Non-US bidders from UK, Europe, Canada, Japan and Australia	Market Model	Various. Maximum from –15 to +15 days	CAR 0.00% for –1 to +1 day (insignificant) CAR –2.71% for –15 to +15 days (insignificant)
Conn and Connell (1990)	1971–1980 35 US Bidders and 38 UK Bidders	US bidders. Targets from UK	DMM	Various. Maximum from –12 to +12 months	11.37% for –12 to +12 months with parameters calculated from post-merger return (significant)
			IMM		10.02% for –12 to +12 months with parameters calculated from post-merger returns (significant)
		UK bidders. Targets from US	DMM		11.33% for –12 to +12 months with parameters calculated from post-merger return (significant)
			IMM		11.16% for –12 to +12 months with parameters calculated from post-merger returns (significant)
Pettway et al. (1993)	1981–1991 53 acquisitions	Japanese bidder. Targets from US	Market Model	Various. Maximum from –21 to 20 days	1.52% for –1 to 0 days (significant) 6.91% for –21 to +20 days (insignificant)
Kang (1993)	1975–1988 119 acquisitions	Japanese bidder. Targets from US	Market Model	Various. Maximum from –20 to +20 days	0.60% for –1 to 0 days (significant) 0.51% for –1 to +1 day (significant)
Markides and Ittner (1994)	1975–1988 276 acquisitions	US bidders. Targets from UK, Canada, Europe and Pacific region	Market Model	Various. Maximum from –10 to +10 days	0.54% for –1 to +3 days (significant) 0.32% for –1 to 0 days (significant) 0.49% for –2 to +3 days (significant)

(Continued)

Table 3.2 (Continued)

Authors	Sample Year and Sample size	Sample Country	Benchmark Return Model Used	Event Window	Main Findings
Manzon et al. (1994)	1975–1983 103 acquisitions	US bidders. Targets are from developed and less developed countries	Market model	–1 day to day 0	Mean CAR 0.01% (significant)
Lin et al. (1994)	1980–1989 119 acquisitions	US bidders. Targets from UK, Europe and Canada	Market Model	–1 day to day 0	1.27% for German targets (significant) –0.45% and –0.25% for UK and Canadian targets, respectively (insignificant)
Mathur et al. (1994)	1984–1988 77 acquisitions	Bidders from Australia, Canada, Europe, Japan, and UK. Targets from US	Market Model	Various. From –15 days to +15 days	–0.263% for –1 to +1 day (significant) –1.692% for –1 to +6 days (significant)
Danbolt (1995)	1986–1991 174 acquisitions	Bidders from US, Canada, Europe, New Zealand, Australia, Asia and Africa	Market Model (MM) and Index Model (IM)	Various. Maximum from –8 months to +5 months	0.44% for –1 to 0 month in IM (significant) –1.03% for –1 to 0 month in MM (significant) –5.34% for –8 to +5 months in IM (significant) –16.46% for –8 to +5 months in MM (significant)
Datta and Puia (1995)	1978–1990 112 acquisitions	US bidders. Targets from UK, Europe, Canada and Australia	Market Model	Various. Maximum from –30 to +30 days	–0.42% for –1 to 0 day (significant) –0.72% for –5 to +5 days (significant)
Doukas (1995)	1975–1989 463 acquisitions	US bidders. Targets from foreign countries	Market Model	–1 to 0 day	0.41% for $q > 1$ firm (significant) –0.18% for $q < 1$ firm (insignificant)

Study	Period	Sample description	Method	Window	Results
Eun et al. (1996)	1979–1990	117 acquisitions	Bidders from Australia, NZ, Canada, UK, Europe and Asia. Targets from US	Mean adjusted return method	−5 to +5 days	−1.20% for −5 to +5 days for the total sample of bidders (significant)
Cakici et al. (1996)	1983–1992	195 acquisitions	Bidders from UK, Canada, Europe and Australia. Targets from US	Market Model	Various. Maximum from −10 to +10 days	1.96% for −10 to +10 days (significant) 1.05% for −10 to +1 day (significant) 0.63% for 0 to +1 day (significant)
Markides and Oyon (1998)	1975–1988	236 acquisitions	US bidders. Targets from UK, Canada and Europe	Market Model	Various. Maximum from −10 to +10 days	0.38% for −1 to 0 days (significant) 0.59% for −1 to +3 days (significant)
Kiymaz and Mukherjee (2000)	1982–1991	112 acquisitions	US bidders. Targets from UK, Europe, Canada, Australia and Japan	International Market Model	Various. Maximum from −10 to +10 days	0.38% for −1 to 0 days (insignificant) 0.50% for −1 to +1 day (insignificant) 0.59% for −10 to +10 days (insignificant)
Corhay and Rad (2000)	1990–1996	111 acquisitions	Dutch bidders. Targets from Europe, US and East Europe	Market Model	Various. Maximum from −40 to +40 days	−1.05% for −40 to +40 days for European targets (insignificant) 4.83% for −40 to +40 days for US targets (significant) −3.74% for −40 to +40 days for East European targets (insignificant)
Eckbo and Thorburn (2000)	1964–1983	394 acquisitions	US bidders. Targets from Canada	Market Model	Various. Maximum from −12 to +12 months	0.41% for −12 to −1 month (insignificant) −0.19% for month 0 (insignificant) −3.72% for +1 to +12 months (insignificant)
Black et al. (2001)	1985–1995	361 acquisitions	US bidders. Targets from UK, Europe, Australia, Asia and South Africa	Market Model CAR	Various. Maximum from −5 to +5 days	1.5% for −5 to +5 days (significant) 0.9% for −5 to +1 days (significant)

(Continued)

Table 3.2 (Continued)

Authors	Sample Year and Sample size	Sample Country	Benchmark Return Model Used	Event Window	Main Findings
Seth et al. (2000)	1981–1990 100 acquisitions	US bidders. Targets from foreign countries	Market Model	–10 to +10 days	0.11% for –10 to +10 days (insignificant)
Kiymaz and Mukherjee (2001)	1982–1991 112 acquisitions	US bidders. Targets from UK, Europe, Canada, Japan, Australia	Market Model	Various. Maximum from –10 to +10 days	1.09% for –5 to +5 days based on post-event parameters (significant). All other returns are insignificant.
Conn et al. (2001)	1984–2000 1065 acquisitions	UK bidders	Size/prior return portfolio BHARs	Various. Maximum 0 to +36 months	Mean BHAR 1.23% in month 0 (significant) 2.12% for 1 to 12 months (insignificant)
Gleason et al. (2002)	1974–1998 351 acquisitions	US bidders. Targets from Pacific Rim countries	Market Model	–1 to +1 days and –1 to 0 days	0.76% for –1 to +1 day (significant) 0.47% for –1 to 0 days (significant)
Goergen and Renneboog (2003, 2004)	1993–2000 185 acquisitions	EU bidders. Targets from EU	CAPM	Various. Maximum from –60 to +60 days	0.7% for –1 to 0 days (significant) 1.18% for –2 to +2 days (significant)
Kiymaz (2003)	1989–2000 148 acquisitions	US bidders. Targets from UK, Europe, Asia Pacific, Latin and Central America and Canada	Market Model	Various. Maximum from –10 to +10 days	0.57% for –1 to 0 days (significant) 0.5% for –1 to +1 day (significant)
Chari et al. (2004)	1988–2002	Bidders from developed countries. Targets from emerging markets	Market Model	–1 to +1 week and –2 to +2 weeks	Raw return of 3.05% for –1 to +1 week (significant) Raw return of 2% for –2 to +2 weeks (significant)
Aw and Chatterjee (2004)	1991–1996 41 acquisitions	UK bidders. Targets from US and Continental Europe	Market adjusted return model Market Model	Various. From +6 months to +24 months	–4.46% for +6 months (significant) –8.07% for +12 months (significant)

Study	Period	Sample	Model	Event window	Results
Campa and Hernando (2004)	1998–2000	80 acquisitions	EU bidders	Market Model	−30 to +30 days	0.05% for −1 to +1 day (insignificant) −0.78% for −30 to +30 days (insignificant)
Lowinski et al. (2004)	1990–2001	91 acquisitions	Swiss bidders	Market Model	Various. Maximum from −63 to +63 days	1.36% for −2 to +2 days (significant) 1.26% for −1 to +1 days (significant)
Moeller and Schlingemann (2005)	1985–1995	383 acquisitions	US bidders. Targets from UK, Canada, France and Germany	Market Model	−1 to +1 day	0.307% for acquisitions from 1985 to 1995 (insignificant) 0.745% for acquisitions from 1985 to 1990 (significant) 0.148% for acquisitions from 1991 to 1995 (insignificant)
Conn et al. (2005)	1984–1998	1140 acquisitions	UK bidders. Targets are from all parts of the world	Market adjusted CAR for short term performance	−1 to +1 day for short run performance	0.33% for all acquisitions from −1 to +1 day (insignificant)
Gregory and McCorriston (2005)	1985–1994	343 acquisitions	UK bidders. Targets are from US, EU and rest of the world	Market Model CAR for short run	−3 to +1 day and −10 to +10 days for short run	−0.00022 for −3 to +1 day (insignificant) −0.0065 for +1 year (insignificant)
Servaes and Zenner (1994)	1980–1989	27 acquisitions	Bidders from UK, Canada, Europe, Asia and Australia. Targets from US	Market Model	Various. Maximum from −20 to 0 days	0.44% for −1 to 0 days (insignificant)
Guo et al. (1995)	1981–1989	82 acquisitions	Japanese bidders. Targets from US	Market Model	Various. Maximum from −5 to +5 days	5.34% on day 0 (significant)

(Continued)

Table 3.2 (Continued)

Authors	Sample Year and Sample size	Sample Country	Benchmark Return Model Used	Event Window	Main Findings
Yook and McCabe (1996)	1979–1989 262 acquisitions	US bidders	Market Model	Various. Maximum from –10 days to +10 days	0.63% on day –1 (significant) 0.22% on day 0 (insignificant)
Block (2005)	1994–2003 298 acquisitions	US bidders	Market Model	Various. Maximum from –10 to +10 days	1.77% for –1 to 0 days (significant)
Morck and Yeung (1992)	1978–1988 322 acquisitions	US bidders	Index Model	Various. Maximum from –2 to +2 days	0.29% on day 0 (significant)
Fatemi and Furtado (1988)	1974–1979 117 acquisitions	US bidders	Market Model	Various. Maximum from –60 to +60 days	2.11% for –1 to 0 day (insignificant)
Seth et al. (2002)	1989–1990 100 acquisitions	US bidders. Targets from UK, Europe, Canada, Australia, Japan and others	Market Model	Various. Maximum from –10 days to +10 days	0.11% for –10 to +10 days (insignificant)

Beside the studies that show positive performance of bidding firms, few other studies show a negative announcement period return for the bidding firms. For example using the market model, Mathur et al. (1994) and Datta and Puia (1995) reported significant negative performance for bidders. Using both the index model and the market model, Danbolt (1995) evaluated bidders from different countries that acquired UK firms and reported that acquirers earn a significant negative abnormal return. Eun et al. (1996) evaluated acquiring firms' return by using the mean adjusted return model and reported that the foreign acquirers of US target firms earn a statistically significant, negative abnormal return.

In addition to positive and negative announcement performance of bidding firms, several other studies have reported insignificant bidder returns for the over-all sample at or around the announcement time of CBM&A. Among those studies, Doukas and Travlos (1988), Fatemi and Furtado (1988), Mathur et al. (1989), Servaes and Zenner (1994), Danbolt (1995), Yook and McCabe (1996), Kiymaz and Mukherjee (2000), Eckbo and Thorburn (2000), Seth et al. (2000), Campa and Hernando (2004) and Gregory and McCorriston (2005) are important.

3.2.3   Long-Term Performance of Developed Country Firms

Several studies have evaluated the long-run performance or more specifically the post-acquisition performance of bidding firms engaged in CBM&A. The time frame used in those studies to evaluate long-term bidder performance varies from one to five years after acquisitions. The most frequently used models are the calendar time, Fama-French three factor model and the size and book to market ratio adjusted model. Among the long-term bidder return studies, Black et al. (2001) for US bidders; Conn et al. (2001), Aw and Chatterjee (2004), Conn et al. (2005) and Gregory and McCorriston (2005) for UK bidders; and Francoeur (2005) and Andre et al. (2004) for Canadian bidders are important.

Table 3.3 shows the results of these studies for long-run performance. Black et al. (2001), Conn et al. (2001), Aw and Chatterjee (2004), Andre et al., (2004) and Conn et al. (2005) have reported that acquiring firms earn significant, negative abnormal return in the long run. However, the returns reported by Gregory and McCorriston (2005) for the UK acquirers and by Francoeur (2005) for Canadian acquirers are insignificant in the long run and are not different from zero.

3.3   COMBINED PERFORMANCE OF DEVELOPED COUNTRY FIRMS

Although much of the attention has been given to evaluating target and bidding firms' performance in CBM&A performance research, there are a number of other studies that have examined the combined firms' performance after the formation of CBM&A events. For example in the study by Eun et al. (1996), the calculation of combined gain shows that US targets and foreign acquirers experienced statistically significant, positive combined wealth gain of US$68 million on average. Seth

Table 3.3 Acquiring Firm Performance (long run) in CBM&A

Authors	Sample Year and Sample Size	Sample Country	Benchmark Return Model Used	Event Window	Main Findings
Black et al. (2001)	1985–1995 361 acquisitions	US bidders. Targets from UK, Europe, Australia, Asia and South Africa	Size/market to book/ prior return portfolio BHARs for long run performance	+1, +3 and +5 years for long run performance	−2.39% one year after merger (insig.) −13.2% 3 years after merger (sig.) −22.9% 5 years after mergers (sig.)
Conn et al. (2001)	1984–2000 1,065 acquisitions	UK bidders	Size/prior return portfolio BHARs	Various. Maximum 0 to +36 months	−2.8% for 13 to 24 months (sig.) −2.06% for 25 to 36 months (insig.)
Aw and Chatterjee (2004)	1991–1996 41 acquisitions	UK bidders. Targets from US and Continental Europe	Market adjusted return model Market model	Various. From +6 months to +24 months	−11.54% for +18 months (sig.) −24.40% for +24 months (sig.)
Conn et al. (2005)	1984–1998 1,140 acquisitions	UK bidders. Targets are from all parts of the world.	Size/market to book ratio BHAR and CTAR for Long-run return	+36 months for long run performance	BHAR of −13.37% for all acquisitions from +1 to +36 months (sig.) CTAR of 0.27% for all acquisitions from +1 to +36 months (sig.)
Gregory and McCorriston (2005)	1985–1994 343 acquisitions	UK bidders. Targets are from US, EU and rest of the world	Size/market to book ratio BHAR for long run	+1, +3 and +5 years for long run performance	−0.0065 for +1 year (insig.) −0.0390 for +3 year (insig.) −0.0929 for +5 year (insig.)
Francoeur (2005)	1990–2000 847 acquisitions	Canadian bidders	Size/book to market ratio adjusted BHAR and Calendar time/FF3FM	Various. Maximum from +1 year to +5 years	All returns are negative and statistically insignificant.
Andre et al. (2004)	1980–2000 90 acquisitions	Canadian bidders	Calendar time /FF3FM	+1 to +3 years	Average return for +1 to +3 years is −1.146% (sig.)

FF3FM = Fama-French three factor model; sig. = significant; insig. = insignificant.

et al. (2000) documented that the value of the combined firm increased after the acquisitions. More specifically, the average increase in the value of the combined firm relative to the pre-offer value of the combined firm is 7.57% and statistically significant. Although majority of the studies have reported positive short-run bidders' performance, it is important to note that others have found that bidding firms have statistically insignificant bidder returns and negative performance. The controversy surrounding bidder's returns also exists in case of long-term bidders' performance, of which researchers have found that the returns are not significantly different from zero and, in some cases, indicate a statistically negative bidder performance. However, one bright side of the analysis is that although there is a controversy regarding short- and long-run bidder performance, there is strong evidence of positive performance of combined firm. A number of studies have concluded that CBM&A do create value for the combined firm shareholders.

3.3.1   Factors Affecting CBM&A Performance of Developed Country Firms

A number of scholars have been suggested that a number of factors may affect the return of target and bidding firms' shareholders. It should be mentioned here that some of these factors are common in the sense that they may affect the return for both the target and bidding firms' shareholders. Moreover, some factors specifically affect either the return of target firms' or the bidding firms' shareholders. Prominent among the factors found in the literature include: method of payment (Wansley et al., 1983; Cebenoyan et al., 1992; Cheng and Chan, 1995; Fuller and Glatzer, 2003; Danbolt, 2004), the origin or nationality of acquiring company (Cakici et al., 1991); lower tax in the target country (Cheng and Chan, 1995; Lessard, 1995; Eun et al., 1996; Kiymaz and Mukherjee, 2000; Goergen and Renneboog, 2003, 2004; Chari et al., 2004). Industry variation of the target may also affect target return. For example, Cakici et al. (1991) have found that abnormal returns to the target firms are significantly higher in the manufacturing, oil and gas industries compared to other industries in the economy such as leisure, entertainment, publishing or textiles. Another important determinant of target return is acquisition type. Danbolt (2004) reported that return to the target firms are higher in vertical acquisitions compared to horizontal or conglomerate acquisitions. Similarly, Cakici et al. (1996) have found that target returns are higher for conglomerate acquisitions followed by horizontal and vertical acquisitions. Exchange-rate variation between target and acquiring firm's country may also affect target return. Harris and Ravenscraft (1991) stated that target return is significantly higher when buyers' currency is stronger relative to targets' currency. Similar views regarding the impact of the exchange rate and the target gain have been put forward by Cebenoyan et al. (1992), Dewenter (1995b), and Kiymaz and Mukherjee (2000). Cultural and industrial relatedness amongst the target and bidding firms constitute an important factor that may enhance the return of the target firm's shareholders. The empirical literature has identified a positive relation between relatedness and target return (Marr et al., 1993; Danbolt, 2004). Target size is also an influential factor that may affect target return. There should be a negative relation between the target size and the target return in the sense that smaller targets are better to manage and therefore should be more attractive to the bidders. Pettway et al. (1993), Marr et al. (1993) and Danbolt (2004) concluded that smaller target earn better return in case of CBM&A. However, Goergen and Renneboog (2003, 2004) could not find significant relationship between target size and target return. Dunne and Ndubizu (1995) have stated that accounting policies and the experience of the acquirers may affect the target return. Moreover, the study concluded that those with previous acquisition experience in the targets' market transfer more wealth to target shareholders than do those entering the targets' market for the first time. Eun et al. (1996) also could not find significant evidence in favour of acquirers' experience as an influencing factor of target return. Lessard (1995) has stated that the timing of acquisition and the proportion of interest acquired can also influence the target return. Kiymaz and Mukherjee (2000) and Servaes and Zenner (1994) have also subscribed the idea that proportion of interest acquired may influence the target return. Sarvaes and Zenner (1994) have reported that the acquisition of whole company provides better a return to the target firms compared to acquisition of a partial interest of target firm. The authors have also pointed out that size of the pre-bid stake of acquiring firm in the target firm can also affect the target return. The higher the pre-bid stake, the lower will be target return. But Danbolt (2004) could not support this finding. Kiymaz and Mukherjee (2000) indicated that economic co-movement between target and bidding firms influence the target return whereas Swenson (1993) has provided support that target firm's possession of intangible assets boosts target return.

3.3.2   Performance of Emerging Economy Firms

Acquisitions studies examining value creation have focus predominantly on the acquirers from emerging economy firms (EEFs) with virtually no attention on target firms. The studies on value creation of EEFS have approached the subject using stock market-based performance measures, case studies and survey techniques to examine value creation. Among these methods, researchers have typically employed the event study methodology (see Boateng et al., 2008; Aybar and Ficici, 2009; Kohli and Mann, 2012; Bhagat et al., 2011; Gubbi et al., 2010). A majority of the studies have reported significant positive abnormal returns for acquirers (see Boateng et al., 2008; Wu and Xie, 2010; Bhagat et al., 2011; Kohli and Mann, 2012; Gubbi et al., 2010) with one study, that is Aybar and Ficici (2009), reporting value destruction for EEFs. Using a sample of 27 acquiring firms from China, Boateng et al. (2008) found that Chinese firms experience significant and positive wealth gains for shareholders. Similarly, Bhagat et al. (2011) examined 678 firms from eight emerging countries, namely Brazil, China, India, Malaysia, Mexico, Philippines, Russia and South Africa, and documented positive and significant returns for acquiring firms. However, a similar study by Aybar and Ficici (2009) of 14 emerging economies using a sample 433 over the 1991–2004 period reported that on average, CBM&A of emerging economies do not create value but point to value destruction for more than half the transactions analysed over two- and three-day event window. The study by Gubbi et al. (2010) on Indian firms reported mean cumulative abnormal returns (CARs) of 2.58% over an 11-day event window for shareholders. It is worth pointing out that these studies look at only the acquirer returns, that no study has investigated the target firm returns and that the paucity research may be due to the difficulty of collecting data on target firms. An important distinction emanating from this review is that overwhelmingly, EEFs engaging in CBM&A tend to create value in the short term, and this is in sharp contrasts to their counterparts in advanced market economies, where several researchers have documented a mixed results for acquirers (see Markides and Ittner, 1994; Datta and Puia, 1995; Cakici et al., 1996; Eun et al., 1996; Corhay and Rad, 2000; Kiymaz, 2003; Aw and Chatterjee, 2004) for positive and negative abnormal returns for the shareholders of acquiring firms.

Similarly, studies using case studies and survey have arrived at same conclusion that CBM&A from EEFs are a value-accretive strategy. Using a case study and s survey, respectively, Deng (2010) and Wu and Xie (2010) reported that CBM&A create value for EEF acquiring firms. Table 3.4 provides a summary of the performance of CBM&A.

3.4   SUMMARY AND FUTURE RESEARCH

The growing importance of CBM&A as an entry mode has attracted a number of researchers to examine the CBM&A performance. This study attempts to evaluate and synthesize the literature of CBM&A performance in the short- and long-run term reported in the earlier studies along with the factors that influence the performance. The study finds some interesting results that are comparable with other earlier review papers on domestic mergers and acquisitions. It is apparent from the review that target firms are clear winners in CBM&A. The review suggests that the abnormal return for the target firm shareholders varies between 4% and 40%. The results for the acquiring firm performance indicate that acquirers are not clear winners. Among the 39 studies (reviewed in this chapter) in respect of acquiring firms, only five reported significant negative bidder performance. Studies that found positive performance of acquiring firms have reported abnormal return between 0.29% and 10% for the shareholders of the acquiring firms. Although the short-run acquiring firms' performance shows mixed results, most of the studies on long run performance have reported statistically negative performance.

Our review identified several important areas relating to CBM&A where there are gaps in research. First, the study found that the CBM&A performance research is heavily skewed to the US sample. Among the 27 target firm performance studies reviewed in this chapter, only four studies (Goergen and Renneboog, 2003, 2004; Danbolt, 2004; Campa and Hernando, 2004) have examined the performance of UK target firms. The study also reveals that among the

Table 3.4 Summary of Studies on Performance of CBM&A by Emerging Economy Firms

Authors	Purpose	Theoretical Perspective	Methodology	Key Findings
Boateng et al. (2008)	Examine performance of Chinese CBM&A	Diversification efficiency theory	Event study: CAR Sample of 27 CBM&A from 2000 to 2004 by Chinese firms	Chinese acquiring firms earn 1.32% for a two-day period (0, +1) and the acquiring firms enjoy an overall average positive CAR of 4.4274%.
Aybar and Ficici (2009)	Examine the firm value of cross-border acquisitions by firms from emerging market	Internalization framework	Event study: CAR and cross-sectional regression of 433 CBM&A in 58 countries	On average, acquisitions do not create value but destroy value for more than half of the transactions analyzed.
Chen and Young (2010)	Examine the performance of Chinese cross-border M&As	Institutional theory	Event Study: CAR Sample of 39 Chinese CBM&A deals from 2000 to 2008	The increased government ownership in the acquiring firms is related with investors viewing cross-border M&As in less favorable terms.
Deng (2010)	Use absorptive capacity to explain performance of Chinese cross-border M&As	Resource-based view	Case study. Sample of two high-profile Chinese CBM&A: Lenovo and TCL	The performance of Chinese firms' outward M&A is substantially influenced by the acquiring firms' absorptive capacity at multiple dimensions.
Gubbi et al. (2010)	Examine the value creation from international acquisitions in India	Resource-based view, institutional theory	Event study of 425 Indian firms over 2000–2007 period; OLS regression	Value creation is higher when the target firms are from advanced economic and institutional environments.
Lin and Lee (2010)	Examine the performance of M&As by Taiwanese financial holding corporations (FHCs)	Size effect	Tobin's Q and regression Sample of 14 FHCs over the period 1997 to 2001 and 2001 to 2006	Overall, there is weak evidence of better performance of M&As for 14 FHCs over time.
Soongswang (2010)	Examine the value creation of M&A in Thailand	Economies of scale and scope, diversification	Event study: CAR and BHAR market-adjusted and market models Sample of 39 acquisitions from 1992 to 2002	Takeovers are wealth-creating for bidding firms' shareholders. Announcement month results in positive abnormal returns of 17% and 10% for the bidders.

Study	Objective	Theory	Method/Sample	Findings
Wu and Xie (2010)	Examine the factors influencing Chinese cross-border M&As	Institutional theory	Survey Sample of 165 cross-border acquisitions in the period of 2000–2006	The pre-acquisition performance and proportion of the state shares have a positive impact on the performance of acquiring firms.
Bhagat et al. (2011)	Examine the characteristics and acquirer returns for emerging country cross-border acquisitions	Diversification, operational efficiency and market power	Event study: CAR and BHAR. Sample of 698 acquisitions over 1991–2008 period Cross-sectional regression	Emerging country acquirers experience a positive and significant market response of 1.09% on the announcement day.
Chi et al. (2011)	Examine the performance and characteristics of Chinese listed acquirers	Value creation, ownership	Market Model (CARs), BHARs, CAPM & cross-sectional regression Sample of 1148 M&As from 1998 to 2003	Significant positive abnormal returns before (6 months) and upon M&A announcement and insignificant returns in the long term (6 months after M&As).
Ismail and Krause (2010)	Examine the post-performance of M&As in Egypt	Value creation	Operating performance: Sample of 9 M&As from 1996 to 2003	Profitability statistically significant gains in the years following M&As.
Kohli and Mann (2012)	Analyze determinants of value creation in Indian domestic and cross-border acquisitions	Internalization theory	Event study and regression Sample of 202 CBM&A and 66 domestic acquisitions by Indian firms	CBM&A create significantly higher wealth gains than domestic ones. Cross-border acquisitions.
Mann and Kohli (2011)	Examine the target shareholders' wealth gains of Indian domestic and cross-border acquisitions	Industrial organizational theory and bid-specific factors theory	Event study and regression analysis Sample of 63 domestic acquires and 43 foreign acquirers, 1997–2008 in India	Both domestic and cross-border acquisitions have created value for the target company shareholders on the announcement.

(Continued)

Table 3.4 (Continued)

Authors	Purpose	Theoretical Perspective	Methodology	Key Findings
Al Rahahleh and Wei (2012)	Examine performance of frequent acquirers from 17 emerging firms		Event study Sample of 2340 merger deals in 17 emerging markets from 1985 to June 2008	Serial acquirers in emerging countries on average experience a declining pattern in returns.
Bertrand and Betschinger (2012)	Investigate long term operating performance of domestic and international acquisitions by Russian firms	Market power and diversification	GMM Sample of 600 domestic firms and 120 Russian foreign acquisitions	Domestic and international acquisitions tend to reduce the performance of acquirers.
Bhaumik and Selarka (2012)	Examine the role of ownership concentration in M&As outcome in India	Agency theory	CAR & regression Sample of 228 events from 1995 to 2004	Significant improvement of post-M&A performance.
Zhou et al. (in press)	Examine the role of state ownership in the M&As performance in China	Institutional theory	CARs, BHARs, Operating Cash Flow Returns Sample of 825 transactions from 1994 to 2008	SOE acquirers outperform POE (privately owned enterprise) in the long-run stock performance and operating performance.
Bhabra and Huang (2013)	Examine the performance of M&As by Chinese listed firms	Efficiency theory	Event study: CAR, OLS regression Sample of 136 M&As from 1997 to 2007	Acquiring firms gain significant positive abnormal returns around the announcement date and over the three-year post-acquisition period.
Nicholson and Salaber (2013)	Compare the motives and performance of CBM&A in China and India	Competitive advantage, culture distance	Event study and cross-sectional regression Sample of 203 Indian CBM&A and 63 Chinese CBM&A from 2000–2010	CBM&A conducted by India and China generate significant shareholder wealth creation.

39 studies that examined short-run bidder performance, only ten studies have examined the performance of UK acquiring firms of which four studies have used UK samples exclusively compared to 20 studies that used US samples. This is against the background that the UK acquirers have been playing a dominant role in the international market for corporate control and since 1985 the UK acquirers have spent $25 for every $100 acquisitions in the global CBM&A market. Second, the evidence regarding performance of UK acquiring firms is mixed and inconclusive. For example Mathur et al. (1994), Cakici et al. (1996) and Eun et al. (1996) have documented that the UK acquirers performed poorly compared to other acquirers from Europe, Japan or Australia. It has also been pointed out by Goergen and Renneboog (2003, 2004) that the UK acquirers have outperformed the continental European acquirers. In light of this controversy, further research should attempt to find out the true picture in terms of profitability/losses accruing to the UK acquiring firms and the reasons for their poor performance compared to acquirers from other merger active countries. Third, although the CBM&A activities have been experiencing a significant growth since late 1990s (UNCTAD, 2000), only a few number of studies have examined the acquiring firm performance using recent data. The lack of performance studies using a recent data set has practically hampered further analysis on the impact of the so-called fifth merger wave on the value of the acquiring firm. Fourth, a number of studies on CBM&A activities have evaluated the motives of international expansion through acquisitions theoretically. But there is paucity of research regarding the empirical examination of CBM&A motives and their link to performance. The achievement of M&A motives has a direct link with the performance. We suggest that further research is required to find out the motives of current wave of CBM&A activities and how they affect the long-run performance of CBM&A activities. Fifth, from the evidence provided in this chapter, it is clear that almost all the studies have used share price performance measures for examining the CBM&A performance. However, it must be pointed out that share price based measures have some inherent limitations. Consequently, a number of authors (e.g. Healy et al., 1992; Sudarsanam, 2003) have suggested profitability measures to evaluate M&A performance. More recently, Schoenberg (2006) pointed out the necessity of using multiple measures of acquisition performance to get a true picture of acquisition performance. In light of this discussion and the recent move towards harmonization of accounting practices around the world, future research should examine the CBM&A performance using both share-price performance measures and operating performance measures to get a comprehensive picture of international acquisition performance.

Regarding the value creation of EEFs, we observed that acquiring firms generally earn positive abnormal returns in the short run. However, the factors influencing short-term abnormal returns are not clear. Given that governments in emerging countries exert considerable influences over business compared to their counterparts in advanced countries, future studies should investigate the political and institutional factors as sources of value creation.

REFERENCES

Al Rahahleh, N. and Wei, P.P. (2012). The Performance of Frequent Acquirers: Evidence from Emerging Markets, *Global Finance Journal*, Vol. 23(1), pp. 16–33.

Andrade, G., Mitchell, M. and Stafford, E. (2001). New evidence and perspectives on mergers, *Journal of Economic Perspectives*, Vol. 15(2), pp. 103–120.

Andre, P., Kooli, M. and L'Her, J.-F. (2004). The Long-Run Performance of Mergers and Acquisitions: Evidence from the Canadian Stock Market, *Financial Management*, Vol., 33(4), pp. 27–43.

Aw, M. and Chatterjee, R. (2004). The Performance of UK Firms Acquiring Large Cross-Border and Domestic Takeover Targets, *Applied Financial Economics*, Vol. 14, pp. 337–349.

Aybar, B. & Ficici, A. (2009). Cross-Border Acquisitions and Firm Value: An Analysis of Emerging-Market Multinationals, *Journal of International Business Studies*, Vol. 40, 1317–1338.

Bertrand, O. and Betschinger, M-A. (2012). Performance of Domestic and Cross-Border Acquisitions: Empirical Evidence from Russian Acquirers, *Journal of Comparative Economics*, Vol. 40(3), pp. 413–437.

Bhabra, H. S. and Huang, J. (2013). An Empirical Investigation of Mergers and Acquisitions by Chinese Listed Companies, 1997–2007, *Journal of Multinational Financial Management*, Vol. 23(3), pp. 187–207.

Bhagat, S., Malhotra, S., & Zhu, P.C. (2011). Emerging Country Cross-Border Acquisitions: Characteristics, Acquirer Returns and Cross-Sectional Determinants, *Emerging Markets Review*, Vol. 12(3), pp. 250–271.

Bhaumik, S.K. and Selarka, E. (2012). Does Ownership Concentration Improve M&A Outcomes in Emerging Markets? Evidence from India, *Journal of Corporate Finance*, Vol. 18, pp. 717–726.

Black, E.L., Carnes, T.A and Jandik, T. (2001). *The Long-Run Success of Cross-Border Mergers Acquisitions*, University of Arkansas Working Paper.

Block, S. (2005). Are International Mergers Value Enhancing to Acquirer Shareholders?, *Journal of Global Business*, Vol. 31(Spring), pp. 73–81.

Boateng, A., Wang, Q. & Yang, T.L. (2008). Cross-Border M&As by Chinese Firms: An Analysis of Strategic Motives and Performance, *Thunderbird International Business Review*, Vol. 50(4), pp. 259–270.

Bruner, R.F. (2002). Does M&A Pay? A Survey of Evidence for the Decision Maker, *Journal of Applied Finance*, Vol. 12(Spring/Summer), pp. 48–68.

Cakici, N., Hessel, C.A. and Tandon, T. (1991). Foreign Acquisitions in the United States and the Effect on Shareholder Wealth, *Journal of International Financial Management and Accounting*, Vol. 3(1), pp. 39–60.

Cakici, N., Hessel, C. and Tandon, K. (1996). Foreign Acquisitions in the United States: Effect on Shareholder Wealth of Foreign Acquiring Firms, *Journal of Banking & Finance*, Vol. 20, pp. 307–329.

Campa, J.M. and Hernando, I. (2004). Shareholder Value Creation in European M&As, *European Financial Management*, Vol. 10(1), pp. 47–81.

Cebenoyan, A.S., Papaioannou, G.J. and Travlos, N.G. (1992). Foreign Takeover Activity in the US and Wealth Effects for Target Firm Shareholders, *Financial Management*, Vol. 21(3), pp. 58–68.

Chari, A., Ouimet, P. and Tesar, L.L. (2004). *Cross-Border Mergers and Acquisitions in Emerging Markets: The Stock Market Valuation of Corporate Control*, University of Michigan Working Paper.

Chen, C. and Findley, C. (2003). A Review of Cross-border Mergers and Acquisitions in APEC, *ASIAN-PACIFIC Economic Literature*, Vol. 17(2), pp. 14–38.

Chen, Y.Y. and Young, M.N. (2010). Cross-Border Mergers and Acquisitions by Chinese Listed Companies: A Principal-Principal Perspective, *Asia Pacific Journal of Management*, Vol. 27(3), pp. 523–539.

Cheng, L.T.W. and Chan, K.C. (1995). A Comparative Analysis of the Characteristics of International Takeovers, *Journal of Business Finance & Accounting*, Vol. 22(5), pp. 637–657.

Chi, J., Sun, Q. and Young, M. (2011). Performance and Characteristics of Acquiring Firms in Chinese Stock Market, *Emerging Market Review*, Vol. 12(2), pp. 152–170.

Conn, C., Cosh, A., Guest, P.M. and Hughes, A. (2001). *Long-Run Share Performance of UK Firms Engaging in Cross-Border Acquisitions*, Working Paper 214, Centre for Business Research, University of Cambridge.

Conn, R.L. and Connell, F. (1990). International Mergers: Returns to US and British Firms, *Journal of Business Finance & Accounting*, Vol. 17(5), pp. 689–711.

Conn, R.L., Cosh, A., Guest, P.M. and Hughes, A. (2005). The Impact on UK Acquirers of Domestic, Cross-Border, Public and Private Acquisitions, *Journal of Business Finance&Accounting*, Vol. 32(5&6), pp. 815–870.

Corhay, A. and Rad, A.T. (2000). International Acquisitions and Shareholder Wealth: Evidence from the Netherlands, *International Review of Financial Analysis*, Vol. 9(2), pp. 163–174.

Danbolt, J. (1995). An Analysis of Gains and Losses to Shareholders of Foreign Bidding Companies Engaged in Cross-Border Acquisitions into the United Kingdom: 1986–1991, *European Journal of Finance*, Vol. 1(3), pp. 279–309.

Danbolt, J. (2004). Target Company Cross-Border Effects in Acquisitions into the UK, *European Financial Management*, Vol. 10(1), pp. 83–108.

Datta, D.K. and Puia, G. (1995). Cross-Border Acquisitions: An Examination of the Influence of Relatedness and Cultural Fit on Shareholder Value Creation in US Acquiring Firms, *Management International Review*, Vol. 35(4), pp. 337–359.

Datta, D.K., Pinches, G.E. and Narayanan, V.K. (1992). Factors Influencing Wealth Creation from Mergers and Acquisitions: A Meta-Analysis, *Strategic Management Journal*, Vol. 13(1), pp. 67–86. Deng, P. (2010). What Determines Performance of Cross-Border M&As by Chinese Companies? An Absorptive Capacity Perspective, *Thunderbird International Business Review*, 52(6), pp. 509–524.

Dewenter, K.L. (1995a). Does the Market React Differently to Domestic and Foreign Takeover Announcement? Evidence from the US Chemical and Retail Industries, *Journal of Financial Economics*, Vol. 37, pp. 421–441.

Dewenter, K.L. (1995b). Do Exchange Rate Changes Drive Foreign Direct Investment, *Journal of Business*, Vol. 68(3), pp. 405–433.

Doukas, J. (1995). Overinvestment, Tobin's Q and Gains from Foreign Acquisitions, *Journal of Banking and Finance*, Vol. 19, pp. 1285–1303.

Doukas, J. and Travlos, N.G. (1988). The Effect of Corporate Multinationalism on Shareholders' Wealth: Evidence from International Acquisitions, *Journal of Finance*, Vol. 43, pp. 1161–1175.

Dunne, K.K. and Ndubizu, G.A. (1995). International Acquisitions Accounting Methods and Corporate Multinationalism: Evidence from Foreign Acquisitions, *Journal of International Business Studies*, Vol. 26, pp. 361–377.

Eckbo, B.E. and Thorburn, K.S. (2000). Gains to Bidder Firms Revisited: Domestic and Foreign Acquisitions in Canada, *Journal of Financial and Quantitative Analysis*, Vol. 35(1), pp. 1–25.

Eun, C.S., Kolodny, R. and Scheraga, C. (1996). Cross-Border Acquisitions and Shareholder Wealth: Tests of Synergy and Internalization Hypotheses, *Journal of Banking and Finance*, Vol. 20, pp. 1559–1582.

Fama, E.F., Fisher, L., Jensen, M.C. and Roll, R. (1969). The Adjustment of Stock Prices to New Information, *International Economic Review*, Vol. 10(1), pp. 1–21.

Fatemi, A.M. and Furtado, E.P.H. (1988). An Empirical Investigation of the Wealth Effects of Foreign Acquisitions, in S.J. Khoury and A. Ghosh (eds.), *Recent Developments in International Banking and Finance*, Vol. 2. Virginia: Lexington Books, pp. 363–379.

Francoeur, C. (2005). *The Long-Run Performance of Cross-Border Mergers and Acquisitions: The Canadian Evidence*, HEC Montreal Working Paper.

Fuller, K.P. and Glatzer, M.B. (2003). Method-of-Payment Choice for International Targets, *Advances in Financial Economics*, Vol. 8, pp. 47–64.

Gleason, K.C., Gregory, D.W. and Wiggins, R.A. (2002). Wealth Effects of US Acquisitions in the Pacific Rim, *Journal of Business & Economic Studies*, Vol. 8(2), pp. 28–47.

Goergen, M. and Renneboog, L. (2003). Value Creation in Large European Mergers and Acquisitions, *Advances in Mergers and Acquisitions*, Vol. 2, pp. 97–146.

Goergen, M. and Renneboog, L. (2004). Shareholder Wealth Effects of European Domestic and Cross-border Takeover Bids, *European Financial Management*, Vol. 10(1), pp. 9–45.

Gregory, A. and McCorriston, S. (2005). Foreign Acquisitions by UK Limited Companies: Short- and Long-Run Performance, *Journal of Empirical Finance*, Vol. 12(1), pp. 99–125.

Gubbi, S.R., Aulakh, P.S., Ray, S., Sarkar, M.B. and Chittoor, R. (2010). Do International Acquisitions by Emerging-Economy Firms Create Shareholder Value? The Case of India Firms, *Journal of International Business Studies*, Vol. 41, pp. 397–418.

Guo, E., Keown, A.J. and Sen, N. (1995). An Explanation of Bidder Returns in Corporate Acquisitions: The Case of Japanese Acquisitions of US Firms, *Japan and the World Economy*, Vol. 7, pp. 145–154.

Harris, R.S. and Ravenscraft, D.J. (1991). The Role of Acquisitions in Foreign Direct Investment: Evidence from the US Stock Market, *Journal of Finance*, Vol. 46(3), pp. 401–417.

Healy, P.M., Palepu, K.G. and Ruback, R.S. (1992). Does Corporate Performance Improve after Merger, *Journal of Financial Economics*, Vol. 31, pp. 135–175.

Ismail, I. and Krause, A. (2010). Determinants of the Method of Payment in Mergers and Acquisitions, *Quarterly Review of Economics and Finance*, Vol. 50(4), pp. 471–484.

Jarrel, G., Brickley, J. and Natter, J. (1988). The Market for Corporate Control: The Empirical Evidence since 1980, *Journal of Economic Perspectives*, Vol. 2(2), pp. 49–68.

Jensen, M.C. and Ruback, R.S. (1983). The Market for Corporate Control: The Scientific Evidence, *Journal of Financial Economics*, Vol. 11, pp. 5–50.

Kang, J.-K. (1993). The International Market for Corporate Control: Mergers and Acquisitions of US Firms by Japanese Firms, *Journal of Financial Economics*, Vol. 34, pp. 345–371.

Kiymaz, H. (2003). Wealth Effect for US Acquirers from Foreign Direct Investments, *Journal of Business Strategies*, Vol. 20(1), pp. 7–21.

Kiymaz, H. and Mukherjee, T.K. (2000). The Impact of Country Diversification on Wealth Effects in Cross-Border Mergers, *The Financial Review*, Vol. 35(2), pp. 37–58.

Kiymaz, H. and Mukherjee, T.K. (2001). Parameter Shifts when Measuring Wealth Effects in Cross-border Mergers, *Global Finance Journal*, Vol. 12(2), pp. 249–266.

Kohli, R. and Mann, B.J.S. (2012). Analyzing Determinants of Value Creation in Domestic and Cross Border Acquisitions in India, *International Business Review*, Vol. 21(6), pp. 998–1016.

Lessard, J.P. (1995). International Acquisition of US Based Firms: Shareholder Wealth Implications, *American Business Review*, Vol. 13(1), pp. 50–57.

Lessard, J.P. and Robin, A.J. (1991). Acquisition of US Firms by Foreign Firms: Wealth Effects, *American Business Review*, Vol. 9(2), pp. 10–17.

Lin, C-Y. and Lee, H-T. (2010). The Bigger the Better? Merger and Acquisition Performance of Financial Holding Corporations; Empirical Evidence from Taiwan, *Emerging Markets Finance and Trade*, Vol. 46(1), pp. 96–107.

Lin, J.W., Madura, J. and Picou, A. (1994). The Wealth Effects of International Acquisitions and the Impact of the EEC Integration, *Global Finance Journal*, Vol. 5(1), pp. 65–74.

Lowinski, F., Schiereck, D. and Thomas, T.W. (2004). The Effect of Cross-Border Acquisitions on Shareholder Wealth—Evidence from Switzerland, *Review of Quantitative Finance and Accounting*, Vol. 22, pp. 315–330.

Mann, B.J.S. and Kohli, R. (2011). Target Shareholders' Wealth Creation in Domestic and Cross-Border Acquisitions in India, *International Journal of Commerce & Management*, 21(1), pp. 63–81.

Manzon, G.B., Sharp, D.J. and Travlos, N.G. (1994). An Empirical Study of the Consequences of US Tax Rules for International Acquisitions by US Firms, *Journal of Finance*, Vol. 49, pp. 1893–1904.

Markides, C. and Ittner, C.D. (1994). Shareholders Benefit from Corporate International Diversification: Evidence from US International Acquisitions, *Journal of International Business Studies*, Vol. 25(2), pp. 343–366.

Markides, C. and Oyon, D. (1998). International Acquisitions: Do They Create Value for Shareholders, *European Management Journal*, Vol. 16(2), pp. 125–135.

Marr, M.W., Mohta, S. and Spivey, M.F. (1993). An Analysis of Foreign Takeovers in the United States, *Managerial and Decision Economics*, Vol. 14(4), pp. 285–294.

Mathur, I., Chhachhi, I. and Sundaram, S. (1989). Shareholder Returns for International Mergers in the US, *Managerial Finance*, Vol. 15, pp. 23–28.

Mathur, I., Rangan, N., Chhachhi, I. and Sundaram, S. (1994) International Acquisitions in the United States: Evidence from Returns to Foreign Bidders, *Managerial and Decision Economics*, Vol. 15(2), pp. 107–118.

Moeller, S.B and Schlingemann, F.P. (2005). Global Diversification and Bidder Gains: A Comparison between Cross-Border and Domestic Acquisitions, *Journal of Banking and Finance*, Vol. 29, pp. 533–564.

Morck, R. and Yeung, B. (1992). Internalization: An Event Study Test, *Journal of International Economics*, Vol. 33, pp. 41–56.

Nicholson, R.R and Salaber, J. (2013). The Motives and Performance of Cross-Border Acquirers from Emerging Countries: Comparison between Chinese and Indian Firms, *International Business Review*, Vol. 22, pp. 963–980.

Parhizgari, A.M. and De Boyrie, M.E. (1995). Return to Shareholders of US Targeted Companies Acquired by Foreign Corporations, *Applied Financial Economics*, Vol. 5, pp. 265–272.

Pettway, R.H., Sicherman, N.W. and Spiess, D.K. (1993). Japanese Foreign Direct Investment: Wealth Effects from Purchases and Sales of US Assets, *Financial Management*, Vol. 22(4), 82–95.

Schoenberg, R. (2006). Measuring Performance of Corporate Acquisitions: An Empirical Comparison of Alternative Metrics, *British Journal of Management*, Vol. 17(4), pp. 361–370.

Servaes, H. and Zenner, M. (1994). Taxes and Returns to Foreign Acquisitions in the United States, *Financial Management*, Vol. 23(4), pp. 42–56.

Seth, A. Song, K.P. and Pettit, R. (2000). Synergy, Managerialism or Hubris? An Empirical Examination of Motives for Foreign Acquisitions of US Firms, *Journal of International Business Studies*, Vol. 31(3), pp. 387–405.

Seth, A., Song, K.P. and Pettit, R. (2002). Value Creation and Destruction in Cross-Border Acquisitions: An Empirical Analysis of Foreign Acquisitions of US Firms, S*trategic Management Journal*, Vol. 23, pp. 921–940.

Shaked, I., Michel, A. and McClain, D. (1991). The Foreign Acquirer Bonanza: Myth or Reality, *Journal of Business Finance & Accounting*, Vol. 18(3), pp. 431–447.

Shimizu, K., Hitt, M.A., Vaidyanath, D. and Pisano, V. (2004). Theoretical Foundations of Cross-Border Mergers and Acquisitions: A Review of Current Research and Recommendations for the Future, *Journal of International Management*, Vol. 10, pp. 307–353.

Soongswang, A. (2010). M&A for Value Creation: The Experience in Thailand, *Interdisciplinary Journal of Contemporary Research in Business*, Vol. 1(11), 28–50.

Sudarsanam, S. (2003). *Creating Value from Mergers and Acquisitions: The Challenges*, London: Pearson Education Limited.

Swenson, D.L. (1993). Foreign Mergers and Acquisitions in the United States, in K.A. Froot (ed.), *Foreign Direct Investment*, Chicago: University of Chicago Press, pp. 255–281.

United Nations Conference on Trade and Development (UNCTAD) (2000). *World Investment Report 2000: Cross-Border Mergers and Acquisitions and Development*, New York and Geneva: United Nations.

Wansley, J.W., Lane, W.R. and Yang, H.C. (1983). Shareholder Returns to USA Acquired Firms in Foreign and Domestic Acquisitions, *Journal of Business Finance & Accounting*, Vol. 10(4), pp. 647–656.

Wu, C. and Xie, N. (2010). Determinants of Cross-Border Mergers and Acquisition Performance of Chinese Enterprises, *Procedia: Social and Behavior Sciences*, Vol. 2(5), pp. 6896–6905.

Yook, K.C. and McCabe, G.M. (1996). The Effect of International Acquisitions on Shareholders' Wealth, *The Mid-Atlantic Journal of Business*, Vol. 32(1), pp. 5–17.

Zhou, B., Guo, J., Hua, J. and Doukas, A.J. (in press). Does State Ownership Drive M&A Performance? Evidence from China, *European Financial Management*.

Part II

Trends, Patterns, Motives and Determinants of UK Cross-Border Mergers and Acquisitions

4 Trends, Patterns and Drivers of UK Cross-Border Mergers and Acquisitions

4.1 INTRODUCTION

The rapid expansion and popularity of CBM&A have attracted the attention of a number of researchers who have examined acquisitions from various theoretical lens including CBM&A as a mode of entry (Brouthers and Brouthers, 2000; Barkema and Vermeulen, 1998; Hennart and Reddy, 1997), shareholders' wealth creation of CBM&A (Harris and Ravenscraft, 1991; Markides and Ittner, 1994; Eun et al., 1996; Seth et al., 2002; Conn et al., 2005; Gregory and McCorriston, 2005), post-acquisition integration of CBM&A (Weber et al., 1996; Lubatkin et al., 1998; Child et al., 2001) and post-acquisition performance of merging firms (Very et al., 1997; Morosini et al., 1998; Moeller and Schlingemann, 2005). However, studies analysing the trends and patterns of CBM&A flows are relatively few in the academic literature. Notable studies that examined the trends and patterns of CBM&A include Sudarsanam (2003), Chen and Findley (2003) and Kang and Johansson (2000). However, none of these studies has analysed the trends in CBM&A from the UK context. For example, Chen and Findley (2003) examined the trends in CBM&A for the APEC countries and the paper focused on CBM&A activities up to 2000. Sudarsanam also explained the trends from an overall global context with some attention to the trends in the UK up to 2001. Kang and Johansson (2000) also did not pay any attention to the UK and examined cross-border acquisitions up to 1998. This is against the background that the overall flow of worldwide CBM&A has changed after 2000. The increased level of participation of the UK in the global market for corporate control warrants special attention. The focus of this chapter is threefold. First, we examine the general trends and patterns of global CBM&A over the last 20 years starting from 1991 and the related forces that influenced those trends and patterns. Second, we then examine the trends and patterns of UK CBM&A over the same period, along with the evidence of the merger waves in the 1990s. Third, we highlight the forces behind the trends and wave patterns in the UK. We draw the data required for examining CBM&A trends from a number of sources, namely the United Nations Conference on Trade and Development (UNCTAD) FDI database, Thomson One Banker deal database and Information available from Office of National Statistics (ONS) UK.

4.2   GLOBAL CBM&A

4.2.1   Worldwide CBM&A Activities

Table 4.1 reports the global CBM&A activities from 1991 to 2010. The figures in Table 4.1 show a massive increase in global CBM&A activities during the 20-year period. For example the total value of global CBM&A in 1991 was US$80,713 million. This figure increased to US$1,022,725 million in 2007, representing a 13-time increase in global cross-border acquisitions activities compared to the figure in 1991. However, the value of CBM&A decreases to US$338,839 million in 2010 due to worldwide economic slowdown. The value of CBM&A activities also reveals that during this 20-year period, the most dramatic increase happened in the 2000 when the total value reached US$1,143,816 million, representing around a 14-times increase compared to the figure in 1991.

Global CBM&A activities in terms of number of deals also reveal an increasing pattern. The number of deals in 1991 was 2,854. This figure rose to 7,018 in 2007, representing two-and-a-half-fold increase compared to the figure in 1991. The gap in increase of global CBM&A activities in terms of total value and in terms of

Table 4.1   Global CBM&A Activities

Year	CBM&A Value (in Million US$)	CBM&A (No.)	CBM&A as % of GDP	CBM&A as % of M&A	CBM&A as % of FDI
1991	80,713	2,854	0.36	23.81	45.18
1992	79,280	2,721	0.31	24.62	43.09
1993	83,064	2,835	0.34	19.10	35.35
1994	127,110	3,494	0.48	24.12	39.22
1995	186,593	4,247	0.64	22.62	53.78
1996	227,023	4,569	0.76	22.63	57.78
1997	304,848	4,987	1.02	20.36	62.92
1998	531,648	5,597	1.80	23.10	77.15
1999	766,044	6,994	2.50	24.94	70.31
2000	1,143,816	7,894	3.63	35.97	88.85
2001	593,960	6,034	1.90	30.15	77.18
2002	369,789	4,493	1.14	49.84	58.00
2003	296,988	4,562	0.82	24.84	53.69
2004	380,598	5,113	0.92	25.65	50.00
2005	716,302	6,134	1.35	31.76	84.52
2006	880,457	6,974	1.78	28.30	60.23
2007	1,022,725	7,018	1.83	24.71	51.89
2008	706,543	6,425	1.15	23.94	40.51
2009	249,732	4,239	0.43	13.45	21.07
2010	338,839	5,405	0.54	17.10	27.25

Source: Author's calculations based on data available from UCTAD FDI database.

number of deals represents an increase in deal value over the years. For example the average deal value in 1991 was US$28 million. The same was US$145.73 million in 2007. This increase in deal value truly represents the sharp competition in the global market for corporate control. Table 4.1 also presents CBM&A as a percentage of global GDP and global M&A. The figures in Table 4.1 show that in 1991, the global CBM&A activities were 0.36% of world GDP. This figure increased to 1.83% in 2007. This increase was more prominent in 2000 when the share was 3.63%. All these figures indicate that the rate of growth in global CBM&A during the last 20 years was much higher than the rate of growth in global GDP. Besides, the share of CBM&A in the total worldwide M&A flow was 23.81% in 1991. This has increased to 31.76% in 2005. This also reveals that global CBM&A has increased faster than the global M&A flows have. It has been stated by a number of scholars that CBM&A have been a dominant mode of worldwide FDI flows. The figures in Table 4.1 support this contention. The proportion of CBM&A in global FDI flows was 45.18% in 1991. This share increased to a massive 85% in 2005. The average share of CBM&A in FDI has been around 55% over this 20-year period. Another important characteristic of global CBM&A activities during the last 20 years is that more and more countries are coming forward to participate in the global market for corporate control. For example, Table 4.2 shows that in the year 1991, 45 countries participated in cross-border purchase activities, of which 19 countries were from the developing world. However, by the end of 2010, 107 countries participated in cross-border purchase activities, of which 65 countries were from the developing world. This means that more and more countries from the developing world are taking part in the worldwide CBM&A activities. In the case of cross-border sales, 61 countries participated in 1991, of which 35 were from developing countries. By the end of 2010, the number of participating countries increased to 142, of which 99 were from developing world. This indicates that during the last 20 years, a large portion of supply for CBM&A activities came from developing countries.

4.2.2   Regional Trends in Global CBM&A

Although it is evident from Table 4.2 that more and more countries are participating in worldwide CBM&A, the fact remains that developed countries dominate

Table 4.2   Participation of Developed and Developing Countries

Activities	Countries	1991	2010	% Increase
Purchase	Developed	26	42	62
	Developing	19	65	242
	Total	*45*	*107*	*138*
Sales	Developed	26	43	65
	Developing	35	99	183
	Total	*61*	*142*	*133*

Source: Author's calculations based on data available from UCTAD FDI database.

Table 4.3   Participation of Developed and Developing Countries in Global CBM&A Activities

Year	% of Developed Purchase in Total	% of Developed Sales in Total	% of Developing Purchase in Total	% of Developing Sales in Total
1991	95.94	91.74	4.04	7.17
1992	92.07	86.21	7.90	10.34
1993	86.86	81.41	12.98	17.17
1994	88.43	87.04	11.30	11.82
1995	92.79	87.86	7.17	8.84
1996	86.66	82.64	13.06	15.74
1997	88.33	76.13	11.55	21.98
1998	95.72	83.36	4.08	15.55
1999	91.48	88.70	8.28	9.66
2000	95.09	92.33	4.24	6.17
2001	89.93	83.53	9.38	14.45
2002	92.25	83.23	7.46	12.04
2003	85.96	80.95	10.52	14.19
2004	89.28	82.99	10.46	14.37
2005	87.44	83.53	11.61	14.05
2006	79.53	84.30	18.38	14.26
2007	82.30	87.20	14.16	09.82
2008	80.31	82.28	14.98	14.83
2009	64.38	81.50	29.63	15.65
2010	63.65	74.28	28.61	24.45

Source: Author's calculations based on data available from UCTAD FDI database.

the international market for corporate control. Table 4.3 shows that in 1991, the share of developed countries in the total CBM&A purchase was 95.94% compared to 4.04% for the developing countries.

Participation of an increased number of developing countries could not shift the dominance of developed countries even by the end of 2010. The share of developed countries in the CBM&A purchase in 2010 was 63.65% compared to 28.61% for the developing countries. The picture is almost the same as in the case of CBM&A sales. In 1991, the share of developed countries in global cross-border sales was 91.74%. The same was 7.17% for the developing countries. In 2010, the share of developed and developing countries in global cross-border sales was 74.28% and 24.45%, respectively. Among the developed countries, which controlled an average of 86% of global cross-border purchase and 80% of global cross border sales, countries from two regions, namely North America[1] and the European Union (EU),[2] dominated the international market for corporate control. Table 4.4 shows the share of North America, EU and other developed countries[3] in global CBM&A purchase and sales for each year from 1991 to 2010.

Table 4.4 Percentage Share of Regional Participation in Global CBM&A Activities

Year	NA Purchase	NA Sales	EU Purchase	EU Sales	OD Purchase	OD Sales
1991	25.65	39.50	49.17	45.86	21.13	6.80
1992	21.68	23.20	55.99	58.71	14.40	6.55
1993	30.74	26.84	48.91	47.17	7.32	8.18
1994	26.44	38.62	50.29	44.26	11.75	4.92
1995	37.43	34.73	43.66	43.22	11.73	12.86
1996	30.61	34.76	42.71	37.54	13.46	11.81
1997	32.71	29.59	47.27	38.27	9.01	8.95
1998	32.55	42.51	53.62	36.01	9.69	5.52
1999	18.13	36.01	67.61	47.62	5.84	6.01
2000	17.39	35.10	70.21	52.58	7.60	5.95
2001	22.73	38.18	55.41	37.33	12.09	9.50
2002	24.72	24.22	57.95	56.46	9.69	6.54
2003	33.14	25.20	40.81	42.43	12.56	14.67
2004	37.85	26.69	43.27	46.97	8.16	9.33
2005	23.74	18.51	53.99	59.91	9.71	5.11
2006	22.16	26.48	41.69	53.31	15.68	4.51
2007	22.16	26.00	52.60	52.00	7.55	9.61
2008	16.18	37.18	43.41	35.55	20.81	9.56
2009	16.21	20.61	35.92	46.54	12.26	14.35
2010	35.10	27.96	5.11	33.51	23.50	12.82

NA = North America; EU = European Union; OD = other developed countries.
Source: Author's calculations based on data available from UCTAD FDI database.

It is evident from Table 4.4 that the EU controlled the largest share of cross-border purchase and sales claiming an average of 48.00% and 46.00% respectively in world cross-border purchase and sales over the last 20 years. The same for the North America region for the same period was 26.36% and 31.00%, followed by other developed countries claiming 10.94% and 8.18% for cross-border purchase and sales, respectively. It is pertinent to mention that among the developing countries and countries from transition economies participating in worldwide CBM&A purchase activities, countries from Asia are ahead of countries from other regions[4] of the world. For example, from Table 4.5, it is evident that from 1991 to 2010, the total amount of purchase by the developing countries and countries from transition economies was US$1,100,466 million (12.39% of total global CBM&A purchase), of which the share of Asian countries was 59% followed by countries from Latin America and the Caribbean (25.33%), Africa (8.35%) and countries from transition economies (7.5%). Countries from Asia also dominate cross-border sales with a share of 44.26%, followed by countries from Latin America and the Caribbean (35.19%) and countries from transition economies (10.89%).

Table 4.5   Share of Developing and Transition Economies in Total Global Cross-Border Purchase and Sales

CBM&A Purchase (1991–2010)		
Region	Total Value	Share in Developing and Transition Economy's Total
World Total	US$ 8,880,935 million	
Developing and Transition Economies	US$ 1,100,466 million	12.39% in World Total
Asia	US$ 645,850 million	59%
Africa	US$ 91,730 million	8.35%
Latin America and Caribbean	US$ 278,735 million	25.33%
Countries in Transition	US$ 82,640 million	7.5%

CBM&A Sales (1991–2010)		
Region	Total Value	Share in Developing and Transition Economy's Total
World Total	US$ 8,880,935 million	
Developing and Transition Economies	US$ 1,262,842 million	14.22% in World Total
Asia	US$ 558,985 million	44.26%
Africa	US$ 113,434 million	8.98%
Latin America and Caribbean	US$ 444,448 million	35.19%
Countries in Transition	US$ 137,498 million	10.89%

Source: Author's calculations based on data available from UCTAD FDI database.

4.2.3   Sectoral Distribution of Global CBM&A

An examination of the sectoral distribution of global CBM&A purchase shows that manufacturing sector dominated over primary and service sectors from 1991 to 1995.

Panel A of Table 4.6 shows that during that time, the total amount of purchase in manufacturing sector was US$283,441 million, representing 50.91% of total cross-border purchase for the same period. The same for the service sector was US$251,321 million (45.14% of total CBM&A purchase) and US$21,673 million (3.90%) for primary sector.

However, this pattern changed in the subsequent years. For example, from 1996 to 2000, the total amount of purchase in service sector was US$1,869,157 million, representing about 63% of total cross-border purchases during that time. The share of the manufacturing sector and the primary sector in total global cross-border purchase for that period declined to 35.95% and 1.16%, respectively. The dominance of the service sector in cross-border purchase remained

Table 4.6   Sectoral Trends in Global Cross-Border Purchases

Panel A: Cross-Border Purchase

Sector	1991–1995	1996–2000	2001–2005	2006–2010
Total	US$556,761 mil.	US$2,973,379 mil.	US$2,357,637 mil.	US$2,943,159 mil.
Primary	US$21,673 mil.	US$34,555 mil.	US$130,385 mil.	US$262,870 mil.
% in Total	3.90%	1.16%	5.53%	8.93%
Manufacturing	US$283,441 mil.	US$1,068,876 mil.	US$696,522 mil.	US$784,669 mil.
% in Total	50.91%	35.95%	29.54%	26.66%
Service	US$251,321 mil.	US$1,869,157 mil.	US$1,529,324 mil.	US$1,895,621 mil.
% in Total	45.14%	62.86%	64.87%	64.41%

Panel B: Top Five Industries (1991–2010)

Industry	Total	% in Total
Finance	US$ 3,112,707 mil.	35.00%
Transport, Storage and Communication	US$ 1,083,545 mil.	12.20%
Chemical and Chemical Products	US$ 668,280 mil.	7.53%
Electricity, Gas and Water	US$ 435,940 mil.	4.91%
Business Services	US$ 534,963 mil.	6.00%
Total	US$ 5,835,435 mil.	66.00%

Source: Author's calculations based on data available from UCTAD FDI database.

almost the same in the year from 2001 to 2005 and from 2006 to 2010. For example the share of the service sector was 64.87% from 2001 to 2005 and 64.41% from 2006 to 2010. Although acquisition activities in the primary sector slightly increased in that period compared to the previous (8.93% of total cross-border purchases in 2006 to 2010), activities in the manufacturing sector declined further to 26.66% of total global cross-border purchase. Panel B of Table 4.6 shows that from 1991 to 2010, the most active industry in the case of cross-border purchase was finance. Other industries that were also considerably active during that period were transport, storage and communication, chemical and chemical products, electricity, gas and water and business services. These five industries together accounted for almost 66% of total global cross-border purchase during the period 1991 to 2010.

In the case of cross-border sales, data from 1991 to 2010 show that the manufacturing sector dominated the global market for corporate control from 1991 to 1995. But this dominance later shifted to the service sector and continued until 2010. Panel A of Table 4.7 shows that during 1991 to 1995, the total amount of sales in the manufacturing sector was US$276,384 million, representing 49.64% of total cross-border sales for the same period. The same for the service sector was

Table 4.7 Sectoral Trends in Global Cross-Border Sales

Panel A: Cross-Border Sales

Sector	1991–1995	1996–2000	2001–2005	2006–2010
Total	US$556,761 mil.	US$2,973,379 mil.	US$2,357,637 mil.	US$2,943,159 mil.
Primary	US$23,019 mil.	US$47,075 mil.	US$171,144 mil.	US$328,860 mil.
% in Total	4.13%	1.58%	7.26%	11.17%
Manufacturing	US$276,384 mil.	US$1,052,850 mil.	US$803,006 mil.	US$1,080,959 mil.
% in Total	49.64%	35.41%	34.06%	36.73%
Service	US$257,233 mil.	US$1,873,014 mil.	US$1,383,487 mil.	US$1,533,341 mil.
% in Total	46.20%	62.99%	58.68%	52.10%

Panel B: Top Five Industries (1991–2005)

Industry	Total	% in Total
Transport, Storage and Communication	US$1,222,213 mil.	13.76%
Finance	US$1,429,158 mil.	16.09%
Business Services	US$923,219 mil.	10.40%
Chemical and Chemical Products	US$738,379 mil.	8.31%
Electricity, Gas and Water	US$564,857 mil.	6.36%
Total	US$4,877,826 mil.	55.00%

Source: Author's calculations based on data available from UCTAD FDI database.

US$257,233 million (46.20% of total CBM&A sales) and US$23,019 million (4.13%) for the primary sector.

However, this pattern had changed in the following years. For example, from 1996 to 2000, the total amount of sales in the service sector was US$1,873,014 million, representing about 63% of total cross-border sales during that time. The share of the manufacturing sector and the primary sector in total global cross-border sales for that period declined to 35.41% and 1.58%, respectively. The dominance of the service sector in cross-border sales remained almost the same in the year from 2001 to 2005 and from 2006 to 2010. During that time, the share of the service sector was 58.68% and 52.10%, respectively, in total global cross-border sales. Although acquisition activities in the primary sector registered a big jump compared to the previous (from 1.58% to 11.17% of total cross-border sales in 2006–2010), activities in the manufacturing sector declined to 36.73% in the years from 2006 to 2010. Panel B of Table 4.7 shows that from 1991 to 2010, the most active industry in case of cross-border sales was finance. Other industries that were also considerably active during that period were transport, storage and communication, business services, chemical and chemical products, electricity and gas and water. These five industries together accounted for almost 55% of total global cross-border sales during the 1991–2010 period.

4.3   TRENDS IN UK CBM& A ACTIVITIES

The rising trends in worldwide CBM&A have also been evident in the UK. During the 20 years starting from 1991 and ending in 2010, the UK's presence in global CBM&A activities is observed in terms of both purchase and sales. Table 4.8 shows the cross-border purchase and sales activities of UK in terms of both value and number of deals. It is clear from Table 4.8 that the UK has been highly active in CBM&A activities during 1991 to 2010. For example, the amount of cross-border purchase made by UK companies was US$8,501 million in 1991. This increased to US$382,422 million in 2000, representing a massive rise of 45 times the initial figure. The purchase activities later fell in the post-2000 period and dropped to US$19,242 million in 2010 in line with the global slowdown of CBM&A activities. The increased participation of the UK in global international acquisition activities is also evident from CBM&A sales figures for the UK. In 1991, the value of inward acquisition activities in UK was US$13,020 million. This increased to US$171,689 million in 2005. The increased involvement of the UK in worldwide CBM&A activities is also apparent from the number of

Table 4.8   The UK's CBM&A Purchases and Sales (values in million US$)

Year	CBM&A Purchase	CBM&A Purchase (No.)	CBM&A Sales	CBM&A Sales (No.)
1991	8,501	397	13,020	332
1992	12,080	366	7,863	293
1993	19,911	392	9,699	343
1994	26,675	500	11,807	400
1995	29,641	570	36,392	468
1996	36,109	580	31,270	497
1997	58,371	714	39,706	630
1998	95,099	711	91,081	725
1999	214,109	955	132,534	784
2000	382,422	982	180,029	844
2001	111,764	789	68,558	595
2002	69,220	537	52,958	458
2003	56,953	525	31,397	459
2004	47,307	602	58,107	470
2005	90,535	720	171,689	587
2006	58,291	681	125,421	537
2007	89,611	814	171,646	689
2008	45,988	600	147,748	632
2009	15,730	231	25,164	317
2010	19,242	336	58,309	474
Average	*74,378*	*600*	*73,220*	*527*

Source: Author's calculations based on data available from UCTAD FDI database.

purchase and sales deals throughout the period from 1991 to 2010. The average value of UK CBM&A purchase and sales during 1991 to 2010 are US$74,378 million and US$73,220 million, respectively. The gap in average purchase and sales figures indicate that UK companies acquired more foreign companies than were sold to foreign acquirers during the selected period.

The relative importance of the UK in the global market for corporate control is represented in Table 4.9, where it is shown that the UK has been a major player in worldwide and EU CBM&A purchase and sales activities. In addition to yearly figures, Table 4.9 shows that from 1991 to 2010, the share of UK CBM&A purchase in global and EU purchase were 16% and 32%, respectively. The share in CBM&A sales both in global and EU sales were 15.20% and 34.16%, respectively. These figures confirm that the UK has been a major player both in the global and EU market for corporate control.

Table 4.10 shows the aggregate figures of CBM&A activities of the four most active countries in the world. These countries are the UK, the US, Germany and France, and together, they control around 51% of global cross-border purchase and 54% of global cross-border sales during the period from 1991 to 2010.

Table 4.9   The UK's Share in Global and EU CBM&A

Year	UK Purchase	Share in World (%)	Share in EU (%)	UK Sales	Share in World (%)	Share in EU (%)
1991	8,501	10.53	21.42	13,020	16.13	35.17
1992	12,080	15.24	27.21	7,863	9.92	16.89
1993	19,911	23.97	49.01	9,699	11.68	24.76
1994	26,675	20.99	41.73	11,807	9.29	20.99
1995	29,641	15.89	36.38	36,392	19.50	45.13
1996	36,109	15.91	37.24	31,270	13.77	36.70
1997	58,371	19.15	40.51	39,706	13.02	34.03
1998	95,099	17.89	33.36	91,081	17.13	47.57
1999	214,109	27.95	41.34	132,534	17.30	36.33
2000	382,422	33.43	47.62	180,029	15.74	29.94
2001	111,764	18.82	33.96	68,558	11.54	30.92
2002	69,220	18.72	32.30	52,958	14.32	25.37
2003	569,053	19.18	46.99	31,397	10.57	24.92
2004	47,307	12.43	28.73	58,107	15.27	32.50
2005	90,535	12.64	23.41	171,689	23.97	40.00
2006	58,291	09.32	22.36	125,421	20.00	37.63
2007	89,611	08.76	16.66	171,646	16.78	32.53
2008	45,988	06.50	15.00	147,748	20.91	58.82
2009	15,730	06.30	17.54	25,164	10.00	21.65
2010	19,242	05.68	20.45	58,309	17.21	51.36
1991–2010	99,983	16.00	32.00	73,220	15.20	34.16

Source: Author's calculations based on data available from UCTAD FDI database.

Table 4.10   Most Active Countries in CBM&A Purchases and Sales, 1991–2010

Country		CBM&A Purchase	CBM&A Sales
World		*US$8,880,935 mil.*	*US$8,880,935 mil.*
UK	Value	US$1,487,259 mil.	US$1,464,400 mil.
	% in Total	16.75%	16.49%
USA	Value	US$1,689,857 mil.	US$2,253,425 mil.
	% in Total	19.03%	25.37%
Germany	Value	US$633,950 mil.	US$713,014 mil.
	% in Total	7.14%	8.03%
France	Value	US$757,367 mil.	US$322,235 mil.
	% in Total	8.53%	3.63%
Share of Four Countries in Total		*51.44%*	*53.52%*

Source: Author's calculations based on data available from UCTAD FDI database.

Table 4.10 reports that among the four countries, the UK has been the second most active in cross-border purchase activities. The share of the UK in global purchase activities was 16.75% for the 20 years starting in 1991. For the US, France and Germany, it was 19.03%, 7.14% and 8.53%, respectively. In the case of cross-border sales, the UK was second to the US, with a share of 16.49% in total global CBM&A sales. For the US, Germany and France, it was 25.37%, 8.03% and 3.63%, respectively. These figures clearly point out that during the 1991–2010 period, the UK was one of the leading countries in the world as a cross-border acquirer and as a target nation. Another interesting aspect of UK CBM&A is that the majority of cross-border purchase and sales transactions were carried out with the US and in EU countries. Table 4.11 shows that almost 85% of UK purchases during 1991 to 2010 were either in the US or in the EU. The same is true for cross-border sales. The figures in Table 4.11 show that 85% of the inward flow of CBM&A activities to the UK came from either the US or from the EU. More specifically, the UK acquired more US companies than EU companies, but EU countries have invested more in the UK than has the US.

Table 4.11   Percentage Share of UK's Cross-Border Purchases and Sales by Region, 1991–2010

Region/Country	Purchase	Sales
US	49.00%	36.18%
EU	37.50%	48.74%
Other Developed Countries	6.81%	8.48%
Developing Countries	6.69%	6.60%

Source: Author's calculations based on data available from UCTAD FDI database.

Table 4.12   Distribution of the UK's Cross-Border Purchases and Sales Activities Based on Number of Completed Deals in Major Industries, 1991–2010

Industry	Cross-Border Purchase (% in Total)	Cross-Border Sales (% in Total)
Consumer Staples	8.73	6.98
Consumer Products and Services	12.22	12.07
Energy and Power	5.19	4.96
Finance	8.74	8.80
High Technology	13.84	12.29
Industrial	16.43	17.66
Material	12.02	9.81
Media and Entertainment	9.02	11.77
Telecommunication	4.31	2.41
Others	9.50	13.25

Source: Author's calculations based on data available from Thomson One Banker Deal database.

4.4   TRENDS OF UK CBM&A BY INDUSTRY

Table 4.12 shows the industrial pattern of UK CBM&A from 1991 to 2010. It is clear from the table that in terms of number of completed deals, the UK acquired most in the industrial sector (16.43%), followed by high technology (14%), consumer products and services (12.22%), material (12%) and media and entertainment (9%). On the other hand, as a target nation, the UK attracted most acquisitions in the industrial sector (17.66%), followed by the high-technology sector (12.29%), consumer products and services (12.07%) and media and entertainment (11.77%).

4.5   THE WAVE PATTERN IN UK CBM&A ACTIVITIES

There is empirical support for the notion that merger and acquisitions come in waves (Mitchell and Mulherin, 1996; Mulherin and Boone, 2000; Andre et al., 2004). The world has seen four distinct time phases of increased M&A activities over the past century (Weston et al., 2004). Generally, merger waves can be defined as the growth in M&A activities in a massive scale in terms of both value and numbers around a specific period. Reid (1968, p. 15) defined M&A waves as the periods characterized by a relatively large number of mergers reported simultaneously in many industries. Based on this definition, Auster and Sirower (2002) stated that merger waves can only occur when companies not previously doing deals begin to do them or when companies active in the merger and acquisitions market are doing more deals. Several authors have tried to detect the existence of merger waves including Nelson (1959), Melicher et al. (1983), Golbe and White (1988), Scherer and Ross (1990), Town (1992), Linn and Zhu (1997), Barkoulas et al. (2001) and Resende (2005). All these studies have found significant M&A activities clustered around a specific period. The main methodology used in those studies varies from simple time-series analysis to the use of the sine curve, the auto-regressive model and the Markov-switching model. Although these studies have discovered that there exists wave patterns in M&A activities over the past century, analysis of wave pattern in CBM&A activities in the 1990s in general and UK CBM&A are scant in the literature (see Gugler et al., 2012). The massive growth in UK CBM&A activities clearly warrants attention, and it will be interesting to see that whether this significant increase in UK CBM&A activities actually follow any wave pattern.

To shed light on the wave pattern in UK CBM&A activities in the 1990s, this study uses the methodology used by Carow et al. (2004). These authors have identified the wave by finding out a peak year for M&A activities and then working backwards in time until they find a year in which the number or value of acquisition is less than three times the peak year activity. The trough year, during which the acquisition activities are less than one-third the peak year's activities, should be the start of a merger wave. To find the end of a merger wave, the authors move forward through time from the peak year to find a year during which the acquisition activities is again one-third of the peak year's. The year before this second or forward trough year is the ending of the merger wave. Following this methodology, and using quarterly average values of cross-border purchase and sales to find yearly values from 1997 to 2006, this study finds that a wave in UK cross-border purchase and sales activities started in 1997 and ended in 2000. Data on CBM&A sales also show that another wave started in 2003 and reached a peak in 2005. These facts are presented in Figure 4.1.

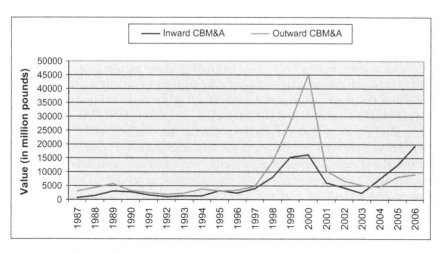

Figure 4.1   Wave in UK CBM&A

4.6   THEORIES OF M&A WAVES

A number of studies have analysed the economic and strategic reasons for M&A. Andre et al. (2004) pointed out that the key reasons for M&A formation include efficiency related reasons that lead to synergistic gains, market power, market discipline, managerialism and diversification. The OLI Paradigm (Dunning, 1992), transaction cost theory (Buckley and Casson, 1976) and the theory of internalization (Rugman, 1980) have also pointed out several reasons to form CBM&A, including internalization and reverse internalization, reduction of transaction cost in the global market for corporate control, taking advantage of suitable and favourable locations and access of proprietary assets to gain competitive advantage (see Chen and Findley, 2003, and UNCTAD, 2000, for a range of reasons to form CBM&A). These theoretical reasons can explain part of the M&A flows but are not sufficient to explain the sudden changes in M&A flows specific to any particular period during which specific reasons become more important for those sudden changes. We discuss in brief the environmental causes of merger waves in the following sub-sections.

4.6.1   Economic Disturbance Theory and Environmental Factors

In an attempt to explain the causes of merger waves, Gort (1969) developed the economic disturbance theory of merger waves. According to this model, merger waves are caused by economic disturbances which create disequilibrium in the product markets. Simply put, economic disturbances cause changes in individual expectation and increase the general level of uncertainty. Thus, the economic disturbances change the ordering of individual expectations in that previous non-owners of assets now place a higher value on these assets than their owners and the converse is true (Trautwein, 1990). The result is a merger wave. Gort's model appears in line with the occurrence of merger waves during the economic growth worldwide. For example, the merger wave from 1916 to 1929 was due to the worldwide economic boom in the post–World War I period and the lenient securities law at that time. The stock market crash in 1929 put an end to this second merger wave. It is important to point out that although economic disturbance may partly explain the wave behaviour, the causes of waves may come from a wider range of influences including political and technological factors (Sudarsanam, 2003). UNCTAD (2000) and Kang and Johansson (2000) pointed out that the spectacular growth in CBM&A activities in 1990s was mainly due to various technology and government related factors. Rapid technological changes in the 1990s and increased liberalization of international capital movements and deregulations in several economic sectors have motivated business enterprises to form partnerships through friendly deals to achieve common business interests. Kang and Johansson have pointed out that technological change has different types of effects in stimulating CBM&A. First, improvement in communication technology has helped to reduce communication and transport costs that have favoured international expansion of firms. Second, new information technology has also helped managers to exercise flexible management techniques in an efficient manner in the international arena. Third, technological change has shortened the product life cycle. This in turn has increased the uncertainty related to technology intensive products and increased R&D costs to find new alternatives. To cope with the uncertainty arising from technological advancements and increased R&D expenditures, firms are forced to form various unions and strategic alliances that have increased the global CBM&A activities. The surge in CBM&A in the service sector in the 1990s was mainly contributed by technological advancements in the telecommunications and media and information industries. A notable extension of technological innovation to explain merger wave come from Jovanovic and Rousseau (2002), who suggested that well-managed companies with high Qs increase their merger activity and lead the merger wave. According to Gugler et al. (2012), a major technological advance increases the profitability of investment and leads to an increase in many companies' Tobin's Qs. These increases in Qs generate a stock market boom and merger wave. Major technological changes affect all companies in an economy, not just those listed on stock exchanges. If the rising stock prices reflect an increased potential for making profitable acquisitions due to common underlying technological factors, then all firms, not just listed firms, will engage in M&A activities. For example, the late 1990s' stock market boom was a result of innovations in information technology that also led to increased opportunities for profitable mergers.

Among the government related factors, liberalization of international capital flows, deregulation of FDI policies, privatization and promotion of regional integration contributed to the global surge in CBM&A. UNCTAD (2000) stated that one of the most important characteristics of the 1990s was the existence of a liberalized capital market around the world. Most of the developed countries have completely liberalized their capital accounts with unrestricted facilities for cross-border loans and credits, foreign currency deposits and portfolio investments. The study also reported that liberalization of capital markets is becoming popular in developing countries and this has opened up greater participation of those countries in global CBM&A activities. UNCTAD (2006) reported that from 1992 to 2005, there were 2,117 regulatory changes relating to FDI, of which 2,078 (98.16%) changes were favourable to FDI. These changes undoubtedly inspired the global expansion of CBM&A activities which is evident from the fact that more and more countries are participating in the global market for corporate control. In fact, the impact of worldwide deregulation to explain global M&A activity was so important that, Andre et al. (2004) stated that the 1990s were the 'decade of deregulation'. Privatization programs, especially in Latin American countries and countries from transition economies have also increased international M&A activities. Privatization programs in those countries increased the supply of target firms in the international market for corporate control. Table 4.5 shows that the share of countries from Latin America and transition economies are more in CBM&A sales (48% and 9%, respectively) than in CBM&A purchase (38% and 4%, respectively). Regional integration such as the European Union also provided opportunities for expansion through CBM&A. The formation of the Single

European Market in 1992 and the introduction of a common currency in the EU zone in 1999 have stimulated global CBM&A in general and within the EU in particular (Sudarsanam, 2003).

4.7   THE DRIVING FORCES OF UK CBM&A

It has been documented that the UK has been keeping pace with the massive growth in global CBM&A activities since 1991. From Table 4.10, it is evident that the UK has been the second-largest acquiring nation and second-largest target nation in the world during the last 20 years, starting from 1991. Along with the common reasons such as technological change, liberalization of capital markets and deregulations that contributed to the global expansion of CBM&A, some other factors have helped the UK take a leading position in the global market for corporate control. The following are some of those important factors that helped the UK to register a massive growth in CBM&A:

1. Acquisitions laws in the UK are more lenient and favourable to the related parties who are interested in mergers or acquisitions. Miller (2000) and Sudarsanam (2003) have pointed out that UK acquisition laws are more liberal compared to any other country in the world and favour the free play of market forces in the takeover context. The UK also imposes limits on available takeover defence strategies that ultimately help increase the level of takeover activities.

2. According to the 2005 Investment Climate Report published by the US Department of State (US Department of State, Bureau of Economic and Business Affairs, 2005), the UK is the most favoured inward investment location in Europe, attracting about a quarter of all direct investment in the EU. About 40% of US, Japanese and Asian investment into the EU goes to the UK, which is the home to more leading global corporations than any other EU nation. The report also states that with few exceptions, the UK does not discriminate between nationals and foreign individuals in the formation and operation of private companies. Once established in the UK, foreign-owned companies are treated no differently than UK firms are. Within the EU, the British government is a strong defender of the rights of any British-registered company, irrespective of its ownership's nationality. The UK's liberal policies and fewer government interventions towards foreign direct investments have also been indicated by the OECD (2002).

3. The US Department of State, Bureau of Economic and Business Affairs (2005) has stated that long-term political, economic and regulatory stability, coupled with relatively low rates of taxation and inflation, make the UK particularly attractive to foreign investors. The UK taxes corporations at a main rate of 30%, with small companies being taxed at a rate of 19%. The UK has a simple system of personal income tax, with one of the lowest top

marginal rates of any EU country (40%). Other marginal tax rates in the UK are 10% and 22%, respectively.

4. The British pound sterling is a free-floating currency with no restrictions on its transfer or conversion. There is no exchange control restricting the transfer of funds associated with an investment into or out of the UK. All exchange controls were repealed in 1987. The non-existence of exchange control and relatively strong position of British currency throughout the 1990s (Daneshkhu, 2007) have helped a greater level of cross-border purchase by British firms.

5. An efficient and sophisticated capital market with world-class facilities is the key for attracting foreign investments and also for making investments abroad. The US Department of State, Bureau of Economic and Business Affairs (2005) and the OECD (2002) have stated that London is one of the world's largest and most comprehensive financial centres. London offers all forms of financial services—commercial banking, investment banking, insurance, venture capital, stock and currency brokers, fund managers, commodity dealers, accounting and legal services, cross-border bank lending, international bond issuance and trading and foreign exchange trading, as well as electronic clearing and settlement systems and bank payments systems. London is highly regarded by investors because of its solid regulatory, legal and tax environment, its supportive market infrastructure and its dynamic and highly skilled workforce. Foreign investors in the UK are able to obtain credit in the local market at normal market terms, and a wide range of credit instruments is available. London's markets have the advantage of bridging the gap between the day's trading in the US market and the opening of the Asian markets. The UK banking sector is the third largest in the world after the US and Japan, with nearly 700 banks authorized to do business in the UK. All these clearly play a vital role for the UK's increased participation in global market for corporate control.

6. The OLI Paradigm (Dunning, 1992) suggests that one of the principal motivations for firms to go abroad is to exploit location advantages of the host country. Labour productivity is one of the most important factors that a firm should consider in making location decisions. The DTI (2006) reported that the UK's labour productivity is behind the labour productivity in the US, Germany or even France. This has led some UK firms to go abroad to ensure the maximum benefit of their investments. According to the DTI (2006), the UK is also behind in terms of wage levels compared to various emerging economies. The wage level of those countries is much lower than that of the UK for a similar level of skills. This has put the UK at a disadvantage, leaving the UK firms to look for investment opportunities abroad. Moreover, the huge economic growth in emerging economies (e.g. in the last decade, the average growth rate in China and the UK was 8.7% and 2.9%, respectively) compared to the UK has also attracted UK firms to go abroad. The UK was also behind the US in terms of economic growth, and this explains a substantial flow of CBM&A to the US from the UK.

7. The investment climate in the UK, in terms of volatility in GDP and volatility in short term interest rates, was favourable throughout the mid 1990s to early 2000. The DTI (2006) reported that both of these two measures, representing the overall investment climate in the UK, were lower throughout the period from 1995 to 2001 compared to major competitor countries such as the US, Germany and France. This has helped the UK to take a leading position in the global CBM&A market.

8. During the 1990s, the UK economy experienced several important shocks in the form of deregulation and privatization, foreign competition and technological innovation in various industries, and these shocks have contributed to an increased level of restructuring activities in the form of CBM&A involving UK companies (Powell and Yawson, 2005). For example, banking, electricity, steel, telecommunication, transport and the water sectors in the UK faced substantial deregulation and privatization during the 1990s (Powell and Yawson, 2005; UNCTAD, 2000, 2006). Privatization also affected the oil and gas, steel and telecommunication industries. The UK aerospace industry faced massive foreign competition in the 1990s due to a shift of concentration of US firms from the UK firms. Foreign competition was also prominent in the automobile, construction and electronics industries. Moreover, falling prices due to technological innovations in electronics and the food processing industry also increased competition in those sectors leading to restructuring activities (Powell and Yawson, 2005).

4.8 CONCLUSION

This chapter has presented an analysis of trends and patterns of UK CBM&A activity for the 20 years starting in 1991 and ending in 2010. An analysis of global trends in CBM&A reveals the following: First, the volume and number of global CBM&A have increased substantially over the 20 years. Second, the average deal value of CBM&A activities has increased tremendously over the 20 years, representing a greater competition in the global market for corporate control. Third, the rate of growth in worldwide CBM&A has been faster than the rate of growth in global GDP and growth in worldwide mergers and acquisitions activities. Fourth, CBM&A have been the most dominant mode of worldwide FDI flows, and this is supported by the fact that during the 20-year period, almost 60% of global FDI flows have been through CBM&A activities. Fifth, more and more countries, especially from the developing world, have come forward to participate in the global market for corporate control. The regional trends in global CBM&A show that developed countries dominated the global market for corporate control both in terms of cross-border purchase and cross-border sales. It is clear from the analysis that EU countries control the largest share in global cross-border purchase and sales (52.06% of global purchase and 46.29% of global sales), followed by countries from North America (27.77% of purchase and 31.58% of sales). Among the developing countries, countries from Asia appear to lead in cross-border purchased and countries from Latin America and the Caribbean are ahead in cross-border sales. An analysis of the sectoral distribution of global CBM&A reveals that the service sector was the most active sector in CBM&A activities from 1996 to 2010, followed by the manufacturing and primary sectors. The most active industries in cross-border purchase and sales for the 1991–2010 period include finance; transport, storage and communications; chemical and chemical products; electricity, gas and water; and business services. This chapter has also found that CBM&A activities in the UK have also kept pace with the huge increase in global CBM&A activities. Data on UK international M&A activities from 1991 to 2010 show that during these 20 years, UK cross-border purchase and sales increased about 11 times and 13 times, respectively. The UK CBM&A flows during that period were so large that it followed the wave pattern as evidenced by the data presented in this study. The analysis reveals that cross-border purchase and sales were particularly higher between 1997 and 2000 and can be compared to wave-like activities. The increased level of participation is also evident from the number of acquisition deals completed over this period. Considering the total flow of cross-border purchase and sales during the period from 1991 to 2010, the UK was the leading country in the case of cross-border purchase, claiming 21.38% of global purchase, and second in terms of cross-border sales, claiming 15.090% of global sales. The UK purchase and sales data also reveal that the US has been the single biggest partner country for both the UK's inward and outward CBM&A activities. Another interesting finding is that from 1991 to 2010, the UK has been most active in industries such as industrial, high technology, consumer product and services, media and entertainment and material.

This study has identified that along with conventional firm- and industry-level factors, technological change, liberalization, deregulation, privatization and regional integration played a vital role for the increased level of global CBM&A activities in the 1990s. In the case of the UK, favourable acquisition laws, non-discriminatory treatment between national and international enterprises, long-term political, economic and regulatory stability along with a lower rate of tax and inflation, sophisticated world-class capital market, uncontrolled exchange regime, labour productivity and wage conditions, overall investment climate and technological change, international competition, deregulation and privatization in various industrial sectors contributed to an increased level of CBM&A activities.

This chapter has analysed the overall and regional trends in global CBM&A activities along with the sectoral trends. CBM&A activities in the UK along with the sectoral distribution and general causes have also been discussed here. The study has found a significant participation of the UK in the international market for corporate control. In fact, the findings suggest that the UK was the leader in the case of both cross-border purchase and sales during the 1991–2010 period. Given this strong position of the UK in the world market for corporate control, it will be interesting to examine the underlying motivations and macroeconomic determinants of this large flow of UK CBM&A. At the same time, it would be worth seeing that how the respective UK corporate entities related with these cross-border acquisition activities performed both in the short run and in the long run. The rest of this book investigates these empirical questions.

NOTES

1. The countries from North America include the US and Canada.
2. The countries from the European Union include all 25 members.
3. The countries from other developed countries include Australia, Greenland, Israel, Japan and New Zealand.
4. The "other region" includes Africa, Latin America and Caribbean and transition economies such as South-East Europe and the CIS.

REFERENCES

Andre, P., Kooli, M. and L'Her, J-F. (2004). The Long-Run Performance of Mergers and Acquisitions: Evidence from the Canadian Stock Market, *Financial Management*, Vol. 33(4), pp. 27–43.

Auster, E.R. and Sirower, M.L. (2002). The Dynamics of Merger and Acquisition Waves: A Three-Stage Conceptual Framework with Implications for Practice, *The Journal of Applied Behavioral Science*, Vol. 38(2), pp. 216–244.

Barkema, H. and Vermeulen, F. (1998). International Expansion through Start-up or Acquisition: A Learning Perspective, *Academy of Management Journal*, Vol. 41(1), pp. 7–26.

Barkoulas, J.T., Baum, C.F. and Chakraborty, A. (2001). Waves and Persistence in Merger and Acquisition Activity, *Economic Letters*, Vol. 70, pp. 237–243.

Brouthers, K.D. and Brouthers, L.E. (2000). Acquisition or Greenfield Start-up? Institutional, Cultural and Transaction Cost Influences, *Strategic Management Journal*, Vol. 21, pp. 89–97.

Buckley, P.J. and Casson, M. (1976). *The Future of Multinational Enterprise*, London: Macmillan.

Carow, K., Heron, R. and Saxton, T. (2004). Do Early Birds Get the Return? An Empirical Investigation of Early-Mover Advantages in Acquisitions, *Strategic Management Journal*, Vol. 25, pp. 563–585.

Chen, C. and Findley, C. (2003). A Review of Cross-Border Mergers and Acquisitions in APEC, *ASIAN-PACIFIC Economic Literature*, Vol. 17(2), pp. 14–38.

Child, J., Falkner, D. and Pitkethly, R. (2001). *The Management of International Acquisitions*, Oxford: Oxford University Press.

Conn, R.L., Cosh, A., Guest, P.M. and Hughes, A. (2005). The Impact on UK Acquirers of Domestic, Cross-Border, Public and Private Acquisitions, *Journal of Business Finance & Accounting*, Vol. 32(5/6), pp. 815–870.

Daneshkhu, S. (2007). The Iron Currency: Britain Learns to Live with a Strong Currency, *The Financial Times*, 12 July.

DTI (2006). *UK Productivity and Competitiveness Indicators 2006*, DTI Economics Paper No.17, Department of Trade and Industry, London.

Dunning, J.H. (1992). *Multinational Enterprises and the Global Economy*, New York: Addison-Wesley.

Eun, C.S., Kolodny, R. and Scheraga, C. (1996). Cross-Border Acquisitions and Shareholder Wealth: Tests of the Synergy and Internalization Hypotheses, *Journal of Banking and Finance*, Vol. 20, pp. 1559–1582.

Golbe, D. and White, L. (1988). Catch a Wave: The Time Series Behavior of Mergers, *Review of Economics and Statistics*, Vol. 79, pp. 493–499.

Gort, M. (1969). An Economic Disturbance Theory of Mergers, *Quarterly Journal of Economics*, Vol. 83, pp. 624–642.

Gregory, A. and McCorriston, S. (2005). Foreign Acquisitions by UK Limited Companies: Short- and Long-Run Performance, *Journal of Empirical Finance*, Vol. 12(1), pp. 99–125.

Gugler, K., Mueller, D.C. and Weichselbaumer, M. (2012). The Determinants of Merger Waves: An International Perspective, *International Journal of Industrial Organisation*, Vol. 30, pp.1–15

Harris, R.S. and Ravenscraft, D.J. (1991). The Role of Acquisitions in Foreign Direct Investment: Evidence from the US Stock Market. *Journal of Finance*, Vol. 46(3), pp. 401–417.

Hennart, J.F. and Reddy, S. (1997). The Choice Between Mergers/Acquisitions and Joint Venture: The Case of Japanese Investors in the United States, *Strategic Management Journal*, Vol. 18(1), pp. 1–12.

Jovanovic, B., and Rousseau, P.L. (2002). The Q-Theory of Mergers, *American Economic Review Papers and Proceedings*, May, pp. 198–204.

Kang, N-H. and Johansson, S. (2000). *Cross-Border Mergers and Acquisitions: Their Role in Industrial Globalization*, STI Working Chapter, OECD.

Linn, S.C. and Zhu, Z. (1997). Aggregate Merger Activity: New Evidence on the Wave Hypothesis, *Southern Economic Journal*, Vol. 64, pp. 130–146.

Lubatkin, M., Calori, R., Very, P. and Veiga, J. (1998). Managing Mergers across Borders: A Two-nation Exploration of a Nationally Bound Administrative Heritage, *Organization Science*, Vol. 9(6), pp. 670–684.

Markides, C. and Ittner, C.D. (1994). Shareholders Benefit from Corporate International Diversification: Evidence from US International Acquisitions, *Journal of International Business Studies*, Vol. 25(2), pp. 343–366.

Melicher, R.W., Ledolter, J. and D'Antonio, L.J. (1983). A Time Series Analysis of Aggregate Merger Activity, *Review of Economics and Statistics*, Vol. 65(3), pp. 423–430.

Miller, G.P. (2000). Takeovers: English and American, *European Financial Management*, Vol. 6(4), pp. 533–541.

Mitchell, M.L. and Mulherin, J.H. (1996). The Impact of Industry Shocks on Takeover and Restructuring Activity, *Journal of Financial Economics*, Vol. 41, pp. 193–229.

Moeller, S.B. and Schlingemann, F.P. (2005). Global Diversification and Bidder Gains: A Comparison between Cross-Border and Domestic Acquisitions, *Journal of Banking and Finance*, Vol. 29, pp. 533–564.

Morosini, P., Shane, S. and Singh, H. (1998). National Cultural Distance and Cross-Border Acquisition Performance, *Journal of International Business Studies*, Vol. 29, pp. 137–158.

Mulherin, J.H. and Boone, A.L. (2000). Comparing Acquisitions and Divestitures, *Journal of Corporate Finance*, Vol. 6, pp. 117–139.

Nelson, R.L. (1959). *Merger Movements in American Industry, 1895–1956*, Princeton, NJ: Princeton University Press.

OECD (2002). *Foreign Direct Investment for Development: Maximising Benefits, Minimising Cost*, Paris: Organisation for Economic Cooperation and Development.

Powell, R. and Yawson, A. (2005). Industry Aspects of Takeovers and Divestitures: Evidence from the UK, *Journal of Banking and Finance*, Vol. 29(12), pp. 3015–3040.

Reid, S.R. (1968). *Mergers, Managers and the Economy*, New York: McGraw-Hill.

Resende, M. (2005). *Mergers and Acquisitions Waves in the UK: A Markov-Switching Approach*, EUI Working Chapter Eco. No. 2005/4, Department of Economics, European University Institute.

Rugman, A.M. (1980). Internalization as a General Theory of Foreign Direct Investment: A Re-appraisal of the Literature, *Weltwirtschaftliches Archiv*, Vol. 116, pp. 365–379.

Scherer, F. and Ross, D. (1990). *Industrial Market Structure and Economic Performance*, 3rd Edition, Boston: Houghton Mifflin.

Seth, A., Song, K.P. and Pettit, R. (2002). Value Creation and Destruction in Cross-Border Acquisitions: An Empirical Analysis of Foreign Acquisitions of US Firms, *Strategic Management Journal*, Vol. 23, pp. 921–940.

Sudarsanam, S. (2003). *Creating Value from Mergers and Acquisitions: The Challenges*, London: Pearson Education.

Town, R.J. (1992). Merger Waves and the Structure of Merger and Acquisition Time-Series, *Journal of Applied Econometrics*, Vol. 7, pp. 83–100.

Trautwein, F. (1990). Merger Motives and Merger Prescriptions, *Strategic Management Journal*, Vol. 11(4), pp. 283–295.

United Nations Conference on Trade and Development (UNCTAD) (2000). *World Investment Report 2000: Cross-Border Mergers and Acquisitions and Development*. New York and Geneva: United Nations.

United Nations Conference on Trade and Development (UNCTAD) (2006). *FDI from Developing and Transition Economies: Implications for Development*, New York: United Nations.

US Department of State, Bureau of Economic and Business Affairs (2005). *2005 Investment Climate Statement: United Kingdom*, accessed from http://200- 2009.state.gov/e/eeb/ifd/2005/42195.htm.

Very, P., Lubatkin, M., Calori, R. and Veiga, J. (1997). Relative Standing and the Performance of Recently Acquired European Firms, *Strategic Management Journal*, Vol. 18(8), pp. 593–614.

Weber, Y., Shenkar, O. and Raveh, A. (1996). National and Corporate Fit in M&As: An Exploratory Study, *Management Science*, Vol. 4, pp. 1215–1227.

Weston, J.F., Mitchell, M.L. and Mulherin, J.H. (2004). *Takeovers, Restructuring and Corporate Governance*, 4th Edition, New Jersey: Pearson-Prentice Hall.

5 Motives for UK Cross-Border Mergers and Acquisitions

5.1 INTRODUCTION

What motivates firms to engage in mergers and acquisitions has been a topic of immense interest to academics and practitioners over the past two decades. This interest stems from the various empirical findings which suggest that more than two-thirds of all merger deals are a financial failure when measured in terms of their ability to deliver profitability (Ravenscraft and Scherer, 1987; Tetenbaum, 1999; Hudson and Barnfield, 2001). In a more boarder context, prior studies suggest that the ability for mergers and acquisitions to create value for acquiring shareholders have been mixed. One stream of research has reported significant positive returns for acquirers (see Kang, 1993; Markides and Ittner, 1994; Kiymaz, 2003). On the other hand, other studies have found negative and insignificant bidders' returns (Eun et al., 1996; Datta and Puia, 1995; Aw and Chatterjee, 2004). Studies such as those by Erez-Rein at al. (2004) and Carleton (1997) have noted that M&A, generally, fail to meet the anticipated goals. Despite the apparent failure of many M&A to meet the expected goals we continue to see a rising trends in merger and acquisition activities. For example, the United Nations Conference for Trade and Development (UNCTAD, 2006) reported that the UK is one of the largest acquiring countries in the world with a share of about 30% of the total value of global CBM&A. The question is, Why do companies continue with this activity given the solid evidence of its relative failure? This paradox is central to the study of mergers and acquisitions.

The goals of this chapter are as follows:

1. To identify the relative importance of the motives for engaging in CBM&A
2. To provide a parsimonious set of factors influencing CBM&A for the sample studied
3. To test hypotheses on the way in which the relative importance of motives for CBM&A vary with the characteristics of the sample

The rest of the chapter is organized into four sections. The next section summarizes the extant literature and develops the hypotheses of the study. The third section sets out the methodology and sample characteristics. The fourth section presents the results and discussion. The study's managerial implications and conclusions are presented in the final section.

5.2   SUMMARY OF MAIN RATIONALE BEHIND CBM&A

Explanations for CBM&A have been offered from two theoretical standpoints: (1) studies that regard CBM&A as an entry mode of foreign direct investment (FDI) and therefore use FDI theories to explain the motivation behind CBM&A (Williamson, 1975; Dunning, 1993; Madhok, 1997; Barkema and Vermeulen, 1998; Vermeulen and Barkema, 2001), and (2) studies that regard M&A as a means of maximizing shareholder wealth and performance. We summarize the two distinct strands of theories explaining why CBM&A take place.

5.2.1   CBM&A as a Mode of Foreign Market Entry

The literature on cross-border mergers and acquisitions as a mode of foreign market entry emphasizes that acquiring an existing foreign business enables the acquiring firm to obtain resources (Baum and Oliver, 1991; Hennart, 1991; Eisenhardt and Schoonhoven, 1996; Madhok, 1997), gain access to new markets (Martin et al., 1998; Datta and Puia, 1995), reduce risk (Seth, 1990; Trautwein, 1990; Shleifer and Vishny, 1992; Markides and Ittner, 1994; Denis et al., 2002), avoid transaction costs and facilitate internalization and reverse internalization (Eun et al., 1996; Morck and Yeung, 1992; Markides and Ittner, 1994) and strategic perspective (Caves, 1990; Schenk, 2000).

5.2.2   Maximizing Shareholder Wealth

The second strand of literature revolves around synergy theory (Seth et al., 2000), valuation theory (Gonzalez et al., 1998) and managerialism (Seth et al., 2000; see Chapter 2 for detail review of the motives).

5.3   HYPOTHESES DEVELOPMENT

5.3.1   The Size of the Acquirer

The size of the acquirer can be an important characteristic that may influence the relative importance of the motives for CBM&A. Large acquirers, which are characterized by multi-plant and multi-product firms, have the benefit of achieving scale and scope economies not available to smaller acquirers. Scherer et al. (1975), UNCTAD (2000), Sudarsanam (2003) and Myers and Majluf (1984) have rendered some support by pointing out that firms enjoy financial benefits because of their size. In the case of CBM&A, Chen and Findley (2003) have stated that size may lead to economies of scale and market power. On the other hand, Ingham et al. (1992) suggest that small acquisitions are more beneficial because they are easier to integrate, thereby leading to managerial, operational and financial synergies. Given that research evidence (see

Carleton, 1997; Erez-Rein et al., 2004) suggests that one of the major reasons for the failure of acquisitions is due to problems of integration, the benefits of easier and effective integration could be significant. This leads to the second hypothesis of the study:

> **Hypothesis 1:** *The relative importance of motives for CBM&A will vary with the size of the acquiring firm.*

5.3.2 The Cash Flow of the Acquirer

The acquirer's cash flow may have a significant impact on the motivation for CBM&A. Using the free cash-flow hypothesis, Jensen (1986), suggested that firms with larger free cash flow are more likely to engage in value decreasing mergers compared with firms with a lower level of free cash flow. Other researchers such as Seth et al. (2000, 2002) and Mathur et al. (1994) suggest that the existence of free cash flow in the hands of management may lead to managerialism. In light of the preceding point, we test the following exploratory hypothesis:

> **Hypothesis 2:** *The relative importance of motives for CBM&A will vary with the level of cash-flow of the acquiring firm.*

5.3.3 The Experience of the Acquirer

Large acquirers that have made multiple acquisitions are clearly more experienced than those acquirers that have made single acquisitions. Consequently, large multiple acquirers are more likely to pursue acquisitions with the expectation of exploiting synergistic gains due their larger size and previous acquisition experiences. Schipper and Thompson (1983), Asquith et al. (1983) and Fuller et al. (2002) have documented that multiple acquirers earn significant positive abnormal returns compared to single acquirers. The return characteristics of multiple acquirers support the notion that multiple acquirers are more efficient in exploiting firm- and industry-specific assets to gain synergy from the acquisition event. On the other hand, multiple acquirers may suffer from overconfidence because of their previous experience gained from conducting multiple acquisitions. This overconfidence may lead to the pursuit of further acquisitions motivated by hubris or managerialism (Roll, 1986). Therefore, it is hypothesized that

> **Hypothesis 3:** *The relative importance of motives for CBM&A will vary with the level of experience of the acquiring firm.*

5.3.4 Intangible Assets

The possession of intangible assets by the acquiring firms may be an important determinant of the relative importance of motives for CBM&A. Based on the internalization hypothesis, Markides and Ittner (1994) argued that the operational benefit of international diversification would be greater for firms possessing intangible assets (such as R&D expenditure, technology, brand names, managerial know-how). Similar conclusions have also been made by Seth et al. (2000, 2002), UNCTAD (2000) and Chen and Findley (2003). Seth et al. (2000) have also pointed out that acquirers with better managerial know-how can make acquisitions with a view to improving the target management efficiency and thereby can create managerial synergy. This discussion leads to the following hypothesis:

> **Hypothesis 4:** *The relative importance of motives for CBM&A will vary with the level of intangible assets possessed by acquiring firms.*

5.4   RESEARCH METHODS AND SAMPLE CHARACTERISTICS

The sources of the data were derived from *Waterlow Stock Exchange Yearbook 2006* (Cole, 2006) and *Hoover's Online* (www.hoovers.com). From the prior literature and data collected from press announcements and interviews with senior managers, a list of 21 motives was derived, and this was used to collect data via a survey from senior managers involved in the UK CBM&A. The questions relating to the motives were ex post assessment of senior managers' perceptions of the relative importance of the motives at the time of M&A formation. Respondents were asked, "As far as your company was concerned, how important were the following motives for the mergers and acquisitions?" Responses were assessed using 5-point Likert-type scales (i.e. not at all important = 1; very important = 5). In August 2006, 325 questionnaires were mailed to the senior managers of the UK listed firms involved in CBM&A. After one reminder, 51 usable questionnaires were returned, representing a response rate of 15.69%. This response rate is comparable to similar studies such as Mukherjee et al. (2004), which evaluated the merger motives of US firms achieved a response rate of 11.8%; Morosini et al. (1998), in which there were 52 usable responses (13%); Brouthers et al. (1998), which used 17 Dutch firms; and Walter and Barney (1990), in which there were 32 usable responses.

5.4.1   Characteristics of the Sample

The characteristics of the sample are summarized in Table 5.1. The size of the M&A is classified into small/medium for those having 750 (43.1%) employees or fewer and large for those having greater than 750 (56.9%) employees. The industry categories of the mergers and acquisitions are as follows: manufacturing (47.1%), non-manufacturing (52.9%). Companies with a single acquisition constitute 43.1%, and those with multiple acquisitions, 56.9%. The companies with low cash flows and intangible assets constitute 51% each in their respective categories.

5.4.2   Statistical Analysis

The hypotheses were tested by considering differences in means of the relative importance of the motives. Given the relatively large sample size, it was reasonable to assume that the sample is from a normal distribution and parametric tests were

Table 5.1   Characteristics of the Sample

	Number	%		Number	%
Sector			*Size*		
Manufacturing	24	47.1	Small/medium	22	43.1
Non-manufacturing	27	52.9	Large	29	56.9
Experience			*Cash flows*		
Single Acquisition	22	43.1	Low	26	51
Multiple Acquisition	29	56.9	High	25	49
Intangibles					
Low	26	51			
High	25	49			
Total	*51*	*100*	*Total*	*51*	*100*

used, that is a two-sample *t*-test or an ANOVA as appropriate. The non-parametric equivalent of the preceding tests (Mann–Whitney *U* and the Kruskal–Wallis tests; the results of non-parametric tests are not presented here) were also conducted to remove any doubt that may stem from the nature of the data used in the study.

5.5   RESULTS AND DISCUSSIONS

5.5.1   Relative Importance of Motives for the UK CBM&A

The rank order of the motivations for the CBM&A based on mean measure of the importance of the 21 motives is shown in Table 5.2. Scores are significantly different on the Friedman two-way ANOVA test ($p < 0.001$). For the full set of motives of CBM&A, the median measure is exceeded by seven motives: revenue/profit enhancement (4.66), increasing the market share/power (3.86), speed of expansion into the foreign market (3.68), achieving economies of scale and scope (3.32), pooling complementary assets and skills (3.28), acquisitions of knowledge from target (3.02) and reducing the dominance of the competitors (3.00). It is clear from the table that the highest-ranked motives for M&A are principally concerned with synergy and market development and power.

It is hardly surprising that 'to increase market share' and 'speed of expansion into new market' are highly ranked. This is because the search for new markets and market power are a constant concern for firms in the increasingly competitive environment (UNCTAD, 2000). M&A represent the fastest means of reaching the desired goals when expanding internationally.

The second- and middle-ranked motives concern (those 8–14) with location advantage and internalization. The lowest-ranked group of motives (those ranked 15–21) is concerned with the pursuit of personal gains, managerial synergy and diversification. This is surprising in that it is expected that CBM&A provide access to important managerial resources and enable firms an opportunity to reduce the

Table 5.2   Relative Importance of Motives for UK CBM&A

Motivation	Rank	Mean	SD
Revenue/profit enhancement	1	4.66	0.66
Increasing market share/market power	2	3.86	1.14
Speed of expansion into foreign market	3	3.68	1.30
Achieving economies of scale and scope	4	3.32	1.24
Pooling complementary assets and skills	5	3.28	1.11
Acquisition of knowledge from target	6	3.02	0.94
Reducing dominance of competitors	7	3.00	1.23
Access to local suppliers and customers	8	2.86	1.44
Better control over foreign operation	9	2.74	1.32
Transfer knowledge to target	10	2.72	1.09
Increasing target management efficiency	11	2.70	1.07
Taking advantage of good location	12	2.66	1.60
Increasing the size of the firm	13	2.60	1.25
Reduce the riskiness of the firm	14	2.44	1.01
Increasing debt capacity	15	1.40	0.76
Reducing exchange rate risk	16=	1.34	0.56
Circumventing trade barriers	16=	1.34	0.80
Availability of excess cash	18	1.32	0.74
Avoiding the need of external capital	19	1.30	0.51
Tax advantage	20	1.22	0.51
Enhancing prestige and job security of managers	21	1.12	0.39

$N = 51$; SD = standard deviation.

Notes: The mean is the average on a scale of 1 (not important) to 5 (very important). Scores are significantly different on the Friedman two-way ANOVA test ($p < .001$).

costs and risks of entering into new foreign markets (Porter and Fuller, 1986; Seth, 1990; Boateng and Glaister, 2003). For example, Manzon et al. (1994), Morck and Yeung (1992) and Seth et al. (2000, 2002) have pointed out that the sources of value such as those associated with exchange rate differences, ability to arbitrage tax regimes are unique to international mergers. It seems that risk reduction and managerial synergy appear not to be the main motivation for the CBM&A. However, it important to point out that the results are consistent with the findings that diversification is not always value enhancing for the firm in that diversification increases the information asymmetry between managers and shareholders and the benefits of diversification can be replicated by the individual investors at a relatively cheaper cost (Kiymaz and Mukherjee, 2000; Ahmed et al., 2003).

5.5.2   Factor Analysis of CBM&A Motives

The correlation matrix of 21 CBM&A motives revealed a number of low to moderate intercorrelations. Due to potential conceptual and statistical overlap, an attempt was made to identify a parsimonious set of variables to determine the underlying dimensions governing the full set of 21 motives. Exploratory factor analysis using varimax rotation was used to extract the underlying factors. The factor analysis produced eight underlying factors which make good sense conceptually and explained a total of 74.41% of the observed variance, as shown in Table 5.3. The eight factors may be summarized as operational synergy, financial synergy, managerial synergy, internalization, location advantage, market power, managerialism and diversification.

To further investigate the underlying nature and pattern of the motives for this sample, the analysis was developed by considering the motives in terms of

Table 5.3   Factor Analysis of the UK CBM&A Motives

Factors	Factor Loads	Eigenvalues	% of Variance Explained	Cumulative %
1. Operational Synergy		4.299	20.473	20.473
Revenue or profit enhancement	0.71			
Economies of scale and scope	0.63			
2. Financial Synergy		2.488	11.847	32.320
Increasing the debt capacity	0.76			
Avoiding the need for external capital	0.88			
Exchange rate differential	0.68			
3. Managerial Synergy		2.037	9.700	42.020
Enhancing target management efficiency	0.70			
Pooling complementary assets and skills	0.82			
Better control over foreign operation	0.59			
4. Internalization		1.932	9.198	51.218
Transfer of knowledge to target firm	0.82			
Acquisition of knowledge from target firm	0.58			
5. Location Advantage		1.418	6.752	57.970
Taking advantage of good location	0.65			
Access to local supplier and customer	0.85			
6. Market Development and Power		1.274	6.067	64.037
Increase market share	0.81			
Reducing the dominance of competitors	0.60			
Speed of expansion	0.83			

(Continued)

Table 5.3   (Continued)

Factors	Factor Loads	Eigenvalues	% of Variance Explained	Cumulative %
7. Managerialism		1.155	5.502	69.539
Enhancing the prestige and job security	0.91			
Availability of excess cash	0.53			
Increasing the size of the firm	0.69			
8. Diversification		1.024	4.875	74.414
Circumventing trade barrier	0.74			
Taking advantage of tax differential	0.58			
Reducing the riskiness of the firm	0.61			

Notes: Principal components factor analysis with varimax rotation. K-M-O Measure of Sampling Adequacy = 0.50; Bartlett Test of Sphericity = 407.471 ($p < .0000$).

the characteristics of the sample. For each of the relevant sample characteristics, Tables 5.4 through 5.7 report the means and standard deviations of the eight factors and the individual motives constituting each factor and the appropriate test statistics for comparing differences in mean scores.

5.5.3   The Size of the Acquirer

The motives for CBM&A by acquirer size are shown in Table 5.4. The size of the acquirer's classification was based on number of employees. To facilitate the statistical testing of the motives, we classified firms with more than 750 employees as large firm and those under 750 employees were treated as small/medium enterprise consistent with standard international classification. The results in Table 5.4 shows that there is some support for Hypothesis 1; that is out of eight factors, the relative importance of motives varies for five factors.

Table 5.4 indicates that relative importance of UK CBM&A varies for five factors—operational synergy ($p < .01$), location advantage ($p < .01$), market development and power ($p < .01$), managerialism ($p < .10$) and diversification ($p < .05$). The results indicate that there is a significant difference in the mean scores for four factors, with the factor scores being higher where the size of the acquirer is large. In the case of managerialism, the factor score is higher for smaller firms. The results provide reasonable support for Hypothesis 2 in that the relative importance of CBM&A motives varies with the size of the acquiring firms. The results suggest that large acquirers are more likely to obtain synergistic gains through the economies of scale and scope, market power and taking advantage of good location. This finding is not surprising in that greater size can be an important factor in achieving economies of scale. Wiggins (1981), UNCTAD (2000) and Chen and

Table 5.4 Motives for CBM&A: Acquirer Size

Motivation	Group	Mean	SD	t-Value
Factor 1: Operational Synergy	Small/medium	3.29	0.81	
	Large	4.09	0.69	2.77***
Factor 2: Financial Synergy	Small/medium	1.90	0.50	
	Large	1.69	0.46	1.12
Factor 3: Managerial Synergy	Small/medium	2.36	1.07	
	Large	2.83	0.95	−1.19
Factor 4: Internalization	Small/medium	3.00	1.26	
	Large	2.84	0.73	0.47
Factor 5: Location Advantage	Small/medium	1.50	0.96	
	Large	2.98	1.31	−3.55***
Factor 6: Market Development and Power	Small/medium	2.43	1.34	
	Large	3.96	0.76	−4.37***
Factor 7: Managerialism	Small/medium	2.00	0.43	
	Large	1.61	0.53	1.84*
Factor 8: Diversification	Small/medium	1.69	0.50	
	Large	2.11	0.46	2.22**

*p < .1. **p < .05. ***p < .01.

SD = standard deviation.

Notes: The mean for the factors is the mean of the factor scores. The mean for the individual motives is the average on a scale of 1 (not important) to 5 (very important).

Findley (2003) suggested that scale economies in raising capital may be achieved by large firms in the presence of significant transaction costs in the capital markets. However, this finding is at variance with Boyd and Graham (1991) and Berger (1995), whose studies concluded that being a larger size does not always mean profitability and consequently efficiency. They indicated that medium-size firms rather than very large firms are the most profitable. It is important to mention that mean score for managerialism factor is higher for small/medium firms compared to large firms. This may be due to the individual motives under the managerialism factor, such as increasing the size of the firm and increasing the prestige of the managers appear to lend themselves readily to small/medium firms as managers of small firms have a huge incentive to expand further in order to increase their prestige and job security.

5.5.4 The Cash Flow of the Acquirer

Following the procedure used by Lang et al. (1991), we adjusted the cash flow for depreciation, tax, changes in investment and working capital and used the resulting figure as a proxy for free cash flow. The median level of cash flow was used as the cut-off point, and the acquiring firm with a cash flow higher than the

Table 5.5 Motives for CBM&A: Level of Acquirer's Cash Flow

Motivation	Group: Cash Flow	Mean	SD	t-Value
Factor 1: Operational Synergy	Low	4.24	0.70	
	High	3.77	0.80	2.05**
Factor 2: Financial Synergy	Low	1.62	0.50	
	High	1.76	0.45	−0.96
Factor 3: Managerial Synergy	Low	3.04	0.72	
	High	2.43	1.02	2.28**
Factor 4: Internalization	Low	3.10	0.64	
	High	2.68	0.87	1.77*
Factor 5: Location Advantage	Low	2.90	1.39	
	High	2.50	1.32	0.98
Factor 6: Market Power	Low	3.86	0.94	
	High	3.68	1.04	0.58
Factor 7: Managerialism	Low	1.59	0.54	
	High	1.70	0.48	−0.71
Factor 8: Diversification	Low	2.18	0.38	
	High	1.89	0.53	2.05**

$^*p < .1.$ $^{**}p < .05.$ $^{***}p < .01.$

SD = standard deviation.

Notes: The mean for the factors is the mean of the factor scores. The mean for the individual motives is the average on a scale of 1 (not important) to 5 (very important).

sample median is classified as cash-rich acquirer. The motivation for CBM&A by acquirer's cash flow is shown in Table 5.5. The results tend to provide a reasonable support for Hypothesis 2, with the mean scores being significantly different for four of the eight factors, namely operational synergy ($p < .05$), managerial synergy ($p < .05$), internalization ($p < .10$) and diversification ($p < .05$). In each case, the factor scores are higher for acquirers with low cash flows, suggesting that low levels of cash flows may motivate firms to make acquisitions to obtain synergistic gains, internalization and diversification compared to cash-rich firms. The finding that low cash flow firms may be motivated to achieve synergistic gains and diversification is not surprising in that it may be argued that low-cash firms have a high probability of financial distress and are not well diversified compared to cash-rich firms. Thus, low-cash firms are more likely to engage in CBM&A to diversify and reduce earnings volatility (Wang and Reuer, 2006). However, it is surprising that low-cash-flow firms are motivated to engage in cross-border investment for internalization. It was expected that cash-rich firms were more likely to use the cash resources to develop their competitive advantage through internalization.

5.5.5 The Experience of the Acquirer

Motives for CBM&A and the acquiring firm's experience are shown in Table 5.6. The results show that the mean scores for firms with acquisition experience have

Table 5.6 Motives for CBM& A: Acquisition Experience

Motivation	Group: Acquisition Experience	Mean	SD	t-Value
Factor 1: Operational Synergy	Low	3.50	0.83	
	High	4.13	0.67	−2.64**
Factor 2: Financial Synergy	Low	1.81	0.50	
	High	1.79	0.46	2.78**
Factor 3: Managerial Synergy	Low	2.70	0.96	
	High	2.78	0.99	−0.21
Factor 4: Internalization	Low	3.04	1.01	
	High	2.81	0.74	0.87
Factor 5: Location	Low	2.42	1.61	
	High	2.88	1.28	−1.00
Factor 6: Market Power	Low	3.00	1.31	
	High	3.99	0.76	−3.20***
Factor 7: Managerialism	Low	1.94	0.46	
	High	1.57	0.53	2.17**
Factor 8: Diversification	Low	1.83	0.46	
	High	2.12	0.48	−1.80*

$^*p < .1.$ $^{**}p < .05.$ $^{***}p < .01.$

SD = standard deviation.

Notes: The mean for the factors is the mean of the factor scores. The mean for the individual motives is the average on a scale of 1 (not important) to 5 (very important).

a mean scores statistically significant for the factors, namely operational synergy ($p < .05$), financial synergy ($p < .05$) market development and power ($p < .01$), managerialism ($p < .05$) and diversification ($p < .10$). This suggests that the firms with multiple acquisitions experience tend to enter into M&A designed to bring in more efficiency and develop the market further compared with firms with single acquisition experience. The results provide support for Hypothesis 3. However, in the case of the managerialism factor ($p < .05$), the factor score is higher for acquirers with single acquisition experience compared to the firms with multiple acquisition experience. This may be explained by the fact that acquirers with single acquisition are more motivated to increase the size of the firm thereby increasing the prestige and job security of the managers.

5.5.6 The Acquirer with Intangible Assets

The motives for CBM&A by acquirers with intangible assets are shown in Table 5.7. Following the studies such as Lang et al. (1991), Servaes (1991) and Doukas (1995), we defined the intangible assets as a ratio of assets to sales. In this study, the acquirer's intangible assets are divided by sales to standardize the value and to measure the firm's intensity of intangible assets. This ratio indicates not only

Table 5.7   Motives for CBM&A: Acquirer's Intangible Assets

Motivation	Group: Intangibles	Mean	SD	t-Value
Factor 1: Operational Synergy	Low	3.91	0.59	
	High	4.10	0.92	−0.78
Factor 2: Financial Synergy	Low	1.62	0.49	
	High	1.77	0.45	−1.07
Factor 3: Managerial Synergy	Low	2.52	0.96	
	High	3.00	0.87	1.73*
Factor 4: Internalization	Low	2.66	0.85	
	High	3.11	0.63	−2.49**
Factor 5: Location	Low	2.95	1.36	
	High	2.48	1.31	1.18
Factor 6: Market Power	Low	3.86	0.69	
	High	3.68	1.20	0.62
Factor 7: Managerialism	Low	1.45	0.48	
	High	1.82	0.47	−2.55**
Factor 8: Other Motivations	Low	2.00	0.48	
	High	2.06	0.47	−0.43

*$p < .1$. **$p < .05$. ***$p < .01$.

SD = standard deviation.

Notes: The mean for the factors is the mean of the factor scores. The mean for the individual motives is the average on a scale of 1 (not important) to 5 (very important).

the intensity of intangible assets but also the quality of management. The study then used the sample median to categorize firms into high intangible asset firms or low intangible asset firms. The results in Table 5.7 tend to provide a moderate support for Hypothesis 4, with the mean scores being significantly different for three of eight factors: managerial synergy ($p < .10$), internalization ($p < .05$) and managerialism ($p < .05$), where mean scores are higher for the acquirers with higher intangible assets. The finding is not surprising in that it is argued that acquirers with higher intangible assets, such as managerial know-how, are more likely to make acquisitions with the motive of creating managerial synergy and obtaining the benefits of internalization as suggested by Seth et al. (2000) and Morck and Yeung (1992). The study also suggests that firms with more intangible assets in the form of managerial know-how may create an opportunity for managerialism.

5.6   SUMMARY AND IMPLICATIONS

The past four decades have witnessed an increasing volume of CBM&A activity. Commensurate with the rising volume of M&As is a number of studies attempting to explain why M&As take place against the backdrop that prior studies have suggested that the failure rate of M&As ranges between 46% to 82% (please see Kitching, 1967; Jensen and Ruback, 1983; Hunt, 1990; Jarrell and Poulsen, 1989; Mueller, 2003).

The chapter makes a significant contribution by providing a rich picture of the motives for CBM&A and explains why senior managers engage in CBM&A despite the evidence of M&A failure rates. We find that the main motives for CBM&A by UK firms appear to be intrinsically linked to profitability/revenue enhancement, market development and power and efficiency gains. Mergers and acquisitions are seen primarily as a means of increasing market share, enabling faster entry into new markets and to obtain economies of scale. This study tends to provide support for the survey findings reported by KPMG Management Consulting (1997/1998), in which 'to increase/protect market share' and have a new presence in other geographical areas were identified as the most important motives for M&As in Europe. A tentative conclusion to be drawn from the results is that mergers in the UK, in general, are used as a competitive weapon designed to obtain market power and synergies to beat off common competitors.

The implication of this research is that the motives and success of M&A events have been traditionally linked to financial gain; this study suggests that strategic reasons now heavily influence the acquisition decisions. The motives such as speed of entering the foreign market, attaining market power and market share, sharing of intangible assets, matching complementary assets and reducing dominance of competitors are found to be significant motives along with traditional operational and financial synergistic motives. This renders support for the observation made by Grinblatt and Titman (2002) that acquisitions in the 1990s and beyond are strategic in nature. The findings that non-financial strategic motives are significant suggests that the success of CBM&A should not only be judged with financial data, such as share price and accounting measures, as has been done in most prior studies. Future research in this field should be encouraged to discover alternative non-financial ways of measuring CBM&A success. More specifically, we suggest that future studies should link the non-financial motives with the assessment of CBM&A performance.

REFERENCES

Ahmed, M.U., Rahim, N. and Uddin, M.M. (2003). The Market Impact of Changes in Corporate Diversification (Focus): Some New Evidence, *Journal of Academy of Business and Economics*, Vol. 1(1), pp. 137–147.

Asquith, P., Bruner, R.F. and Mullins, D.W. (1983). The Gains to Bidding Firms from Merger, *Journal of Financial Economics*, Vol. 11, pp. 121–139.

Aw, M. and Chatterjee, R. (2004). The Performance of UK Firms Acquiring Large Cross-Border and Domestic Takeover Targets, *Applied Financial Economics*, Vol. 14, pp. 337–349.

Barkema, H.G. and Vermeulen, G.A.M. (1998). International expansion through start up or through Acquisitions: An Organisation Learning Perspective, *Academy of Management Journal*, Vol. 41(1), pp. 7–26.

Baum, J. and Oliver, C. (1991). Institutional Linkages and Organization Morality. *Administrative Science Quarterly*, Vol. 36, pp. 187–218.

Berger, A.N. (1995). The Profit-Structure Relationship in Banking: Test of Market Power and Efficient Structure Hypotheses, *Journal of Money, Credit and Banking*, Vol. 27(2), pp. 404–432.

Boateng, A., and Glaister, K. W. (2003). Strategic Motives for International Joint Venture Formation in Ghana. *Management International Review*, Vol. 43(2), pp. 107–128.

Boyd, J.H. and Graham, S. (1991). Investigating the Bank Consolidation Trend, *Quarterly Review (Federal Reserve Bank of Minneapolis)*, (Spring), pp. 3–15.

Brouthers, K., Hastenburg, P.V. and Van den van, J. (1998). If Most Mergers Fail Why Are They So Popular?, *Long Range Planning*, Vol. 31(3), pp. 347–358.

Carleton, R.J. (1997). Cultural Due Diligence, *Training*, Vol. 34, pp. 67–80.

Caves, R.E. (1990). *Corporate Mergers in International Economic Integration*, Working Paper, Centre for Economic Policy Research, Harvard University.

Chen, C. and Findley, C. (2003). A Review of Cross-border Mergers and Acquisitions in APEC, *Asian-Pacific Economic Literature*, Vol. 17(2), pp. 14–38.

Cole, M. (2006). *Waterlow Stock Exchange Yearbook 2006*, London: CaritasData.

Datta, D.K. and Puia, G. (1995). Cross-Border Acquisitions: An Examination of the Influence of Relatedness and Cultural Fit on Shareholder Value Creation in US Acquiring Firms, *Management International Review*, Vol. 35(4), pp. 337–359.

Denis, D.J., Denis, D.K. and Yost, K. (2002). Global Diversification, Industrial Diversification and Firm Value, *Journal of Finance*, Vol. 57, pp. 1951–1979.

Doukas, J. (1995). Overinvestment, Tobin's Q and Gains from Foreign Acquisitions, *Journal of Banking and Finance*, Vol. 19, pp. 1285–1303.

Dunning, J.H. (1993). *Multinational Enterprises and the Global Economy*, Reading, MA: Addison-Wesley Publishers.

Eisenhardt, K.M. and Schoonhoven, C.B. (1996). Resources Based View of Strategic Alliance Formation: Strategic and Social Effects in Entrepreneurial Firms. *Organisational Science*, Vol. 7(2), pp. 136–150.

Erez-Rein, N., Erez, M. and Maital, S. (2004). Mind the Gap: Key Success Factors in Cross-Border Acquisitions, in A.L. Pablo and M. Javidan (eds.), *Mergers and Acquisitions: Creating Integrative Knowledge*, Oxford: Blackwell Publishing, pp. 20–42.

Eun, C.S., Kolodny, R. and Scheraga, C. (1996). Cross-Border Acquisitions and Shareholder Wealth: Tests of the Synergy and Internalization Hypotheses, *Journal of Banking and Finance*, Vol. 20, pp. 1559–1582.

Fuller, K., Netter, J. and Stegemoller, M. (2002). What Do Returns to Acquiring Firms Tell Us? Evidence from Firms that Make Many Acquisitions, *Journal of Finance*, Vol. 57(4), pp. 1763–1793.

Gonzalez, P., Vasconcellos, G.M. and Kish, R.J. (1998). Cross-Border Mergers and Acquisitions: The Undervaluation Hypothesis, *The Quarterly Review of Economics and Finance*, Vol. 38(1), pp. 25–45.

Grinblatt, M. and Titman, S. (2002). *Financial Markets and Corporate Strategy*, 2nd edition, Boston, MA: McGraw-Hill Irwin.

Hennart, J.F. (1991). The Transaction Cost Theory of Joint Ventures: An Empirical Study of Japanese Subsidiaries in the United States, *Management Science*, Vol. 37, pp. 483–497.

Hudson, J and Barnfield, E. (2001). Mergers and Acquisitions Requires Social Dialogue, *Strategic Communications Management*, Vol. 5, pp. 207–239.

Hunt, J. (1990). Changing Pattern of Acquisition Behaviour in Takeovers and Consequences for Acquisition Process, *Strategic Management Journal*, Vol. 11, pp. 66–71.

Ingham, H., Kran, I. and Lovestam, A. (1992). Mergers and Profitability: A Managerial Success Story, *Journal of Management Studies*, Vol. 29(2), pp. 195–209.

Jarrell, G.A and Poulsen, A.B. (1989). The Returns to Acquiring Firms in Tender Offers: Evidence from Three Decades, *Financial Management*, Vol. 18(3), pp. 12–19.

Jensen, M.C. (1986). Agency Costs of Free Cash-Flow, Corporate Finance and Takeovers, *American Economic Review*, Vol. 76, pp. 323–329.

Jensen, M.C. and Ruback, R.S. (1983). The Market for Corporate Control: The Scientific Evidence, *Journal of Financial Economics*, Vol. 11, pp. 5–50.

Kang, J-K. (1993). The International Market for Corporate Control: Mergers and Acquisitions of US Firms by Japanese Firms, *Journal of Financial Economics*, Vol. 34, pp. 345–371.

Kitching, J. (1967). Why Do Mergers Miscarry? *Harvard Business Review*, November–December, pp. 84–101.

Kiymaz, H. (2003). Wealth Effect for US Acquirers from Foreign Direct Investments, *Journal of Business Strategies*, Vol. 20(1), pp. 7–21.

Kiymaz, H. and Mukherjee, T.K. (2000). Impact of Country Diversification on Shareholders' Wealth in Cross-Border Mergers, *Financial Review*, Vol. 35(2), pp. 37–58.

KPMG Management Consulting (1997/1998). *Mergers and Acquisitions in Europe*, Research Report.

Lang, L.H.P., Stulz, R.M. and Walkling, R.A. (1991). A Test of Free Cash Flow Hypothesis: The Case of Bidder Return, *Journal of Financial Economics*, Vol. 29, pp. 315–335.

Madhok, A. (1997). Cost, Value and Foreign Market Entry: The Transaction and the Firm. *Strategic Management Journal*, Vol. 18(1), pp. 39–63.

Manzon, G.B., Sharp, D.J. and Travlos, N.G. (1994). An empirical study of the consequences of US tax rules for international acquisitions by US firms, *Journal of Finance*, Vol. 49, pp. 1893–1904.

Markides, C. and Ittner, C.D. (1994). Shareholders Benefit from Corporate International Diversification: Evidence from US International Acquisitions, *Journal of International Business Studies*, Vol. 25(2), pp. 343–366.

Martin, X., Swaminathan, A. and Mitchell, W. (1998). Organizational Evolution in the Interorganizational Environment: Incentives and Constraints on International Expansion Strategy, *Administrative Science Quarterly*, Vol. 43, pp. 566–601.

Mathur, I., Rangan, N., Chhachhi, I. and Sundaram, S. (1994). International Acquisitions in the United States: Evidence from Returns to Foreign Bidders, *Managerial and Decision Economics*, Vol. 15(2), pp. 107–118.

Morck, R. and Yeung, B. (1992). Internalization: An Event Study Test, *Journal of International Economics*, Vol. 33, pp. 41–56.

Morosini, P. Shane, S. and Singh, H. (1998). National Cultural Distance and Cross-Border Acquisition Performance, *Journal of International Business Studies*, Vol. 29, pp. 137–158.

Mueller, D.C. (2003). The Finance Literature on Mergers: A Critical Survey, in M. Waterson (ed.), *Competition, Monopoly and Corporate Governance, Essays in Honour of Keith Cowling*, Cheltenham, UK: Edward Edgar, pp. 161–205.

Mukherjee, T.K., Kiymaz, H. and Baker, H.K. (2004). Merger Motives and Target Valuation: A Survey of Evidence from CFOs, *Journal of Applied Finance*, Vol. 14 (Fall/Winter), pp. 7–24.

Myers, S.C. and Majluf, N.S. (1984). Corporate Financing and Investment Decisions When Firms Have Information that Investors Do not Have, *Journal of Financial Economics*, Vol. 13, pp. 187–221.

Porter, M.E. and Fuller, M.B. (1986). *Coalitions and Global Strategy*, in M.E. Porter (Ed.), *Competition in Global Industries*, Boston, MA: Harvard Business School, pp. 315–344.

Ravenscraft, D.J. and Scherer, F.M. (1987). *Mergers, Sell-offs and Economic Efficiency*, Washington, DC: The Brookings Institution.

Roll, R. (1986). The Hubris Hypothesis of Corporate Takeover, *Journal of Business*, Vol. 59, pp. 197–216.

Schenk, H. (2000). Are International Acquisitions a Matter of Strategy Rather than Wealth Creation? *International Review of Applied Economics*, Vol. 14(2), pp. 193–211.

Scherer, F.M., Beckenstein, A., Kaufer, E. and Murphey, R.D. (1975). *The Economics of Multi-plant Operation: An International Comparison Study*, Cambridge, MA: Harvard University Press.

Schipper, K. and Thompson, R. (1983). Evidence on the Capitalized Value of Merger Activity for Acquiring Firms, *Journal of Financial Economics*, Vol. 11, pp. 85–119.

Servaes, H. (1991). Tobin's Q and the Gains from Takeovers, *Journal of Finance*, Vol. 46, pp. 409–419.

Seth, A. (1990). Sources of Value Creation in Acquisitions: An Empirical Investigation, *Strategic Management Journal*, Vol. 11, pp. 431–446.

Seth, A., Song, K.P. and Pettit, R. (2000). Synergy, Managerialism or Hubris? An Empirical Examination of Motives for Foreign Acquisitions of US Firms, *Journal of International Business Studies*, Vol. 31(3), pp. 387–405.

Shleifer, A. and Vishny, R.W. (1992). Asset Liquidity and Debt Capacity, *Journal of Finance*, Vol. 47, pp. 1343–1366.

Sudarsanam, S. (2003). *Creating Value from Mergers and Acquisitions: The Challenges*, London: Pearson Education Limited.

Tetenbaum, T.J. (1999). Beating the Odds of Mergers and Acquisition Failure: Seven Key Practices that Improve the Chance for Expected Integration and Synergies, *Organizational Dynamics*, Autumn, pp 22–35.

Trautwein, F. (1990). Merger Motives and Merger Prescriptions, *Strategic Management Journal*, Vol. 11(4), pp. 283–295.

United Nations Conference for Trade and Development (UNCTAD) (2000). *World Investment Report 2000: Cross-Border Mergers and Acquisitions and Development*, New York and Geneva: United Nations.

United Nations Conference for Trade and Development (UNCTAD) (2006). "FDI from Developing and Transition Economies: Implications for Development", New York and Geneva: United Nations.

Vermeulen, F. and Barkema, H.G. (2001). Learning through Acquisitions, *Academy of Management Journal*, Vol. 44, pp. 457–476.

Walter, G.A. and Barney, J.B. (1990). Management Objectives in Mergers and Acquisitions, *Strategic Management Journal*, Vol. 11, pp. 79–86.

Wang, H. and Reuer, J. (2006). Risk Reduction through Acquisitions: The Roles of Firm-Specific Investments and Agency Hazards. In C.L. Cooper and S. Finkelstein (eds.), *Advances in Mergers and Acquisitions*, Vol. 5, pp. 25–29.

Wiggins, S.N. (1981). A Theoretical Analysis of Conglomerate Mergers, in R.D. Blair and R. Lanzilotti (eds.), *The Conglomerate Corporation*, Cambridge, MA: Oelgeschlager, Gunn & Hain, pp.16–22.

Williamson, O.E. (1975). *Market and Hierarchies: Analysis and Antitrust Implications*, New York: The Free Press.

6 Macroeconomic Determinants of Cross-Border Mergers and Acquisitions
Evidence from the UK

6.1 INTRODUCTION

Over the past two decades, CBM&A have grown substantially and become one of the most important vehicles for firms seeking to internationalize their operations. Data and analysis presented in Chapter 4 based on the information available from the United Nations Conference on Trade and Development (UNCTAD) database and the database of UK National Statistics revealed that the total share of CBM&A as a percentage of world FDI flows rose from 45.18% in 1991 to 84.52% in 2005. The ratio of world CBM&A activities as a percentage of GDP is also impressive. For example, the share of global value of CBM&A increased from 0.36% of worldwide GDP in 1991 to more than 1.35% in 2005, representing a growth of 275%. In similar vein, the UK CBM&A activity has seen a rising trends in the recent years. For example in 1991 the value of UK's cross-border purchases and sales were US$8,501 million and US$13,020 million, respectively. These values increased to US$90,535 million and US$171,689 million in 2005. This represents a growth of 965% in cross-border purchases and a more than 1,200% growth in cross-border sales over this 15-year period. In terms of relative ranking among the participating countries in the international market for corporate control, UK has been the top acquiring nation in the world over the 1991–2005 period and next to the top as a target nation for the same period.

Despite the sheer volume and scale of CBM&A in the UK, relatively few studies have investigated specifically the reasons for the rising trends in CBM&A activities in the UK. This is against the backdrop that researchers have not been able to develop a coherent theory explaining the increasing trends of CBM&A activity. The few studies investigating the relationship between merger activity and macroeconomic factors have produced mixed results. For example the study by Melicher et al. (1983) suggests a weak relationship between merger activity and economic conditions. On the other hand, studies such as McCann (2001), Ali-Yrkko (2002) and Nakamura (2004) provide some support for the relationship between the pattern of merger activity and selected macroeconomic factors. Given the conflicting results from the various studies, it is imperative, we investigate the driving forces behind the rising trends of the UK CBM&A. Building on prior studies, this study attempts to extend the few existing studies by analysing the effects of macroeconomic influences on the UK CBM&A over the 1988–2005 period. The next section discusses the literature underpinning CBM&A and formulates hypotheses of the study. Section 6.3 focuses on data collection and analytical methods used in the study. Section 6.4 presents the results and discussions. The last section provides a summary of the study's conclusions.

6.2   LITERATURE REVIEW AND HYPOTHESES DEVELOPMENT

Most of the growth in international production over the past decade has been via cross-border mergers and acquisitions (UNCTAD, 2000). Commensurate with the increasing trends in CBM&A activities is the mounting interest by researchers in finance and management attempting to provide a coherent explanation of why CBM&A activity takes place. Prominent among the factors identified in the extant literature include synergy (Seth et al., 2002), global diversification (Markides and Ittner, 1994), difference in valuation (Gonzalez et al., 1998), hubris (Seth et al., 2002), managerialism (Seth et al., 2002), existence of tax differential between countries (Manzon et al., 1994), and strategic reasons such as the quickest way of entering the foreign market (UNCTAD, 2000) and to counteract a rival's move. A similar argument has also been put forward by Caves (1996) whose research found that international M&A may be undertaken to gain access to new opportunities and to limit the opportunities of the competitors. In addition, rapid changes in technology have intensified the competitive pressure on the firms and as a result CBM&A formation are used as a way of sharing the costs of innovation and accessing new technological assets to enhance firms' capabilities (UNCTAD, 2000). It is also important to mention that changes in the regulatory environment and massive liberalization of worldwide FDI policies have also facilitated the growth of CBM&A.

6.2.1   Macroeconomic Determinants and CBM&A

The motivations discussed earlier are more driven by a firm's quest to gain synergy, a competitive edge over rivals and market power. These factors are therefore, internal and the extent to which they explain why mergers take place are more applicable to particular firms and the sectors in which they operate. Vasconcellos et al. (1990) have argued that industry- or firm-specific variables help to explain whether CBM&A are more common for certain industry or firms with particular characteristics. In order to explain the rising pattern of aggregate CBM&A activities, it will be more useful to examine the exogenous variables or macroeconomic factors. This is because managers of individual firms make the acquisition decision as a response to industry-specific shocks that have been created by the influence of macroeconomic factors. Given the importance of macroeconomic factors in influencing the aggregate level of M&A activities, several authors have attempted to identify the macroeconomic determinants and the nature of their influences on the M&A activities. The various macroeconomic factors used in existing studies include gross domestic products (Ali-Yrkko, 2002), share prices (Nelson, 1959; Geroski, 1984), interest rates (Diebold and Lindner, 1996), stock market capitalization (Ali-Yrkko, 2002), changes in the total investment in the economy (Yagil, 1996), real money supply (Resende, 2005), inflation rate (Evenett, 2003), macro-level liquidity (Harford, 2005) and bond yield (Melicher et al., 1983). This chapter attempts to evaluate a set of selected macroeconomic variables to explain rising trends of CBM&A activities in the UK which, to the best of our knowledge, two studies have been done partially in this area (see Vasconcellos et al., 1990, and McCann, 2001).

6.2.2 GDP

GDP may be one of the important determinants of M&A activities. GDP is an indicator of the size of the economy. The higher the GDP, the bigger will be the economy. Ali-Yrkko (2002) contended that the bigger economy as reflected by the size of GDP should engage in more acquisition activities compared to the countries with lower level of GDP. Higher size of absolute GDP or higher level of GDP growth signifies greater demand in the economy, and an increased level of demand may lead the economy to reallocate its resources in order to ensure the optimum use. The urge for reallocation of resources increases the possibility of M&A formation in the economy. The impact of GDP on the aggregate flow of M&A has been supported by Resende (2005), Nakamura (2004) and Crook (1995). The general conclusion of these studies is that there exists a positive relation between GDP and aggregate domestic M&A activities. In addition, Anand and Kogut (1997) suggested that there is a positive relation between FDI and growth of the host country's GDP. It has been argued by Globerman and Shapiro (1999) that higher GDP in the host country will attract more FDI, of which CBM&A is a part, because of the possibility of higher demand and higher profitability within the economy. In case of higher level of GDP in the home country, numerous authors contend that the relation might be positive on the ground that higher GDP may result in higher level of cash reserve in the hands of local firms, and those firms may end up spending the excess funds in foreign countries to increase the size of their companies and to gain market power. On the other hand, the relationship may be negative because a higher GDP level can encourage local firms to acquire domestic companies as a result of greater potential of market demand within the home country rather than to go abroad to get control of the foreign firms. As a part of FDI, CBM&A may also be influenced by GDP. This has been pointed out by several authors such as Kish and Vasconcellos (1993), Vasconcellos and Kish (1996) and Manchin (2004). Therefore, there a strong theoretical basis for linking the surge in UK CBM&A activities and the growth in GDP, which has increased from US$834 billion to US$1,110 billion over the past10 years. It is therefore hypothesized that

> **Hypothesis 1:** *There will be a positive relationship between the UK GDP and CBM&A (inflows and outflows) activities.*

6.2.3   Share Price

Share price is an important macroeconomic variable that may influence the aggregate M&A flow. Nelson (1959) was among the few pioneers who examined changes in quarterly merger activities in the US market during 1895–1920 and found high positive correlation between changes in the merger activities and changes in the stock prices. There are several explanations about this relationship. Melicher et al. (1983) and Benzing (1991) have argued that higher stock prices indicate the prospects of future economic growth and therefore a higher level of M&A activities. Gort (1969) argued that rapid change in stock prices may create economic disturbance through the expectational gap between stockholders and non-stockholders, and this disturbance may lead to higher level of M&A activities. Shleifer and Vishny (2003) and Rhodes-Kropf et al. (2005) suggested that higher stock prices may lead to overvaluation of firms and that this overvaluation may lead to M&A formation. Vasconcellos and Kish (1998) have examined the impact of stock prices on the number and direction of CBM&A between the US and each of the four major European countries: the UK, Germany, Italy and France. The study found that a depressed US stock market relative to foreign stock market encourages foreign acquisitions of US companies. Kish and Vasconcellos (1993) from US–Japan context contend that higher stock prices in Japan and lower stock prices in the US encourage Japanese firms to acquire US firms.

Unlike the previously mentioned studies, Golbe and White (1988) found a negative relationship between stock price and M&A. Based on the concept of Tobin's Q the authors postulate that when replacement costs are higher than market value (Q ratio is less than one) due to lower level of stock prices, there can be a surge in M&A activities as the assets could be acquired more cheaply from the market. The study by Geroski (1984) also finds weak relationship between stock prices and M&A. McCann (2001) found that the lower the UK stock market index, the more the UK inward CBM&A but the relationship is not statistically significant. In light of the earlier discussions, it is hypothesized that

> **Hypothesis 2:** *The relationship between UK stock prices and UK CBM&A (outflow and inflow) will not be independent.*

6.2.4   Interest Rates

Interest rate is another macroeconomic variable that may affect the number and the size of M&A. The relationship between M&A and interest rate lies with the fact that lower interest rate reduces the cost of financing and encourages more M&As formation. Melicher et al. (1983) argue that the expansion of cash-financed acquisitions may be an outcome of lower cost of financing reflected by lower levels of interest rates. The inverse relation between interest rate and M&A formation has also been supported by Yagil (1996) and Haque et al. (1995). On the other hand, Golbe and White (1988) and Steiner (1975) suggest that higher interest rates may cause a liquidity problem for the small firms which may become takeover targets by the bigger firms with better access to the capital markets. On the relationship between CBM&A and interest rate, Kish and Vasconcellos (1993) and Vasconcellos and Kish (1998) suggest that higher interest rate in the host country discourage inflow of CBM&A. This reasoning leads to the following hypothesis:

Hypothesis 3: *The relationship between UK money market interest rate and CBM&A (outflow and inflow) is not independent.*

6.2.5   Money Supply

Aggregate M&A activities may also be affected by the liquidity position of the economy. Harford (2005) contends that liquidity position in the economy have a positive effect on the aggregate level of M&A activities. Resende (2005), Clarke and Ioannidis (1994) and Fishman (1989) also point to the role of liquidity as a motivator of aggregate M&A activities. From the perspective of CBM&A, higher liquidity in the economy, as reflected by increased money supply, should have a negative impact on outward CBM&A on the grounds that increased money supply should boost the national economy and lead to high demand in the economy making it attractive for local firms to seek new opportunities such as M&A other than going abroad. On the other hand, it may be argued that higher liquidity may also discourage the inward CBM&A because competition among bidding companies are likely to put prices up thereby making it more expensive in acquiring new firms due to potential overvaluation of target firms. Based on the previous discussion, it is hypothesized that

Hypothesis 4: *The relationship between liquidity (money supply) in UK economy and UK CBM&A (outflows and inflows) will be independent.*

6.2.6   Exchange Rate

The exchange rate theory of FDI states that countries with strong currency tend to invest in the foreign countries and countries with weak currency tend to be recipients of the foreign direct investments (Aliber, 1970; Caves, 1988; Froot and Stein, 1991). As a popular mode of FDI entry, CBM&A is also affected by the changes in the foreign exchange rates. Harris and Ravenscraft (1991), Kang (1993), Dewenter (1995) and Goergen and Renneboog (2004) studies lend support to this notion and point out that firms from countries with appreciating currency should act as acquirers whereas firms from countries with depreciating currency should be targets on the grounds that strong currency will reduce the acquisition price and transaction costs. This implies that an appreciation of local currency may increase outward and decrease inward CBM&A. The converse is true for depreciating local currency. But considering the effect of strong currency on the repatriated profit, Vasconcellos and Kish (1996) suggest there might be a negative relation between the exchange rate and aggregate flow of CBM&A. That is, an appreciation of local currency may increase (decrease) inward (outward) CBM&A. In the light of the this discussion, it can be hypothesized that

> **Hypothesis 5:** *The relationship between UK exchange rate and UK CBM&A (outflows and inflows) will not be independent.*

6.2.7   Inflation

Inflation rate has been identified as one of the determinants of CBM&A. For example, Black (2000) stated that a lower inflation rate is a strong determinant of the growth of CBM&A in the late 1990s. A lower inflation rate leads to lower prices of the targets and lower cost of debt, thereby encouraging higher flow of CBM&A activities. Thus, if the inflation rate of a country is low, it should attract more CBM&A. On the other hand, higher inflation in the home country will make domestic targets expensive and will encourage potential acquirers to go to foreign countries where inflation rates are low. Although the role of inflation in explaining aggregate CBM&A flow is important, there are few studies on this issue in the UK context. Given the consistently lower rates of inflation in the UK over the past decade, it is important we investigate the relationship between inflation and the rising trends of CBM&A in the UK. This leads to the following hypotheses:

> **Hypothesis 6:** *The low level of UK inflation rate and CBM&A outflows and inflows will not be independent.*

6.3   DATA AND METHODOLOGY

6.3.1   Sources of Data

The data which compose the UK CBM&A (inwards and outwards) deals completed between 1988 and 2005 were derived from Thomson One Banker database and compared with data provided in *Acquisitions Monthly*. In terms of the data relating to macroeconomic variables used in the model, namely UK real GDP, UK money market interest rate, exchange rate between the UK pound sterling and the US dollar, total value of UK export and import, the UK money supply, the UK all share price index and the UK consumer price index were collected from the Economist Intelligence Unit (EIU) country database and were cross-checked with data available from the UK national statistics database. The data were then organized to form a quarterly time series, covering the period from the second quarter of 1988 to the third quarter of 2005, creating 70 observations.

6.3.2   Data Analysis

To examine the hypothesized relationship, regression analysis was employed to assess the relationship between the UK CBM&A inflows and outflows (dependent variables) and selected UK macroeconomic factors (independent variables). Several assumptions checked before running the test. First, the multicollinearity appears not to be a problem in this study, as evident by the low levels of VIF (variance inflation factor) for all the independent variables. The results for all predictor variables showed no pattern of increasing and decreasing residuals thereby confirming the assumption of homoscedasticity. Independent variables were lagged for one quarter to cover the possibility that CBM&A decisions may be subject to a delayed response of any major macroeconomic policy change.

6.3.3 Definitions of Variables in the Model

Dependent Variables

CBMAOUT = CBM&A outflow. This is the number of purchase of foreign target firms by UK companies.

CBMAIN = CBM&A inflow. This is the number of purchase of UK target companies by foreign bidding companies.

Independent Variables

RGDP = Real GDP. This is the absolute value of real GDP of UK at constant 2001 market price.

INTRATE = Interest rate. This is the percentage interest rate on three-month UK treasury bills.

EXRATE = Exchange rate. This is the value of US dollars against UK pound.

M4 = M4 is the total money supply in UK economy.

FTSEALL = This is the UK all share price index (1962 index = 100).

INFLATION = Absolute value of consumer price index (CPI) is used to represent inflation (CPI of 1996 = 100). An increase in CPI should represent inflation and a decrease represents deflation.

Given the previously described dependent and independent variables, the following models have been used to assess the impact of independent variables on the dependent variables.

$$CBMAOUT_t = \alpha + \beta_1\,RGDP_{t-1} + \beta_2\,INTRATE_{t-1} + \beta_3\,EXRATE_{t-1} \\ + \beta_4\,M4_{t-1} + \beta_5\,FTSEALL_{t-1} + \beta_6\,INFLATION_{t-1} + e_t$$

$$CBMAIN_t = \alpha + \beta_1\,RGDP_{t-2} + \beta_2\,INTRATE_{t-2} + \beta_3\,EXRATE_{t-2} \\ + \beta_4\,M4_{t-2} + \beta_5\,FTSEALL_{t-2} + \beta_6\,INFLATION_{t-2} + e_t$$

6.4 RESULTS AND DISCUSSION

Table 6.1 presents the descriptive statistics of the dependent and independent variables. The reported descriptive statistics includes maximum and minimum values of two dependent variables and seven independent variables used in the study. It reports the mean values of the variables and standard deviation of each of the

Table 6.1 Descriptive Statistics

Variables	Minimum	Maximum	Mean	SD
CBMAOUT	62	275	146.77	48.84
CBMAIN	60	248	126.86	40.01
DIFFOUTIN	−64	73	19.91	28.50
GDP	190,046	282,657	228,548.9	30,155.90
INTRATE	3.50	15.14	7.09	3.31
EXRATE	1.42	1.95	1.64	0.13
M4	330,201	1,275,136	723,913	250,389.10
FTSEALL	927	3,111	1,926.01	656.69
CPI	71.90	113.90	97.82	11.54

SD = standard deviation.

Note: Number of quarterly observations n = 70 (April 1988 to September 2005).

variables. These statistics are reported for 70 observations of each of the variables ranging from the second quarter of 1988 to the third quarter of 2005. The table shows that the value of mean difference between outward and inward CBM&A is positive, which suggests that, on average, the number of outward UK CBM&A is higher than the number of inward UK CBM&A.

The regression results shown in Table 6.2 suggest that the UK CBM&A activities can be explained by the chosen macroeconomic variables, that is, RGDP, INTRATE, RXRATE, M4, FTSEALL and CPI. The regression results for model 1; that is outward CBM&A activities show that four factors, namely GDP ($p < .05$), exchange rate ($p < .01$), money supply ($p < .01$) and share prices ($p < .01$) have significant impact on the level of outward UK CBM&A and render support for Hypotheses 1, 2, 4 and 5. However, CPI, and INTRATE were found to not be statistically significant in explaining the outward UK CBM&A. The total amount of variation explained by the model 1 (adjusted R^2 = 0.79754), and F-value was significant ($p < .01$) is substantial and compares favourably to other similar CBM&A studies such as Nakamura (2004) and Ali-Yrkko (2002). The result that there is a positive and statistically significant relationship between the real GDP of UK and the UK outward CBM&A is surprising in that no other previous study has found positive significant relationship between GDP and outward CBM&A. The result may be due to the economic prosperity being enjoyed in the UK in recent years as reflected by the growing level of its GDP, and this might have led to the rising trend of CBM&A activity. The result also suggest positive and significant relationship between the exchange rate and outward CBM&A of UK and is consistent with the conclusion drawn by Vasconcellos et al. (1990), Froot and Stein (1991), Harris and Ravenscraft (1991) and Kang (1993), but it varies from that found by McCann (2001). This finding supports the notion that a strong pound sterling (UK currency) with respect to foreign currencies should result in upward trends in the acquisition of foreign firms by the UK firms in

Table 6.2 Regression Results

Variables	Outward CBM&A Model: 1	Inward CBM&A Model: 2
Intercept	−426.1965 (−1.9644)*	−752.7195 (− 3.7249)***
RGDP_1	0.0023173 (2.4353)**	0.0022717 (2.5632)**
INTRATE_1	0.34720 (0.16433)	9.7049 (4.9316)***
EXRATE_1	89.8942 (2.9898)***	43.5495 (1.5551)
M4_1	−0.4476 E-3 (−4.0779)***	−0.3218 E-3 (−3.1475)***
FTSEALL_1	0.073624 (7.9843)***	0.052661 (6.1316)***
CPI_1	−0.16426 (−0.11678)	4.4988 (3.4339)***
Adjusted R^2	0.79754	0.75452
F-Values	39.2659***	30.8576***
N	69	69

*$p = .10$. **$p = .05$. ***$p = .01$.

Note: t-values are presented in parentheses.

that the level for funds required to acquire foreign targets will be less. The study also find that the UK stock prices influence the UK outward CBM&A and this renders support for the conclusion drawn by Shleifer and Vishny (2003) and Rhodes-Kropf et al. (2005) that higher stock valuation leads to overvaluation of firms, and this overvaluation may consequently lead to more M&As formation. This result also lends support to the finding by Kish and Vasconcellos (1993) but inconsistent with the findings of McCann (2001), who reported insignificant relationship between these two variables. As expected, there is a negatively significant association between money supply and outward UK CBM&A. This finding suggests that more liquidity in the economy may not lead to investment outflows but may rather lead to domestic acquisitions or investments to meet the demand created by more liquidity at home. It is important to point out that out of top 50 outward CBM&A deals completed worldwide during the 1987–1999 period, the UK firms led with 22% ahead of the US with 20% and that this may be explained by the combination of various macro economic variables identified in model 1.

The regression results for model 2 suggest that GDP ($p < .05$), interest rates ($p < .01$), share price ($p < .01$) and consumer price index ($p < .01$) have a positive impact on the UK CBM&A inflows, providing support for Hypotheses 1, 2, 3 and 6. However, the money supply ($p < .01$) is statistically significant and negatively related to CBM&A inflows, providing support for Hypothesis 4. The significant positive relationship between GDP and inward CBM&A may be due to the booming UK economy, and this supports the findings by Kish and Vasconcellos (1993) and Vasconcellos and Kish (1996), which suggest that growth in GDP tends to attract more foreign investments. The results of this study also indicate a positive relationship between interest rate and inward CBM&A. Perhaps this result may be explained by the relatively lower interest rates prevailing in the UK in that lower interest rates lower the costs of raising funds for all cash offers; hence, lower interest rates are associated with more inwards acquisitions in the UK. However, this finding is inconsistent with the research finding by Kish and Vasconcellos (1993). The study also finds a statistically significant positive relationship between the UK share prices and inward CBM&A suggesting that the higher stock prices help attract foreign acquirers. This may be due to massive liberalization and deregulation of the London Stock Exchange making it easier for foreign companies to raise capital and becoming biggest capital market for non-domestic shares. The study also finds statistically significant positive relationship between CPI and inward CBM&A. The result is not surprising in that lower inflation in the host country should attract foreign acquirers (Black, 2000). Perhaps the consistently low levels of inflation in the UK throughout most of the period examined may explain the increase in inward acquisitions in UK. The significantly negative relationship between the money supply and inward CBM&A is not surprising in that an increased money supply in an economy is likely to raise competition among bidders, push target price up and discourage the foreign acquirers from taking over local companies.

6.5   CONCLUSION

The purpose of this chapter has been to examine the influence of selected macroeconomic variables on the rising trends of the UK CBM&A inflows and outflows. The overall regression results indicate that macroeconomic variables have a bearing on CBM&A inflows and outflows in the UK. It was found that GDP, the exchange rate and share prices have a significant positive impact on the outflow of UK CBM&A whereas money supply has a significant negative impact. In case of UK CBM&A inflows, the overall surge can be explained by GDP, the interest rate, the exchange rate, the money supply, share prices and inflation. The overall results suggest the important role played by macroeconomic factors in explaining the surge in overall UK CBM&A. The decision to engage in CBM&A activities is one of the most important decisions firms faced in that it has a direct impact on the level of capital and human resources to be committed as well as, consequently, the overall competitive ability of the firm. A wrong decision here could not only be very expensive but often difficult to reverse and therefore has to be approached with care. In making the acquisition decision, managers usually consider various industry specific factors such as industry consolidation, industry profitability, industry growth, industry concentration, industry deregulation and capital intensity (Schorenberg and Reeves, 1999; Shimizu et al., 2004). The study suggests that it is not only industry and firm specific factors which may influence CBM&A activities, but in addition, factors such as GDP, interest rates, exchange rates, the money supply, stock prices and inflation are major contemporaneous causal factors that drive CBM&A activities. The implication of this study is that managers should consider macroeconomic determinants at the time of making international acquisition decisions. The large explanatory power of the models used in the study suggests the managers that they should thinks carefully regarding the acquisitions decision at and in particular pay attention to changes in macroeconomic variables to ensure a pioneering position rather than becoming follower of their competitors. Another important conclusion to be drawn from this chapter is that GDP and stock prices influence both inflows and outflows of CBM&A. The implication of this to policy makers is that GDP has an impact not only on inward capital flows but also on outward investments, and therefore, they should have this mind when designing their policies.

REFERENCES

Aliber, R.Z. (1970). A Theory of Direct Foreign Investments, in C.P. Kindleberger (ed.), *The International Corporation: A Symposium*, Cambridge, MA: MIT Press, pp. 17–34.

Ali-Yrkko, J. (2002). Mergers and Acquisitions: Reasons and Results, *Discussion Paper Series, No. 792*, The Research Institute of the Finnish Economy (ETLA).

Anand, J. and Kogut, B. (1997). Technological Capabilities of Countries, Firm Rivalry and Foreign Direct Investments, *Journal of International Business Studies*, Vol. 28(3), pp. 445–467.

Benzing, C. (1991). The Determinants of Aggregate Merger Activity before and after Celler-Kefauver, *Review of Industrial Organization*, Vol. 6, pp. 61–72.

Black, B.S. (2000). Is This the First International Merger Wave? *M&A Lawyer* (July/August), pp. 20–26.

Caves, R.E. (1988). Exchange Rate Movements and Foreign Direct Investment in United States, in D.B. Audretsch and M.P. Claudon (eds.), *The Internationalisation of US Markets*, New York: New York University Press, pp. 199–228.

Caves, R.E. (1996). Corporate Mergers in International Economic Integration, in A. Giovannini and C. Mayer (eds.), *European Financial Integration*, Cambridge: Cambridge University Press.

Clarke, R. and Ioannidis, C. (1994). Mergers and Excess Deposits: Some Evidence for the UK, *International Journal of the Economics of Business*, Vol. 1, pp. 377–385.

Crook, J. (1995). Time Series Explanations of Merger Activity: Some Econometric Results, *International Journal of Applied Economics*, Vol. 9, pp. 58–85.

Dewenter, K.L. (1995). Do Exchange Rate Changes Drive Foreign Direct Investment? *Journal of Business*, Vol. 68(3), pp. 405–433.

Diebold, F.X. and Lindner, P. (1996). Fractional Integration and Internal Prediction, *Economic Letters*, Vol. 50(3), pp. 305–313.

Evenett, S.J. (2003). The Cross-Border Mergerand Acquisitions Wave of Late 1990s, *NBER Working Paper No. 9655*, Cambridge, MA.

Fishman, M.J. (1989). Preemptive Bidding and the Role of Medium of Exchange in Acquisition, *Journal of Finance*, Vol. 44, pp. 41–57.

Froot, K. and Stein, J.C. (1991). Exchange Rates and Foreign Direct Investment: An Imperfect Capital Markets Approach, *Quarterly Journal of Economics*, Vol. 106, pp. 1191–1217.

Geroski, P.A. (1984). On the Relationship between Aggregate Merger Activity and the Stock Market, *European Economic Review*, Vol. 25, pp. 223–233.

Globerman, S. and Shapiro, D.M. (1999). The Impact of Government Policies on Foreign Direct Investment: The Canadian Experience, *Journal of International Business Studies*, Vol. 30(3), pp. 513–532.

Goergen, M. and Renneboog, L. (2004). Shareholder Wealth Effects of European Domestic and Cross-border Takeover Bids, *European Financial Management*, Vol. 10(1), pp. 9–45.

Golbe, D. and White, L. (1988). Catch a Wave: The Time Series Behavior of Mergers, *Review of Economics and Statistics*, Vol. 70, pp. 493–499.

Gonzalez, P., Vasconcellos, G.M. and Kish, R.J. (1998). Cross-Border Mergers and Acquisitions: The Undervaluation Hypothesis, *The Quarterly Review of Economics and Finance*, Vol. 38(1), pp. 25–45.

Gort, M. (1969). An Economic Disturbance Theory of Mergers, *Quarterly Journal of Economics*, Vol. 83, pp. 624–642.

Haque, M., Harnhirun, S. and Shapiro, D. (1995). A Time Series Analysis of Causality Between Aggregate Merger and Stock Prices: The Case of Canada, *Applied Economics*, Vol. 27, pp. 563–568.

Harford, J. (2005). What Drives Merger Waves? *Journal of Financial Economics*, Vol. 77, pp. 529–560.

Harris, R.S. and Ravenscraft, D.J. (1991). The Role of Acquisitions in Foreign Direct Investment: Evidence from the US Stock Market, *Journal of Finance*, Vol. 46(3), pp. 401–417.

Kang, J-K. (1993). The International Market for Corporate Control: Mergers and Acquisitions of US Firms by Japanese Firms, *Journal of Financial Economics*, Vol. 34, pp. 345–371.

Kish, R.J. and Vasconcellos, G.M. (1993). An Empirical Analysis of Factors Affecting Cross-Border Acquisitions: US-Japan, *Management International Review*, Vol. 33(3), pp. 227–245.

Manchin, M. (2004). Determinants of European Cross-Border Mergers and Acquisitions, *Economic Paper No. 212*, Directorate General for Economic and Financial Affairs, European Commission.

Manzon, G.B., Sharp, D.J. and Travlos, N.G. (1994). An Empirical Study of the Consequences of US Tax Rules for International Acquisitions by US Firms, *Journal of Finance*, Vol. 49, pp. 1893–1904.

Markides, C. and Ittner, C.D. (1994). Shareholders Benefit from Corporate International Diversification: Evidence from US International Acquisitions, *Journal of International Business Studies*, Vol. 25(2), pp. 343–366.

McCann, M. (2001). Cross-Border Acquisitions: The UK Experience, *Applied Economics*, Vol. 33, pp. 457–461.

Melicher, R.W., Ledolter, J. and D'Antonio, L.J. (1983). A Time Series Analysis of Aggregate Merger Activity, *Review of Economics and Statistics*, Vol. 65(3), pp. 423–430.

Nakamura, R.H. (2004). To Merger and Acquire When the Times are Good? The Influence of Macro Factors on the Japanese M&A Pattern, *Working Paper No. 197*, The European Institute of Japanese Studies, Stockholm School of Economics, Sweden.

Nelson, R.L. (1959). *Merger Movements in American Industry, 1895–1956*, Princeton, NJ: Princeton University Press.

Resende, M. (2005). *Mergers and Acquisitions Waves in the UK: A Markov-Switching Approach*, EUI Working Chapter Eco. No. 2005/4, Department of Economics, European University Institute, Italy.

Rhodes-Kropf, M., Robinson, D. and Viswanathan, S. (2005). Valuation Waves and Merger Activity: The Empirical Evidence, *Journal of Financial Economics*, Vol. 77, pp. 561–603.

Schorenberg, R. and Reeves, R. (1999). What Determines Acquisition Activities within an Industry? *European Management Journal*, Vol. 17(1), pp. 93–98.

Seth, A., Song, K.P. and Pettit, R. (2002). Value Creation and Destruction in Cross-Border Acquisitions: An Empirical Analysis of Foreign Acquisitions of US Firms, *Strategic Management Journal*, Vol. 23, pp. 921–940.

Shimizu, K., Hitt, M.A., Vaidyanath, D. and Pisano, V. (2004). Theoretical Foundations of Cross-Border Mergers and Acquisitions: A Review of Current Research and Recommendations for the Future, *Journal of International Management*, Vol. 10, pp. 307–353.

Shleifer, A. and Vishny, R. (2003). Stock Market Driven Acquisitions, *Journal of Financial Economics*, Vol. 70, pp. 295–311.

Steiner, P.O. (1975). *Mergers, Motives, Effects, Policies*, Ann Arbor: University of Michigan Press.

United Nations Conference on Trade and Development (UNCTAD) (2000). *World Investment Report 2000: Cross-Border Mergers and Acquisitions and Development*, New York and Geneva: United Nations.

Vasconcellos, G.M. and Kish, R.J. (1996). Factors Affecting Cross-Border Mergers and Acquisitions: The Canada-US Experience, *Global Finance Journal*, Vol. 7(2), pp. 223–238.

Vasconcellos, G.M. and Kish, R.J. (1998). Cross-Border Mergers and Acquisitions: The European-US Experience, *Journal of Multinational Financial Management*, Vol. 8(4), pp. 431–450.

Vasconcellos, G.M., Madura, J. and Kish, R.K. (1990). An Empirical Investigation of Factors Affecting Cross-Border Acquisitions: The US/UK Experience, *Global Finance Journal*, Vol. 1(3), pp. 173–189.

Yagil, J. (1996). Mergers and Macroeconomic Factors, *Review of Financial Economics*, Vol. 5(2), pp. 181–190.

Part III

Integration and Performance of Cross-Border Mergers and Acquisitions

7 Managing the Post-Acquisition Integration Process
An Examination of Accounting Task Integration

7.1 INTRODUCTION

Mergers have become part of the business landscape and a popular strategic choice for companies' growth and expansion. To Jemison and Sitkin (1986b, p. 107), "the use of acquisitions to redirect and reshape corporate strategy has never been greater". Yet despite the popularity and strategic importance of M&A, several major consulting, advisory services firms and academics have reported that, most acquisitions are financial failure in the long-term (KPMG, 1999; Mergerstat, 2000; PricewaterhouseCoopers, 2000; Henry, 2002). The issue of M&A's performance is central to research in M&A studies. Both academic research and anecdotal evidence indicate that one of the reasons attributed to M&A's failure to create value for shareholders is lack of effective and successful integration of the two companies. Researchers have addressed the issue of post-acquisition integration process from human resources, cultural and corporate points of view (see Haspeslagh and Jemison, 1991; Birkinshaw et al., 2000). In the context of accounting, we know very little about what accountants do when two companies are merged and the process involved in finance and accounting system integration. We believe that the ability to recognize the importance of the acquisition integration process itself is a key to a successful integration. This is consistent with the views of Jemison and Sitkin (1986b), who suggested that the lack of careful research attention on the issues of post acquisition integration appears to reflect the difficulty of recognizing the process itself as part of the problem and solution. To fully understand how M&A create value, it is important to study not only the actions that led up to the acquisition decision but also the integration of management activities that follow the decision (Jemison and Sitkin, 1986a). We contribute to this direction by examining the actions that are taken to manage the task involved in accounting integration which are a key to successful performance. This study attempts to examine and develop management accounting task performance model prior to, during and after the M&A of the two companies involved and the factors influencing the integration process. The main purpose of this chapter is to examine and map out the task performance of management accountants in the integration process of accounting system (FAS) in mergers and acquisitions.

The chapter is organized as follows: the next section reviews the literature of accounting integration. Section 7.3 outlines methodology of the study, followed by section 7.4, which deals with the phases of M&A integration process. Section 7.5 discusses the factors influencing the choice of MAS integration. The implications and conclusions are discussed in the final section.

7.2   LITERATURE REVIEW

7.2.1   Management Accounting and M&A Integration

Normative management accounting research suggests that changes in an organization's external environment lead to changes in an organization's management accounting systems. This is because managers need specific forms of management accounting information to facilitate decision making brought about by the organization's change in order maintain the reliability of accounting information for the firm to remain competitive. It is therefore not surprising that the debate relating to management accounting change has heightened in recent years. The environment in which management accounting is practised has changed, particularly, the growing level of global competition and advances in information technology (Burns and Scapens, 2000; Baines and Langfield-Smith, 2003). In the context of M&A, when two companies merge, this represents a new development which requires new organizational structures, hence the need to ensure that management accounting systems change to meet the information needs of the new organization.

7.2.2   Approaches to Management Accounting Change

7.2.2.1   Contingency Theory

A number of scholars such as Anthony et al. (1972), Jones (1985a, 1985b), Burns and Scapens (2000) and Bromwich and Bhimani (1989) have attempted to investigate management accounting change. One of the theories advanced to explain management accounting change is contingency theory. The contingency approach to the design of MAS is based on the premise that there is no universally appropriate accounting system which applies equally to all organizations in all circumstances (Emmanuel and Otley, 1990). Rather, it is argued that the particular features of an appropriate accounting system will depend on the specific circumstances in which an organization finds itself. This line of reasoning is consistent with the views of Otley (1980) and Anthony et al. (1972), who pointed out that as the specific circumstances of an organization change, the management accounting system should adapt or modify with due regard to such changes to remain effective. A number of authors, including Khandwalla (1972), Jones (1985b) and Drury (2000) have rendered some support to this view and suggested that the variation of MAS depends on various contingent factors such as environment, organization structure and technology; intensity of competition and strategic mission; business unit; firm; and industry variables. In addition, several other internal variables, such as the choice by the dominant coalition, audit, legal and stakeholder requirements and cost of information may influence the design of MAS. Supporting this line of thinking, Haldma and Lääts (2003) provided a theoretical framework which grouped contingencies into two categories, namely external and internal factors. According to Haldma and Lääts (2003), external environmental factors affect both the internal characteristics of an organization and its management accounting practice (MAP). They suggested that increased competition influences the choice of strategy, organization structure and the application of cost management and control. Internal factors which affect MAPs consequently influence the effectiveness of performance measurement and evaluation. It is argued that the contingency-based approach assumes that MAS is adopted in order to assist managers in achieving some desired goals and outcomes. This is because if MAS is found to be appropriate, then it is likely to provide enhanced information for managers to help make better decisions and achieve the organizational goals effectively.

Child and Mansfield (1972) point out that, as an organization grows, the needs for managers to handle large volume of information increases to the point where they have to put in place controls, extend hierarchies and further decentralize down the hierarchical structure to maintain effectiveness. This suggests that management accounting practices are associated with shifts in business and environment. Acquisition increases organizational size and changes the environment within which an organization operates, and hence, it is argued that the management accounting system implemented should support the particular strategic priorities. Based on this argument, Jones (1985a) suggests that contingency theory provides a logical approach to the study of post-acquisition management accounting systems and as such, a study utilizing this approach may shed more light on the practical application of the theory.

7.2.3   The Process Approach to Management Accounting Change

Another approach which may be relevant to this research is the process approach to change. Process approach involves the managerial activities inherent in shaping expectations, goals and facilitating the work of an organization in achieving these goals (Simons, 1990). A number of authors, including Barnard (1938), Andrew (1980) and Pettigrew (1985a), have written extensively on how business leaders use the process approach to gain competitive advantage. Pettigrew (1985a) defines the process of change as actions, reactions and interactions from the various interested parties as they seek to move the firm from its present to its future. Pettigrew (1985a, 1985b) posits that formulating the content of strategic change involves managing its context and process. It is also important to point out that actions, reactions and interactions among the interested parties have effects on the implementation and how management accounting change should proceed. As management accounting change in M&A integration process entails moving management accounting system from its present form to what will best serve the new organization information needs in future, the process approach to change provides an important basis on which to ground this study. Simply put, the process perspective focuses on the

Table 7.1 Summary of Research on MAS Integration in M&A

Author	Objectives of the Study	Methodology	Results
Jones (1985a)	1. How important MAS became as a means of effecting post-acquisition control 2. How acquiring companies modified and used MAS to establish control 3. The dysfunctional effects of change	Sample of 30 firms interviews	MATS assumed significant importance after acquisition. Inappropriate changes in MAS caused considerable undesirable effects.
Jones (1985b)	1. Examined whether MAS are best perceived as universal or unique in nature in conditions of rapid change 2. The willingness to accept variations in MAS between the acquirer and acquired	Sample of 3 firms interviews	The acquirer is likely to replace the MAS of the acquired firm with its own MAS. Dominant individual preferences may not coincide with the needs of the overall organization. Dominant individuals or coalitions tended to enforce conformity in MAS and limit any willingness to accept changes in acquirer's system. MAS tended to bear the characteristics of the universalistic theory of MAS.
Jones (1986)	Examined the changes introduced in the accounting control systems from acquisitions	Case study of 2 acquisitions made by the same company	Dominant person or coalitions determined the form of ACS appropriate for their particular style of running the business. Acquired ACS was destroyed either deliberately or by default.
Roberts (1990)	Explore the relationship between the use of accounting information for performance reporting and control and the formulation and implementation of business and corporate strategy in a UK conglomerate	Case study of 1 acquisition	Removal of power from the acquired management to the acquirer management. Individuals dominate the development of MAS.
Granlund (2003)	Examined how MAS developed after acquisition Provides new insights into management control problems in M&A	Longitudinal case study Sample of 2 firms	Every acquisition is a special case with many contextually divergent issues. Large acquirers are likely to replace MAS of smaller acquired companies. Problems of post-acquisition management control seem to vary a lot in different contexts.

actions taken by management to guide the post-acquisition integration process. Greenwood et al. (1994), Haspeslagh and Jemison (1989, 1991) and Jemison and Sitkin (1986a) argue that strategic and organizational fit offers potential synergies; however, their realization depends ultimately on the ability of management to manage the post-acquisition integration process in an effective and efficient manner. To this end, Galpin and Hendon (2000) argue that leadership, human resources issues, communication, planning and timing of the process are important variables to achieve integration success.

7.2.4   M&A Integration and Value Creation

Management accounting system which encompasses accounting systems designed to provide information for use by managers within an organization, is regarded as the most important formal source of information for all aspects of business planning and control. In the context of mergers and acquisitions, it is argued that successful integration of two merging firms or between the acquired and acquiring firms is essential for value creation in any merger or acquisition. Therefore, a clear understanding of integration process is essential for conducting effective integration. According to Haspeslagh and Jemison (1991), there are several key components of a successful integration process. These are transfer of strategic capabilities which include operational resource sharing, transfer of functional skills, transfer of general management skills, combination of benefits, creating appropriate atmosphere which include reciprocal organizational understanding, willingness to work together and capacity transfer. The proper functioning of these processes has a significant influence on the extent of value creation from the acquisition event. Appropriate caution must be taken at each stage because the integration is full of uncertainties and complexities. Schweiger et al. (1994) suggest that M&As integration involve adapting the firms' value-generating activities, altering bureaucratic mechanism of authority, control and transforming systems of value, beliefs and practices.

In order to carry out these changes and make integration process effective, various approaches of integration have been suggested by researchers (e.g. Bastien and Van de Ven, 1986; Haspeslagh and Farquar, 1987; Buono and Bowditch, 1989; Lubatkin et al., 1998; Schweiger, 2002). The approaches are consolidation, standardization, coordination and intervention. In the case of consolidation, the separate functions and activities of both acquirer and target firms are physically consolidated into one. Standardization refers to standardizing and formalizing the separate functions and activities of both the acquired and acquiring firms, whereas coordination refers to the extent to which functions and activities of both firms are coordinated. Intervention involves intervening in different activities of acquired firms to revitalize synergistic potentials. In addition to selecting the appropriate integration approach, successful integration entails selection of appropriate level of integration as over or under integration may impede and adversely impact on value creation from M&A (Pablo, 1994).

To make the M&As integration successful, the role of management accountants is inseparable. In explaining the process of integration, Haspeslagh and

Jemison (1991) pointed out that interaction between the merging companies is at the heart of integration. Interaction includes substantive, administrative and symbolic interactions. To make the interactions effective, common accounting system and control procedures are necessary and these can happen even before the consolidation. To facilitate smooth interactions, management accountants can help by providing relevant information and setting appropriate goals and standards that are to be followed by the related parties. The same conclusion regarding the role of accountants, especially management accountants, has also been made by Pitkethly et al. (2003) and Bruner (2004). Likewise, Jones (1985a, 1985b, 1986), Granlund (2003) and Beusch (2005) have also emphasised the role of management accounting in the M&As integration process.

Table 7.1 provides a summary of prior studies.

7.3   RESEARCH DESIGN

To map out the tasks performed by management accountants in the M&A integration process, a qualitative approach was adopted. Adopting qualitative approach is significant for the following reasons. First, qualitative research goes beyond the measurement of observable behaviour (the 'what') and seeks to understand the meaning and beliefs underlying action (the 'why and how') (Yin, 1994). Because our research questions concern the tasks involved in integrating MAS and the factors influencing integration, qualitative approach is deemed the most appropriate for this research. Another reason for the choice of qualitative approach is because each merger or acquisition is a unique event and therefore the use of standardized questionnaire may not capture adequately in quantitative data analysis. In addition, this chapter adopts multi-case study design, due to the complexity of M&A integration processes, one single-case company cannot represent the image of the whole. The evidence from multiple cases is more persuasive, and the overall analytical results are regarded as more robust (Herriot and Firestone, 1983). Finally, multiple cases enable the researcher to conduct multiple experiments applying 'replication' logic (Yin, 1994).

The design of the questions for the interview was heavily influenced by the recommendations of Dilman (1978) and Oppenheim (1992), who both presented comprehensive reviews of literature on questionnaire design. The interview questions generated were based on the aims of the study and literature review. The questionnaire for the interviews was divided into three main parts as follows:

The *first* part was concerned with the company's background (for example, company's products and markets, size etc.) as well as information about the motivation for the company's decision to merge.

The *second* part of the questionnaire had questions about the task performance of management accountants in M&As integration process of MAS.

The *third* part dealt with questions relating to factors influencing MAS integration and the success of integration process.

7.3.1   Data Collection

The sample of interest for this study was a cross section of the UK companies involved in mergers and acquisitions between 2002 and 2007. The research population of interest was obtained from FAME and Thomson One Banker deal database. This information was further cross-checked with the information provided by *Acquisitions Monthly*, which publishes information on all mergers and acquisitions worldwide. The respondents are drawn from the acquirer firms and the merged firms. The reason for this is that, when two companies merged, the existing firms ceased to exist and a new company is created. However, in the case of acquisition, it is only the acquired company which ceases to exist.

To obtain data, the researcher must be "on-site observing, talking with people and going through programme records" (Patton, 1990, p. 244). Consequently, the data for this study was collected via in-depth interviews with senior managers in eight companies. Between July and September, eight open and semi-structured interviews—88% face-to-face and 12% through pre-arranged telephone calls—were conducted with senior managers who were key decision makers involved in the management accounting integration process during M&As. The interviews lasted between 1 and 1.5 hours, and as the participants agreed, all the interviews were recorded by digital recorder. An examination of the job titles of the respondents revealed that 12% of the respondents were merger and acquisition managers, and 88% were finance directors/management accountants. It is pertinent to note that all the respondents have more than 5 years of prior experience involving in the integration process of MAS relating to M&A in their respective companies. What makes the data more valuable is that together, the respondents have previously integrated more than 50 acquisitions among themselves. Secondary data were also collected from company reports, internal company documents and reports, industry reports and previous research on the subject area. Using several sources of information allows us to triangulate data and thus improve the reliability and validity of the findings derived from the case material.

7.3.2   Characteristics of the Sample

The characteristics of the sample are summarized in Table 7.2. The size of the mergers are classified into small/medium with no more than 500 employees (37.5%) (Brouthers and Nakos, 2004) and large with more than 500 employees (62.5%). The industry categories of the mergers and acquisitions are as follows: leisure (25%), services (25%) and real estate, brewing and retailing, plumbing and heating and higher education (12.5%) each. The merger types included horizontal (75%), unrelated (12.5%) and vertical (12.5%).

7.3.3   Data Analysis

The interviews were recorded, transcribed, organized and grouped into meaningful categories. It was then coded in the NVivo software to help in the process of

Table 7.2   Sample Characteristics

Industry	Number	%	M&A Type	Number	%
Leisure	2	25	Horizontal	6	75
Service	2	25	Vertical	1	12.5
Real Estate	1	12.5	Unrelated	1	12.5
			Total	*8*	*100*
Brewing and Retail	1	12.5	**Size**		
Plumbing and Heating	1	12.5	Small/ Medium	3	37.5
Higher Education	1	12.5	Large	5	62.5
Total	*8*	*100*	*Total*	*8*	*100*

creating labelling and layering the connection between the identified categories. The researchers applied the rules of "pattern matching" and comparative methods to draw conclusions (Yin, 1994). To derive further in-depth inferences, the complex relationships among the variables were studied for each acquisition, using the content analysis and explanation building modes of analysis.

7.4   RESULTS

From our analysis, we propose a four-staged integration framework which captures the activities performed and goals of each of the four phases shown in Figure 7.1. Our framework for MAS integration encompasses the following:

1. Pre-integration stage designed to communicate, audit and foster cooperation, trust and understanding of the acquired MAS to help plan the integration
2. Integration planning stage to develop a blueprint and to decide the integration option to follow
3. The choice of integration option to achieve speed of integration, hold on to or retain customers and key staff members, provide relevant and reliable information for performance evaluation and the achievement of synergies
4. Review and evaluation designed to learn from and rectify problems arising out of implementation

7.4.1   Phase 1: Pre-Integration

The first stage—pre-integration—involves the acquirer preparing the ground for the integration to take place. This involves information gathering with a view to develop trust through various means of communication. It is important to point out that, it is in this stage where employees of the acquired and acquirer will have to work with

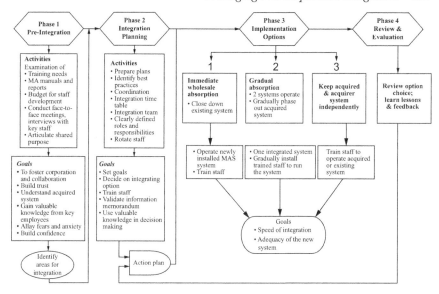

Figure 7.1 Framework for MAS Integration in M&A

Source: Boateng and Bampton (2010)

each other in order to obtain information to accomplish the goal of successful integration. As a result, communication is intense and done mostly on face-to-face basis when feasible and, in some cases, through telephone calls and e-mails. This point was emphasized by a number of respondents. A respondent indicated that "at the early stages of the integration process, communication cannot be done remotely on the telephone, and it is a lot easier if people spend some time with the person who hands it over to you." This is supported by another respondent, who said that "trying to get people from the acquired company on board by communicating carefully actually helps." Communication with key management accounting staff, and continuous communication with all employees and unions to clarify issues such as possible redundancies at the early stage is therefore central to the achievement of the effective integration and reduction of employees' resistance. The extent of the acquired accounting employees' participation at this stage has a tremendous influence on the integration outcome hence it is important that the acquirer's management accounting team acknowledges the importance of the acquired accounting employees' role and handles it through continuous and face-to-face interaction. During this phase, the following activities are carried by the management accounting staff:

• The acquirer management accounting staff undertakes regular on-site visits to:

    conduct face-to-face meetings, interviews with key members of accounting staff;
    examine MAS manual and reports;

distribute and collect an information request form (also called information memorandum) from management accountants giving details about the acquired company MAS;

articulate shared purpose through regular meetings with the management accounting staff; and

engage in jobs rotation—when key members of staff in both target and acquired firms exchange jobs and/or work together to familiarize themselves with the management accounting systems in both companies

These activities are carried out to foster cooperation and build trust, and to facilitate understanding of the acquired MAS. More important, this phase helps to draw a list of priority areas to take immediate control of, to ensure continuous flow of information for customer retention, facilitate the identification of training needs, preserve quality of data and areas to integrate, increase shareholder confidence, ensure costs are controlled and integration synergies are capable of being measured and achieved during the integration.

7.4.2   Phase 2: Integration Planning

The second phase aims at creating a plan for integration. Integration planning is a very important task and determines how the integration process will proceed. A respondent indicated that "as soon as it's announced that we've bought the business, we'll be down at head office fairly quickly trying to get to grips with what's happening, putting a plan together." Another respondent commenting on their latest acquisition said that

> When you're doing an acquisition you only know a certain part about that business and about what you've been given etc. what's in the public domain, and afterwards once you've bought it and you start to put a business plan together you're making assumptions on things that you know and afterwards it's about finding out whether the assumptions you've made were correct or not correct. If they're not correct it's about finding out what to do, you still have to do a business plan, it just shows a bit about what we do and the depth you have to go into.

Other respondents concur and pointed out that planning acquisition integration is a key to successful integration. It may be argued that every merger deal is unique and may involve different sets of problems, however, it should be recognized that the performance of certain common activities will result in a higher level of synergy and will promote the eventual success of the integration. Prominent among the activities performed at this stage are

1. selection of integration/installation team,
2. validation of information memorandum,
3. setting of integration goals,

4. preparation of the blueprint for integration with time schedules,
5. preparation of the training plan with checklist,
6. clear definition of the roles and responsibilities of the installation team,
7. establishment of the reporting lines, and
8. decision on the integration options to be used for implementation.

7.4.3 Phase 3: Implementation and Choice

At this stage, the integration strategy has to be decided as well as how the MAS is going to be integrated with structure and control systems. We found that three integration strategies/options are used by management accountants:

1. Immediate absorption
2. Gradual integration
3. Two management accounting systems operate independently

The key activities normally performed at this phase are coordination, standardization, absorption of the acquired management accounting system and the closing down of the acquired MAS system.

7.4.3.1 *Option 1: Immediate Absorption*

The primary aim of this approach is to consolidate completely the MAS of both firms through assimilating the target firm MAS into that of the acquiring firm. Here the acquired MAS are replaced with the acquirer or, in rare cases, with the target system. As this method of integration involves a significant degree of change in the target firm, it is important to prepare a preliminary plan for key integration issues, transitional structures, techniques for continuous communication, coordination and preparation of a time table for the closure of the acquired management accounting department and its eventual movement to the acquirer's system. The change is carried out in a relatively quick manner to reduce the level of disruption resulting from the delay in the integration of MAS. It is pertinent to point out that the communication tool employed is predominantly face-to-face and more intense in nature.

7.4.3.2 *Option 2: Gradual Integration*

This option involves the following activities: training of staff/development, coordination, standardization of documents and consolidation and regular review. In addition, many of the activities involved in the immediate absorption will also be undertaken. This option is relatively slow and may take about 6 to 18 months to complete depending upon the size of the firm and the complexity of the management accounting system. This is the most popular option for the organizations surveyed in this research.

7.4.3.3   *Option 3: Two Systems Operating Independently*

This option involves operating each system independently after acquisition. This approach is necessitated by a need for operational autonomy with the acquirer and target systems being kept at arm's length. The most important activity here is staff development, in particular, the use of job rotation to help accounting staff of the two companies to understand both systems and improve quality of information needed for decision making.

7.4.4   Phase 4: Review and Evaluation

Following the implementation of one of the options is the review and evaluation of outcomes. Here lessons are learned and fed back into the process for future management accounting integration. A respondent commented,

> We are continually learning and reviewing and every time we do an acquisition we learn new things. For me, the main key area is the people issue, to have the people onside and I think that's been overlooked especially when looking at acquisitions beforehand, what you don't realise till you get there. It's very difficult to do unless you've got the people onboard. So I think that's something we've learnt quite a bit over the years, you can't just expect that the accountants can go in and the company you've acquired will play ball and that they will be able to get the data, they might not be able to get the data in the format required.

Similar point was made by another respondent. "Communication's my biggest learning of it, the first time we did it and it depends on the location to some extent. The last one was in Hartlepool which was a trek but unless you actually sit down there and talk face to face you won't understand the problems, so it's face to face contact." Another respondent commented, "We found what works well is to have an installation team that reports back weekly to the accounting teams ahead to keep them briefed, even if it is something that doesn't particularly relate to their area just so they know the full picture and the story of what's going on and that's come out of the last couple of acquisitions that we've done." These remarks indicate that review and evaluation are important part of the MAS integration process.

7.5   FACTORS INFLUENCING THE CHOICE OF MAS INTEGRATION OPTION

Our guiding question regarding the factors influencing the choice of MAS integration option was "What factors influence the management's decision to choose the MAS integration option used?" Given the predisposition of the companies interviewed towards these three options, namely immediate absorption, gradual integration of the acquired companies or the two systems operate

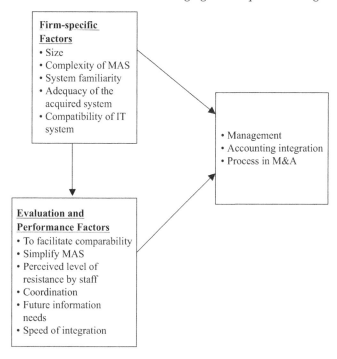

Figure 7.2   Factors Influencing MAS Integration Process
Source: Boateng and Bampton (2010).

independently, we expected that a number of factors may influence the choice of integration strategies. We find that the two sets of factors influence the choice of integration approach: firm-specific factors and performance-evaluation factors in Figure 7.2.

7.5.1   Firm-Specific Factors

Firm-specific factors relate to the unique characteristics of the acquired firm and the extent to which they differ from the acquirer system. These include

- the size of the acquired company,
- the complexity of the management accounting system,
- the similarity of the acquiring firm with the target firm,
- the reporting requirements,
- the adequacy of the acquired system and
- the compatibility of the information technology (IT) systems

The firm-specific factors have an impact on both the effectiveness of performance evaluation and the management accounting system integration. For example, the complexity of the production system influences the extent to which the

MAS can be simplified and consequently the choice of management accounting implementation option to be adopted.

7.5.2   Performance-Evaluation Factors

This is driven by factors which facilitate good evaluation and performance. These include

- facilitating comparability,
- the speed of integration,
- simplifying MAS to ensure adequate and timely production of information,
- perceiving the level of resistance by the acquired staff,
- the future information needs and
- the level of coordination and communication required.

It is pertinent to note that the list of factors identified in our framework cannot be considered exhaustive since we were unable to identify and include all factors.

7.5.3   Discussion

On factors influencing the post-acquisition integration process, we found that size is the single most important factor. One respondent pointed out that "whether to replace the acquired system immediately or integrate on gradual basis is 'very dependent on the size of acquisition.'" Supporting this view, another respondent said, "[I]t very much dependent on the size and the similarity of the systems to be integrated." This point was highlighted by the rest of the respondents. The conclusion emanating from this is that whereas the acquiring firm tends to replace the MAS of small acquisitions, in a case in which the acquired is large, the integration process tends to be gradual over a 6- to 18-month period, or the management accounting system is allowed to operate autonomously. This finding renders some support for the conclusion drawn in the earlier studies by Jones (1985b) and Granlund (2003) that large acquirers are likely to replace the management accounting system of considerably smaller acquired companies.

Regarding the performance evaluation factors, the respondents indicated that the speed at which the integration process carried out is crucial to the success and realization of the operational synergies. A respondent pointed out that "as soon as the acquisition is announced that we have bought the business, we'll be down at head office fairly quickly trying to get grips with what's happening, put a plan together, working out when we need to close down the office fully. Of course the quicker we do that the more money we save." Another respondent echoed similar point: "We define success as being as quick as we can get it back into business as usual, because if it's not business as usual, the management team are focused on the integration and not the customer and the quicker you can get it back to what we define as business as usual, then you know that the acquisition has been successful." This finding is not surprising in that it is consistent with the observation made by

Jones (1985b) that the consequences of delay in implementing group-wide control systems may led to uncertainty and undesirable outcomes and consequently the non-achievements of the expected synergies. Another important finding of this study is that the role of management accountants in the MAS integration is focused on task aspects rather human aspects of the integration. This point was highlighted by most of the respondents who indicated that "there were no human resources [HR] issues concerned with MAS integration." This suggests that HR issues are handled by the HR team. However, the tasks to be undertaken are dependent on the approach used.

Another important conclusion to be drawn from the preceding discussion is that the decision whether to integrate or not is ultimately driven by the desire to achieve better performance and gain synergies at the point of acquisition.

7.6   IMPLICATIONS AND CONCLUSION

The study has examined the tasks performed by management accountants in MAS integration process of mergers and acquisitions. This study represents one of the first attempts to provide a framework for MAS integration and therefore makes a significant contribution to an under-researched area of management accounting. The study finds that the role of management accountants in the MAS integration is focused on task aspects of the MAS integration process with relatively little attention on human aspects of integration. The emphasis of task integration process by the management accountants is not surprising in that the activity segmentation during acquisitions creates a process in which managers focus on the job they have been given rather than on the whole (Birkinshaw et al., 2000); hence, management accountants may focus on task to get the job done.

We find that MAS integration goes through four-staged phases, namely pre-integration, integration planning, implementation options, review and evaluation. The study also finds that all the acquirers (regardless of the size industry and implementation strategy to be used) follow the similar activities outlined in the first two stages of the MAS integration framework, that is pre-integration and integration planning. However, at the implementation phase, the activities to be performed are contingent on the implementation option adopted. Companies adopting immediate absorption tend to undertake minimal changes, whereas companies adopting gradual integration tend to perform a number of activities ranging from coordination, standardization of documents and consolidation. In addition, this study finds that large acquirers are more likely to immediately absorb the MAS of relatively smaller acquired system. This is not surprising given that integrating a relatively small firm tends to be easier However, when the acquired system is unrelated, the acquirer is more likely to retain the MAS and to allow it to operate independently.

Notwithstanding the common activities we documented and that are normally performed by all management accountants, it is pertinent also to point out that we also find that each acquisition tends to be unique and different with many contextually divergent issues influencing the integration approach to be adopted or used.

Another important conclusion to be drawn from this study is the importance of communication. We identified communication as a major tool for reducing the uncertainty among the people involved. Gathering important information about the target MAS is a key to stabilizing volatile situations and reduce the dysfunctional effects likely to undermine the integration process.

An examination of the framework for the integration process we have put forward in this study indicates that the integration of MAS in M&A involves task integration activities with a number of common activities being performed by management accountants during the integration process. The implication of this for management accountants is that certain common activities are important for the successful integration of MAS in M&As. We suggest that managers should pay attention to these activities, particularly those relating to the first and second phases of the integration process.

Another important implication of the finding is that management accountants of the companies examined place more emphasis on the task aspects of MAS integration process in M&A with relatively little attention on the human aspects of integration. Although, it is acknowledged that the concentration on task integration can lead to the achievement of synergies but that this may also result in poor employee motivation. Given that the integration of MAS involve people, who in some cases, are about to lose their jobs, lack of full and proper attention in this vital aspects of integration may result in uncooperative attitudes towards the integration process with potential negative consequences. However, the important implication here is that although task integration and human integration require separate and different management actions, efforts must be made by management accountants to give equal attention to both task integration and human integration because they both constitute important elements for successful integration. This is because for the process to generate maximum benefits both task and human integration issues should be at the core of MAS integration process. Specifically, we suggest that there should be personnel among the management accounting integration team charged with the responsibility of dealing with human aspects of the integration far beyond just taking actions to get cooperation and information of the target employees.

REFERENCES

Andrew, K.R. (1980). *The Concept of Corporate Strategy*, Homewood, IL: Irwin.

Anthony, R.N. Dearden, J.and Vancil, R.F. (1972). *Management Control Systems*, Homewood: Richard D. Irwin.

Baines, A. and Langfield-Smith, K. (2003). Antecedents to Management Accounting Change: A Structural Equation Approach, *Accounting, Organisation and Society*, Vol. 28, pp. 675–698.

Barnard, C.I. (1938). *The Functions of the Executive*, Cambridge, MA: Harvard University Press.

Bastien, D.T. and Van de Ven, A.H. (1986). *Managerial and Organizational Dynamics of Mergers and Acquisitions*, Discussion Paper No. 36, Strategic Research Center, University of Minnesota, Minneapolis.

Beusch, P. (2005). *A Tentative Model of Management Accounting and Control in the Integration Process of Mergers and Acquisitions*, paper presented at Research Conference on the Changing Roles of Management Accounting as a Control System, University of Antwerp, Belgium.

Birkinshaw, J., Bresman, H. and Hakanson, L. (2000). Managing the Post-Acquisition Integration Process: How the Human Integration and Task Integration Processes Interact to Foster Value Creation, *Journal of Management Studies*, Vol. 37(3), pp. 395–425.

Boateng, A. and Bampton, R. (2010). Mergers and Acquisition Integration Process: The Role of Management Accountant, *Chartered Institute of Management Accountants, Report 187, RES*, Vol. 6(5), pp. 1–3.

Bromwich, M. and Bhimani, A. (1989). *Management Accounting: Evolution not Revolution*, London: CIMA.

Brouthers, K.D. and Nakos, G. (2004). 'SME Entry Mode Choice and Performance: A Transaction Cost Perspective, *Entrepreneurship Theory and Practice*, Vol. 28, pp. 229–247.

Bruner, R.F. (2004). *Applied Mergers and Acquisitions: Workbook*, Hoboken, NJ: John Wiley & Sons.

Buono, A.F. and Bowditch, J.L. (1989). *The Human Side of Mergers and Acquisitions: Managing Collusions between People and Organizations*, San Francisco: Jossey-Bass.

Burns, J. and Scapens, R.W. (2000). Conceptualizing Management Accounting Change: An Institutional Framework, *Management Accounting Research*, Vol. 11(1), pp. 3–25.

Child, J and Mansfield, R. (1972). Technology, Size and Organisation Structure, *Sociology*, Vol. 6, pp. 369–393.

Dilman, D.A (1978). *Mail and Telephone Surveys*, New York: Wiley.

Drury, C. (2000). *Management and Cost Accounting*, 5th Edition, London: Thomson Learning.

Emmanuel, C. and Otley, D. (1990). *Accounting for Management Control*, 2nd Edition, London: Van Nostrand Reinhold.

Galpin, T.J and Hendon, M. (2000). *The Complete Guide to Mergers and Acquisitions: Process Tools to Support M&A Integration at Every Level*. San Francisco: Jossey-Bass.

Granlund, M. (2003). Management Accounting System Integration in Corporate Mergers: A Case Study, *Accounting, Auditing and Accountability Journal*, Vol. 16(2), pp. 208–243.

Greenwood, R., Hinings, C.R. and Brown, J (1994). Merging Professional Service Firms, *Organisation Science*, Vol. 5(2), pp. 23–35.

Haldma, T. and Lääts, K. (2003). Contingencies Influencing the Management Accounting Practices of Estonian Manufacturing Companies, *Management Accounting Research*, Vol. 13, pp. 379–400.

Haspeslagh, P.C. and Farquar, A.B. (1987) *The Acquisition Integration Process: A Contingent Framework*, paper presented at the Seventh Annual International Conference of the Strategic Management Society, Boston.

Haspeslagh, P.C. and Jemison, D.B. (1989). Acquisitions, Myths and Reality, *Sloan Management Review*, Winter, pp. 53–58.

Haspeslagh, P.C. and Jemison, D.B. (1991). *Managing Acquisitions: Creating Value through Corporate Renewal*, New York: The Free Press.

Henry, D. (2002). Mergers: Why Most Big Deals Don't Pay Off, *Business Week*, 14 October, pp. 60–70.

Herriott, R.E. and Firestone, W.A. (1983). Multisite Qualitative Policy Research Optimizing Description and Generalizability, *Educational Researcher*, Vol. 72(2), pp. 14–19.

Jemison, D. and Sitkin, S.B. (1986a). Corporate Acquisitions: A Process Perspective, *Academy of Management Review*, Vol. 11(1), pp. 145–163.

Jemison, D. and Sitkin, S.B. (1986b). Acquisitions: The Process Can Be a Problem, *Harvard Business Review*, March–April, pp. 107–116.

Jones, C.S. (1985a). An Empirical Study of the Role of Management Accounting Systems Following Takeover or Merger, *Accounting, Organization and Society*, Vol. 10, pp. 177–200.

Jones, C.S. (1985b). An Empirical Study of the Evidence for Contingency Theories of Management Accounting Systems in Conditions of Rapid Change, *Accounting, Organizations and Society*, Vol. 10(3), pp. 303–328.

Jones, C.S. (1986). Organizational Change and the Functioning of Accounting, *Journal of Business Finance & Accounting*, Vol. 13(3), pp. 283–310.

Khandwalla, P. (1972). *The Design of Organizations*, New York: Harcourt, Brace & Jovanovich.

KPMG (1999). *Unlocking Shareholder Value, the Key to Success*, Mergers and Acquisitions: A Global Research Report, November.

Lubatkin, M., Calori, R., Very, P. and Veiga, J. (1998). Managing Mergers Across Borders: A Two Nation Exploration of a Nationally Bound Administrative Heritage, *Organization Science*, Vol. 9(6), pp. 670–684.

Mergerstat (2000). Two Tales Can Be Told about the M&A Market in 2000, *PR Newswire*, December 28.

Oppenheim, A.N. (1992). *Questionnaire Design, Interviewing and Attitude Measurement*, New Edition, London: Printers Publication.

Otley, D.T. (1980). The Contingency Theory of Management Accounting: Achievement and Prognosis, *Accounting Organization and Society*, Vol. 5(4), pp. 413–428.

Pablo, A.L. (1994). Determinants of Acquisition Integration Level: A Decision-Making Perspective, *Academy of Management Journal*, Vol. 37, pp. 803–836.

Patton, M.Q. (1990). *Qualitative Evaluation and Research Methods*, 2nd Edition, London: Sage.

Pettigrew, A. (1985a). *The Awakening Giant: Continuity and Change in ICI*, Oxford: Blackwell.

Pettigrew, A. (1985b). Contextualist Research: A Natural Way to Link Theory and Practice, in E.E. Lawler (ed.). *Doing Research that is Useful in Theory and Practice*, San Francisco: Jossey-Bass, pp. 222–248.

Pitkethly, R., Faulkner, D. and Child, J. (2003). Integrating Acquisitions, *Advances in Mergers and Acquisitions*, Vol. 2, pp. 27–57.

PricewaterhouseCoopers (2000). PricewaterhouseCoopers Forecast. While M&A Outlook Remains Strong for 2001, Acquirers Look for More than Size as They Struggle with New Economy Growth Model, *Business Wire*, (December 18).

Roberts, J. (1990). Strategy and Accounting in UK Conglomerate, *Accounting, Organization and Society*, Vol. 15, pp. 107–126.

Schweiger, D.M. (2002). *M&A Integration: A Framework for Executives and Managers*, New York: McGraw-Hill.

Schweiger, D.M., Csiszar, E.N. and Napier, N.K. (1994) A Strategic Approach to Implementing Mergers and Acquisitions, in G.V. Krogh, A. Sinatra and H. Singh (eds.), *Managing Corporate Acquisitions: A Comparative Analysis*, London, Macmillan, pp. 23–49.

Simons, R. (1990). The Role of Management Control Systems in Creating Competitive Advantage: New Perspectives, *Accounting, Organisation and Society*, Vol. 15(1/2), pp. 127–143.

Yin, R.K (1994). *Case Study Research Design and Methods*, Applied Social Research Methods Series, Newbury Park, CA: Sage.

8 Short-Run Performance of Cross-Border Mergers and Acquisition of UK Acquiring Firms

8.1 INTRODUCTION

Cross-border mergers and acquisitions (CBM&A) activity has become an increasingly important phenomenon and has been at the centre of business and management research over the last two decades. The increasing integration of the world economy and the accompanying liberalization of restrictions on international capital flows have heightened the global market for corporate control (Eun et al., 1996). Evidence of spectacular growth of worldwide CBM&A activities is available from various data sources including the investment reports of the United Nations Conference for Trade and Development (UNCTAD) and OECD. In a particular, CBM&A activity in the UK has witnessed a substantial increase over the past decade. According to UNCTAD (2000), the UK is one of the largest acquiring countries in the world with a share of about 31% of the total value of global CBM&A.

Despite the massive participation in the global market for corporate control, the CBM&A research in the UK has received relatively little attention by the researchers in corporate finance. This view is endorsed by Gregory and McCorriston (2005) who pointed out that the literature on the UK CBM&A is fairly scant. This is against the backdrop that, the results of existing studies in finance and strategy support the view that wealth effects on shareholders of acquiring firms are mixed and more puzzling. For example Conn and Connell (1990), Pettway et al. (1993), Kang (1993), Markides and Ittner (1994), Cakici et al. (1996), Kiymaz (2003) and Block (2005) have reported positive abnormal return for the shareholders of acquiring firms. On the other hand, Datta and Puia (1995), Eun et al. (1996), Corhay and Rad (2000), and Aw and Chatterjee (2004) have reported negative returns for the acquiring firm shareholders. Following from the observation of phenomenal growth, dearth of research and mixed results, there is a need for further research regarding the performance of acquiring firms engaged in CBM&A. Another important aspect of merger and acquisition activities is the size of the acquisition deals. Over the past decade, we witnessed an increasing volume of large deals involving huge amounts of money such as Akzo Nobel's US$14.4 billion sale of its pharmaceutical business to ScheringPlough; Vodafone US$13 billion deal for mobile operator Hutchison Essar. Large deals raise a number of issues ranging from integration problems, method of payment and agency problems which have implications for performance of the acquiring firms. For example, managers may embark on such deals to maximize their own utility at the expense of shareholders. Large deals provide a fertile ground for managers to seek growth in assets which is tied to managerial compensation, increased power and reputation (see Marris, 1964). In addition, large deals are likely to be financed by stock rather than cash (UNCTAD, 2000) and this has implications for performance as a number of studies have suggested that cash acquisitions perform better than stock acquisitions. In fact, the majority of large deals do not meet expected results (Schmidt and Ruhli, 2002). However, no study has explicitly investigated the impact of deal size on the returns of acquiring firm's performance of UK CBM&A. The aim of this chapter is to consider the short-run performance of UK firms acquiring foreign target firms over the 1994–2003 period and to explore the impact of deal size and other firm specific factors on performance. Specifically, this study attempt to address the following research questions:

1. What is the short-run share price performance of UK acquiring firms engaged in CBM&A?
2. What are the factors that determine the short-run performance of UK acquiring firms?
3. What is the impact of the deal size on the short-run performance of UK acquiring firms?

The rest of the chapter is organized as follows. The next section presents the hypotheses of the study. Section 8.3 describes the data and the method used in this study. Section 8.4 comprises the results and discussion, and this is followed by the conclusions of the study (Section 8.5).

8.2   HYPOTHESES

8.2.1   CBM&A Performance and UK Acquiring Firms

An important source of positive performance for acquiring firm shareholders engaged in acquisitions activities of CBM&A is the possibility of internalization and reverse internalization. Eun et al. (1996) suggested the possibility of achieving internalization and reverse internalization by acquiring foreign target firms (that is, the creation of synergy which ultimately ends up with positive market reaction about the participating firms). The value-creation effect of internalization and of reverse internalization has also been supported by Morck and Yeung (1992) and Seth et al. (2000, 2002). The possibility of global or international diversification of the firm through cross-border mergers and acquisitions can also create value for the participating firm (Markides and Ittner, 1994; Shimizu et al., 2004). Other possible sources of benefits include the exchange rate variations among the countries (Markides and Ittner, 1994), tax differentials (Manzon et al., 1994) and differences in accounting methods (Dunne and Ndubizu, 1995). On the other hand, researchers such as Moeller and Schlingemann (2005) suggested that increased integration in the market for corporate control may lead to increased competition in this market and that this increased competition may in turn reduce the gains for the bidding firm. The increased integration may also contribute to the reduction of the cost of CBM&A which may increase the hubris and agency problem of the firm. Denis et al. (2002) find that global diversification is associated with discount which is mostly similar in magnitude to the industrial diversification discount as suggested by Berger and Ofek (1995). Thus, if the international diversification is not beneficial as suggested by Denis et al. (2002), the profitability of CBM&A should also be in question. The existence of managerialism and hubris in the CBM&A as suggested by Seth et al. (2000, 2002) and the liability of foreignness, such as unfamiliarity of foreign environment, cultural, political and economic difference and coordination problems due to geographical distance, may actually destroy the value of the acquiring firms acquiring foreign targets (Zaheer, 1995). Based on these arguments, a number of studies have examined the performance of acquiring firms. However, relatively few studies have examined the short-run performance of UK acquiring firms. Among the studies examining the short-run performance of UK acquiring firms, Conn and Connell (1990), Conn et al. (2001) and Conn et al. (2005) have reported statistically significant positive return in the short-run for the UK acquirers, whereas Aw and Chatterjee (2004) reported statistically significant negative abnormal return. Gregory and McCorriston (2005) have also reported negative bidder return but the result is not statistically significant. In addition, whereas Mathur et al. (1994) and Eun et al. (1996) suggested the UK acquirers and acquirers from other countries earned statistically significant negative abnormal return, Goergen and Renneboog (2003, 2004) reported statistically significant positive abnormal return for the UK acquiring firms. Based on the preceding discussion, it is clear that the theoretical literature on the performance of CBM&A is indeed divided. Whereas one strand of literature suggests positive contribution of CBM&A on the value of the firm, the other strand suggests that CBM&A are value destroying in nature. To further test this relationship, the study examines the following hypothesis:

> **Hypothesis 1:** *The shareholder of UK acquiring firms engaged in CBM&A will earn positive abnormal return in the short-run.*

8.2.2   Payment Method and Acquiring Firm Performance

Prior literature suggests that the method of payment may influence the performance of the acquiring firm. A number of scholars argue that acquisitions that are financed through cash create more value than acquisitions that are financed by non-cash methods (e.g. stock or combination of cash and stock). A number of studies involving CBM&A including those of Wansley et al. (1983), Cebenoyan et al. (1992), Cheng and Chan (1995), Fuller and Glatzer (2003) and Danbolt (2004) have provided some support for the proposition that cash transactions produced higher returns compared with the stock or other method of payment transactions; however, the results are not statistically significant in some of the studies. On the other hand, Chang (1998), Chatterjee and Kuenzi (2001) and Fuller et al. (2002) reported superior performance for stock acquisition compared to cash acquisition. Moreover, Conn et al. (2005) suggest that the signalling effect of cash transactions may not have the same force in the case of CBM&A in that other factors have influence on the means of payment. For example, it is suggested that the use of equity by cross-border acquirers may be due to greater uncertainty associated with information problems associated with acquiring abroad. Moreover, the payment of cash may be an outcome of the reluctance of foreign target firms to accept overseas equity as suggested by Gaughan (2002), and this might neutralize the signalling impact of a cash acquisition. In the light of these arguments, it becomes less clear that cash acquisitions will outperform stock acquisitions in case of CBM&A. The apparent controversy in the empirical literature regarding the profitability of cash and non-cash acquisitions leads to our second hypothesis:

> **Hypothesis 2:** *In the short-run, cash acquisitions will produce more value than non-cash acquisitions to the UK acquiring firms engaged in CBM&A.*

8.2.3   Public versus Private Target and Performance of Acquiring Firm

A number of studies have suggested that the nature and form of target firms (public or private target) may influence the performance of the acquiring firm. Draper and Paudyal (2006) suggested that managerial motives may be one of the reasons for higher returns of bidding firms that acquire private targets. The managerial motive hypothesis is premised on the assumption that acquisitions tend to increase the private benefit of managers, which is positively related with the size and the reputation of the target. As public companies are relatively bigger in size and more reputed in the market than private firms, managers are willing to pay more for those targets leaving the shareholders in a vulnerable position. However, acquisitions of private targets will not provide the managers with any of these benefits and hence will not result in overpayment for those targets. Consequently, acquisitions of private targets are most likely to improve the wealth of acquiring firms' shareholders. Fuller et al. (2002) also argue that private firms are less liquid than are public firms. This illiquidity reduces the private firm owners bargaining power in terms of price likely to be obtained during the sale. Therefore, acquiring firms enjoy a price discount at the time of purchasing private targets, which ultimately increases the return for the acquiring firm.

On the other hand, Draper and Paudyal (2006) have stated that private firms are often held by a family or by a small group of people and that this ultimately reduces the agency problem. The absence of the agency problem gives the owners of private firms the control of setting the time to sell and selecting the appropriate buyer. This enhanced bargaining power favours the target firm in charging higher prices from the prospective acquirer, leaving the latter at a relatively disadvantaged position. In addition, if the private firm managers use the acquisition as an exit strategy and become uninterested in performing the monitoring role then the superiority of acquiring a private target might be violated (Chang, 1998; Fuller et al., 2002). The theoretical controversy regarding the performance of acquiring firms that acquire private targets and firms that acquire public targets is even more complex in the context of international acquisitions due to the higher information search costs and limited information availability regarding foreign private companies. It may be argued that the transaction cost involved in acquiring private companies may severely affect the performance of the acquiring firm. In the light of preceding discussion, it is hypothesized that

> **Hypothesis 3:** *In the short-run, the performance of the UK acquiring firms that acquire foreign private targets will be better than the acquirers that acquire foreign public targets.*

8.2.4 Relatedness of Target and Acquiring Firms and Performance of Acquirers

It has been documented in the M&A literature that the relatedness between target and acquiring firms may have an impact on the performance of the acquiring firm. Singh and Montgomery (1987) pointed out that value creation in related acquisitions may arise from three sources. These are economies of scale, economies of scope and market power. Singh and Montgomery further suggested that the market power benefit is more prevalent in the case of related acquisitions where the size of the firm may be increased through horizontal acquisition in order to be able to exert pressure on the market. Seth (1990) pointed out that two merging firms competing in the same product market have a higher potential for market-power-related gains than will two firms competing in dissimilar product markets. Based on this reasoning, Singh and Montgomery (1987), Shelton (1988), Morck et al. (1990), Hubbard and Palia (1999) and Walker (2000) examined the performance of related acquisitions and found evidence that relatedness between merging firms positively affect the bidder's return.

On the other hand, there is evidence in the M&A literature that unrelated acquisitions may also be value-creating events. The main sources of value in the case of unrelated acquisitions come from the possibility of a diversification effect. Diversification at corporate level is a major stimulus for domestic mergers and acquisitions (Trautwein, 1990). Corporate diversification through mergers and acquisitions helps the participating firms to get the benefit of coinsurance (Lewellen, 1971; Kim and McConnell, 1977; Asquith and Kim, 1982), a reduction of risk (Hughes et al., 1980; Reed and Luffman, 1986), a reduction of the firm's default risk and an increase in the debt capacity (Halpern, 1983; Shleifer and Vishny, 1992) and the creation of an internal capital market (Stulz, 1990). Unrelated acquisitions may also create market power for the acquiring firm by increasing the absolute size and breadth of the firm (Singh and Montgomery, 1987). However, scholars suggest that the benefits of unrelated acquisitions may be overshadowed by the possibility of being implemented by managers to achieve their own objectives at the expense of the shareholders' benefit (Morck et al., 1990). More specifically, unrelated acquisitions may help managers rather than stockholders by decreasing managers' employment risk (Amihud and Lev, 1981), entrenching managers (Shleifer and Vishny, 1989) and by enhancing managers' salaries by increasing the firm size (Kroll et al., 1990). Moreover, unrelated acquisitions may have a detrimental effect on R&D output (Hitt et al., 1991) and total stock risk (Lubatkin and O'Neill, 1987). Despite the existence of several sources of value destruction in the case of unrelated acquisitions compared to related acquisitions, it is not always clear that related acquisitions will always outperform unrelated acquisitions (Elgers and Clark, 1980; Chatterjee, 1986; Singh and Montgomery, 1987). The effect of relatedness on the value of the firm has also been investigated in the case of CBM&A. For example, studies by Markides and Ittner (1994), Eun et al. (1996), Markides and Oyon (1998), Corhay and Rad (2000), Gleason et al. (2002), Gregory and McCorriston (2005) and Francoeur (2005) have found superior performance of related acquisitions compared to unrelated acquisitions. However, Datta and Puia (1995) and Pettway et al. (1993) have concluded that the influence of relatedness on the value creation of acquiring firm is unclear. To further examine this area, the study proposes the following hypothesis:

Hypothesis 4: In the short run, UK acquirers that acquire related foreign target firms perform better than the acquirers that acquire unrelated foreign target firms.

8.2.5   Geographical Origin of Target and Acquiring Firms' Performance

One of the important sources of benefit from CBM&A is the inter country diversification that may help to reduce riskiness of the acquiring firm and enable the bidder to use its strategic advantages in international financial and product markets because of the differences in tax structure, governance system, level of development in the market for corporate control and technology (Kiymaz and Mukherjee, 2000). The benefits to the acquiring firms arising from country diversification are not the same for all countries where the acquiring firms purchase the targets. Hisey and Caves (1985) support this line of thinking and suggest that the target firm's country may be an important determinant of the benefits of an international acquisition. For example, Doukas and Travlos (1988) found that acquiring firms' shareholders will gain if the target firms are from less developed countries and acquiring firm diversify simultaneously across geographic and industry space. Similar conclusions have been drawn by Manzon et al. (1994), Doukas (1995) and Chari et al. (2004). However, the findings of Conn et al. (2001) suggest that acquiring firms earn more when they acquire European targets. Gleason et al. (2002) reported that CARs for the acquiring firms are positive when the firms acquire targets from countries with less restrictive tax regulations, open banking climate and lower level of government regulations and interventions. Corhay and Rad (2000), Kiymaz (2003), Goergen and Renneboog (2004), Campa and Hernando (2004), Gregory and McCorriston (2005), Moeller and Schlingemann (2005) and Francoeur (2005) have also pointed out that target country variation affects bidder return, whereas Fatemi and Furtado (1988) and Yook and McCabe (1996) could not find significant evidence on the relation between country variation of target firms and bidder returns. In the context of UK, Conn et al. (2001) found that announcement month return for acquiring firms is higher for European targets compared to targets from the US and the rest of the world or non-US English-speaking countries. Gregory and McCorriston (2005) found that the return for acquiring US targets is higher than the return for acquiring European Union (EU) or rest of the world targets. However, Aw and Chatterjee (2004) also found return difference when targets are from either the US or the EU but the results are not statistically significant. Given these inconsistencies in the prior literature, we hypothesised that

> **Hypothesis 5:** *The return to the UK acquiring firms engaged in CBM&A will not be the same irrespective of geographical origin of target firms.*

8.2.6   Deal Size and Acquiring Firm Performance

Besides the preceding five hypotheses, we test one additional hypothesis which is exploratory in nature. The hypothesis is related to the impact of deal size on the performance of acquiring firms engaged in cross-border acquisitions. The size of the deal may have an impact on the acquiring firm's performance for several reasons. First, a larger deal size may indicate that the size of the target is large. The managerialism hypothesis posits that managers of the acquiring firms invest in the purchase of other firms to maximize their own benefits. If this is the case, then larger targets are more likely to contribute to the benefits maximization compared to smaller targets. Acquiring larger targets will give the acquiring firm's managers greater power, more reputation, higher salary and social recognition (Firth, 1980). Therefore, a larger deal size may be a source of empire building or a pursuit of managerialism behaviour. It is also documented in the M&A literature that managers of acquiring firms may suffer from hubris in making the acquisition deal (Roll, 1986; Seth et al., 2000). If the deal size is large, then the effect of hubris is likely to have more of an impact on the return of the acquiring firm. Third, larger deals are more likely to be financed by stock rather than cash (UNCTAD, 2000, p. 113). Travlos (1987), Asquith et al. (1990), Servaes (1991), Andrade et al. (2001) and Dong et al. (2005) have found evidence that cash acquisitions perform better than stock acquisitions. Therefore, smaller deals that are more likely to be financed by cash should perform better than larger deals. Moreover, Ingham et al. (1992) pointed out that integration of smaller acquisitions is easier and that this can be done without the possibility of loss of control.

On the other hand, larger deals might reduce the free cash flows in the hands of acquiring firms' managers as suggested by Jensen (1986), and reduction of free cash flow might bring some added benefits to the acquiring firm. Moreover, UNCTAD

(2000) and Sudarsanam (2003) have indicated that large acquisitions can have the benefit of economies of scale and scope. Myers and Majluf (1984) support this view by pointing out that large acquisitions are beneficial for attaining financial synergy. These theoretical arguments clearly indicate that deal size may have both a positive and a negative impact on the return of the acquiring firm. However, no such study has explicitly investigated the impact of deal size on the returns of acquiring firm of CBM&A in the UK. To fill this gap, we hypothesise that

> **Hypothesis 6:** *The return to the UK acquiring firms engaged in CBM&A will not be the same irrespective of deal size.*

8.3   DATA AND METHODOLOGY

8.3.1   Data Source

The initial sample information was collected from Thomson One Banker deal database. This database provides information regarding the initial announcement date and effective completion date of acquisition. It also provides the following information: name of the companies, public status, country of origin, primary US Standard Industrial Classification (SIC) codes, mid- and macro- industry of acquiring and target firms, information regarding deal status, consideration offered and rank value of each deal. The information was further checked with the information provided by the *Acquisitions Monthly* magazine, which is specialized in publishing worldwide deal data. Share price information was collected from Datastream database, which provides daily share prices of various listed companies across the world. The daily data on LSE All share price index was also collected from Datastream database. Information on announcement of any significant event for each of the firms included in the initial sample frame was collected from Thomson One Banker company analysis. This database provides information on equity and bond issue of all the companies listed in any major stock exchange in the world.

8.3.2   Sample Selection

The sample selection procedure for examining the UK acquiring firms' performance starts with the universe of UK acquirers who are engaged in acquiring foreign targets. Thomson One Banker deal database for UK CBM&A reported 14,956 acquisitions of foreign targets by UK firms from January 1985 to June 2006. The following restrictions were imposed on the acquiring firms to become part of sample:

1. The samples are restricted to those acquisitions that involve UK public limited companies as acquirer because companies of that type are obliged by the Companies Act to keep proper records that facilitate proper data collection.

2. Acquisitions that were announced and completed between 1994 and 2003 have been included in the sample. This restriction has been imposed to allow sufficient time for calculating returns before and after the acquisition event

3. Acquisitions in the financial sector (e.g. banks, insurance, life assurance, investment companies, real estate investment trusts, speciality and other finance and investment) are excluded from the sample. This criterion has been imposed in selecting sample because of the different nature of assets and liabilities of financial firms and the different financial reporting system of the same.

4. To avoid insignificant impact on the performance of acquiring firm acquisition events that are valued less than US$5 million and acquisitions that represent less than 50% interest in the target firm are excluded.

The imposition of these restrictions has produced a sample of 994 acquisitions undertaken by 485 UK public companies. As the objective of this study was to examine the short-run share-price performance of acquiring firms, we calculated the normal returns using standard market model parameters and compared the normal returns with actual returns to detect the abnormal returns of acquiring firms. To calculate the individual company returns, we used daily adjusted share prices for each individual sample companies. Although, in a number of cases, merger performance has been analysed by using monthly share prices, using daily share prices are more common. Brown and Warner (1980) pointed out that using daily return data allows a researcher to more effectively isolate the market's reaction to a particular event with a known event date. Lubatkin (1987) reinforced this view by stating that daily return data allow abnormal returns to be computed over short horizons. The shorter the time horizon, the less likely the estimated returns will be biased by extraneous events. These considerations led to the choice of daily share-price data to examine the short-run (announcement-period) performance of UK CBM&A. This requirement compels the researchers to impose additional restrictions in selecting the final sample firms. The following additional restrictions were imposed on the initial sample firms to become part of final sample firms:

1. The dividend adjusted daily closing share-prices spanning 200 trading days before the acquisition to at least 20 days after the acquisition must be available for the sample firms.

2. To separate out the effect of each acquisition properly, acquisitions that took place within three months are excluded from the final sample. If a firm has any such event, that is, a series of acquisitions happened within a three months interval, then only the first acquisition is considered.

3. To avoid possible information contamination or the confounding effect as described by McWilliams and Siegel (1997), firms that undertake any significant event (e.g. equity issue, bond issue or share repurchase) within 30 days prior and after the acquisition are also excluded from the final sample list.

Table 8.1   Derivation of Final Sample

Description	No. of Firms	No. of Acquisitions
Initial Sample	485	994
Less Unavailability of daily share price	293	544
Less Announcement of significant event	11	25
Less Acquisitions within less than three months		52
Total for final sample	181	373

The imposition of these restrictions produced a final sample of 373 acquisitions by 181 UK acquiring firms. The derivation of the final sample considering the above additional restrictions is shown in Table 8.1.

It is important to note that the sample in this study is free from survivorship bias. Survivorship bias can be defined as the tendency for failed companies to be excluded from performance studies because they no longer exist. Survivorship bias can cause the results of the study to skew higher because only companies successful enough to survive until the end of the period are included. The study selected sample firms from the Thomson One Banker deal database which revises the deal data on a daily basis. As the sources of data collection report acquisition events almost instantly irrespective of the future status of the acquiring companies, a sample drawn from those sources should be free from survivorship bias.

8.3.3   Sample Statistics

Panel A of Table 8.2 reveals that majority of the acquisitions were consummated in the manufacturing (48%) and service (29%) sectors.[1] Another important characteristic of the sample acquisition events is that most of the acquisitions were consummated during 1998–2000 with the highest number of acquisitions in 2000. This is consistent with the observations provided in UNCTAD (2000).

Panel B of Table 8.2 presents some individual characteristics of the sample acquisition events. For example, the majority of targets are from North America (56%) followed by Europe (44%). Distribution of related (i.e. acquirer and target firms belong to the same sector based on the first two digits of US SIC codes for both the target and bidding firms) and unrelated acquisitions are 51% and 49%, respectively. Another important sample characteristic is that sample acquisitions events are dominated by private targets, with almost 70% targets being private firms. It is also important to note that out of 373 acquisitions, 206 acquisitions are financed by cash consideration with the remaining financed by non-cash considerations. The table also shows that the majority of the deals (69%) were small and medium-size deals representing deal values less than US$50 million, with the remaining 31% of deals valued at more than US$50 million.

Table 8.2 Sample Characteristics

Panel A: Year and Sector wise Distribution of Sample Acquisition Events

Year	No.	% in Total	Sector	No.	% in Total
1994	14	3.75	Agriculture, Forestry and Fishing	1	0.27
1995	24	6.43	Mining	8	2.15
1996	28	7.51	Construction	4	1.07
1997	36	9.65	Manufacturing	186	49.87
1998	46	12.33	Transport, Communication,	35	9.38
1999	59	15.82	Electric, Gas and Sanitary Services		
2000	67	17.96	Wholesale Trade	17	4.56
2001	44	11.80	Retail Trade	9	2.41
2002	20	5.36	Real Estate	4	1.07
2003	35	9.38	Services	109	29.22
Total	*373*	*100*	*Total*	*373*	*100*

Panel B: Sample Characteristics of Acquisition Events

Description	Sample Characteristics	No. of Acquisitions	% in Total
Target Region	North America[1]	210	56
	Europe	163	44
Total		*373*	*100*
Related vs. Unrelated	Related	189	51
	Unrelated	184	49
Total		*373*	*100*
Form of Target	Private	262	70
	Public	111	30
Total		*373*	*100*
Payment Method	Cash	206	55
	Non-cash[2]	167	45
Total		*373*	*100*
Deal Size	Small and medium deals[3]	256	69
	Larger deals[4]	117	31
Total		*373*	*100*

[1] North America includes targets from the US and Canada.

[2] Non-cash payment methods predominantly include stock and a combination of cash and stock.

[3] Small and medium-size deals are deals that are valued at less than US$50 million.

[4] Larger deals are deals that are valued at more than US$50 million.

8.3.4   Data Analysis

The study uses event study to analyse short-run share price performance of UK acquiring firms engaged in CBM&A. The event date for this study is set to be the date of the announcement of the respective merger and acquisition event. McWilliams and Siegel (1997) have stated that the most crucial research design issue is the length of the event window used in an event study. In deciding the length of the event window, researchers should bear in mind that it should be short enough to increase the power of the test and that, at the same time, it should be long enough to incorporate the full effect of the event in question. Following this argument and considering the trends in earlier studies of CBM&A performance regarding the length of the event window,[2] this study utilized both a short event window ranging from announcement day to 1 day after the announcement date and a long event window ranging from 10 days before the announcement date to 10 days after the announcement date. The estimation period used in this study started from the 200th day before the announcement of the acquisition event and ended on the 21st day before the date of the announcement. To calculate the normal return for the sample of UK firms, the standard market model has been used. The superiority of the market model over the other statistical models has been supported by researchers including Brown and Warner (1980), Beaver (1981), Bowman (1983), Armitage (1995) and Strong (1992). The FTSE All Share Index is used as a proxy for the market portfolio. The FTSE All Share Index is a capitalization-weighted index, composed of companies traded on the London Stock Exchange.[3] The study used the following standard market model equation to calculate the normal return of the sample firms' common stock:

$$R_{jt} = \alpha_j + \beta_j R_{mt} + \varepsilon_{jt},$$

where

t = day measured relative to event,

R_{jt} = return on security j on day t,

R_{mt} = FTSE All Share Index (a proxy for the market portfolio of risky assets),

α_j = estimated period intercept of firm j,

β_j = OLS estimates of firm j's market model parameters and

ε_{jt} = the error term of security j on the sample event day t

The abnormal returns (AR) for each sample event j on day t are obtained as follows:

$$AR_{jt} = R_{jt} - (\alpha_j - \beta_j R_{mt}),$$

where

t = day measured relative to event,

AR_{jt} = excess return to security j for day t,

R_{jt} = return on security j during day t,

R_{mt} = FTSE All Share Index (a proxy for the market portfolio of risky assets),

α_j = estimated period intercept of firm j and

β_j = OLS estimates of firm j's market model parameters

Daily abnormal excess returns are calculated for each sample event in the study over the event window. For a sample of N sample events, the daily average abnormal return for each day t is estimated as

$$AR_t = \sum_{j=1}^{N} AR_{jt}/N.$$

The expected value of AR_{jt} is 0 by definition.

Analysis of statistical significance of the abnormal returns calculated above requires the standardization of abnormal return to reflect statistical errors in the determination of expected returns. To determine whether the average daily abnormal return is statistically significantly different from 0, the average standardize abnormal returns (ASAR$_t$) are calculated as follows:

$$ASAR_t = 1/N \sum_{j=1}^{N} AR_{jt}/S_{jt}$$

where

$$S_{jt} = \left\{ S_j^2 \left[1 + \frac{1}{T} + \frac{(R_{mt} - R_m)^2}{\sum_{i=1}^{T}(R_{mi} - R_m)^2} \right] \right\}^{1/2}$$

and

S_{jt} = standard error of the forecast for security j in period t in the event period,

S_j^2 = the residual variance for security j from the market model regression,

N = the number of observations in the estimation period,

R_m = the average return of the market portfolio for the estimation period,

R_{mt} = the returns on the market portfolio for the day t,

R_{mi} = the market return for period j within the estimation period,

T = number of periods employed in the regression equation for parameter estimation (180 days),

T = number of periods in the event window (41 days),

i = sub-script for estimation period and

j = sub-script for the event window.

The cumulative abnormal return (CARs) for each security j, CAR_j, is calculated by summing average abnormal returns over the event period as follows:

$$CAR_{j,K,L} = \sum_{t=K}^{L} AR_{jt}$$

where the $CAR_{j,K,L}$ is for the period from t = day K to t = day L.

The cumulative average abnormal returns (CAARs) over the event period from day K to day L are calculated as

$$CAAR_{K,L} = \frac{1}{N} \sum_{j=1}^{N} CAR_{j,K,L}$$

Then the average of the above standardized cumulative abnormal return over the interval K to L is obtained as follows:

$$ASCAR_{K,L} = \sum_{K}^{L} \frac{ASAR_{K,L}}{\sqrt{K-L+1}}$$

Finally, to find out the statistical significance of ARs and CARs for each day of event window, Z-score and corresponding p-values were used.

8.4 RESULTS AND DISCUSSION

8.4.1 Univariate Analysis

Table 8.3 shows the abnormal return (AR) for the 373 UK acquiring firms that made acquisitions abroad. The individual returns from10 days prior to the acquisition announcement to10 days after the acquisition announcement shows that acquiring firms earned negative ARs prior to the announcement of the acquisition. Following the announcement, the ARs become mostly positive up to tenth day after the event. Almost all the returns that are positive after the announcement are statistically significant. The ARs on the announcement days and the day following the announcement are 0.0059% and 0.13%. Both of them are statistically significant at 5% and 1% level respectively. These results show that announcement of UK acquisitions abroad produced value for the shareholders of the acquiring firm in the short run.

Table 8.4 reports the CAR for the UK acquiring firms for four different windows. The results show that acquiring firms produced negative CARs for event windows (−10, 10), (−5, 5) and (−1, 1) days. But all these returns are statistically insignificant indicating that returns are not different from zero. But CAR for event window (0, 1) days shows a positive CAR of 13.69% which is statistically significant at the 1% level. Similar to AR results, CAR results also show that UK acquiring firms purchasing foreign targets earns statistically significant positive return on the announcement of those events.

Table 8.3   Abnormal Returns (ARs) for the UK CBM&A Acquirers

Event Days	AR (%)	Z-Statistic	p-Value
−10	0.0330	2.1338	0.0329
−9	−0.0180	−0.2829	0.7773
−8	−0.1359	−1.3706	0.1705
−7	−0.4513	−4.1162	0.0000
−6	0.0186	−0.1032	0.9178
−5	−0.0876	−0.6066	0.5441
−4	−0.0618	−0.1453	0.8845
−3	−0.2443	−2.4810	0.0131
−2	−0.0393	−1.5217	0.1281
−1	−0.3578	−3.8407	0.0001
0	0.0059	1.9623	0.0497
1	0.1310	2.6689	0.0076
2	−0.0221	0.0453	0.9638
3	0.2798	2.9555	0.0031
4	0.0700	1.8721	0.0612
5	0.1190	2.2740	0.0230
6	−0.1746	−1.1547	0.2482
7	−0.1568	−1.6195	0.1053
8	−0.0557	0.1217	0.9031
9	0.0795	1.8703	0.0614
10	0.0544	0.6113	0.5410

Table 8.4   Cumulative Abnormal Returns (CARs) for the UK CBM&A Acquirers

Event Window	CAR (%)	Z-Statistic	p-Value
CAR (−10, 10)	−1.0145	−0.1596	0.8732
CAR (−5, 5)	−0.2074	0.9589	0.3376
CAR (−1, 1)	−0.2209	0.4560	0.6484
CAR (0, 1)	0.1369	3.2745	0.0011

In addition to the previous two tables, the overall trend of ARs and CARs for the UK acquiring firms over the 21-day period surrounding the foreign acquisition announcement is shown in Figure 8.1. The figure shows that ARs are mostly positive from the day of the announcement to the fifth day after the announcement. The CAR line in Figure 8.1 shows that CARs over the 21 days surrounding the announcement are clearly negative. The figure therefore indicates the fact that the announcement period benefit of the acquiring firm disappears with the passage of time, a view which is appropriate for a highly competitive market for corporate control such as the UK.[4]

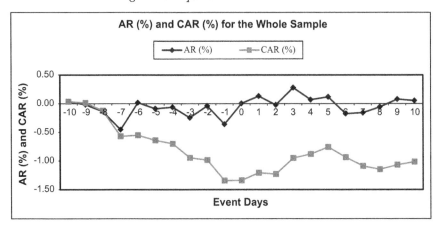

Figure 8.1   ARs and CARs for the UK CBM&A Acquirers

Besides measuring the abnormal and cumulative abnormal returns for the whole sample, this study looked at the abnormal return performance of UK acquiring firms based on various characteristics of the acquisition transactions. Table 8.5 shows the performance of UK acquiring firms based on the payment methods used in foreign acquisitions. Results provided in Table 8.5 reasonably support Hypothesis 2 suggesting cash acquisitions perform better than do non-cash acquisitions. The CARs for cash acquisitions for event windows (–10, 10) and (–1, 1) days are negative and statistically insignificant. However, CARs for the event windows (–5, 5) and (0, 1) days are positive and statistically significant. Thus, it can be concluded that cash acquisitions produced value for UK acquirers. On the other hand, CARs for the UK acquirers in non-cash acquisitions produced negative return for event windows (–10, 10), (–5, 5) and (–1, 1) days, although returns are not statistically significant. The only significant return for non-cash acquisition is in event window (0, 1) days and is consistent with the overall value

Table 8.5   Payment Method

Event Window	CAR (%) Cash Acquisitions	Z-Statistic	CAR (%) Non-Cash Acquisitions	Z-Statistic	Difference	Z-Statistic
CAR (–10, 10)	–0.0327	1.1769	–2.2401	–1.5937	2.2075	9.0361***
CAR (–5, 5)	0.3267	1.7127*	–0.9253	–0.6045	1.2520	5.2909***
CAR (–1, 1)	–0.0940	0.7650	–0.3795	–0.1784	0.2854	1.1162
CAR (0, 1)	0.1760	2.3920**	0.0912	2.2164**	0.0848	–0.0659

*p = .10. **p = .05. ***p = .01.

creation effect of UK acquirers in the short run. Table 8.5 also shows the relative performance of cash and non-cash acquisitions. The results indicate that for all the event windows, cash acquisitions outperformed non-cash acquisitions, and the performance difference is statistically significant at the 1% level for $(-10, 10)$ and $(-5, 5)$ days event windows and not significant for $(-1, 1)$ and $(0, 1)$ event windows. The finding that, in the case of UK CBM&A, cash acquisitions paid for by cash perform better than non-cash acquisitions is consistent with various theoretical arguments in favour of cash acquisitions, prominent among those are the information asymmetry hypothesis (Myers and Majluf, 1984), signalling hypothesis (Leland and Pyle, 1977), valuation hypothesis (Fishman, 1989) and benefit of debt hypothesis (Peterson and Peterson, 1991) and supports the earlier findings provided by Wansley et al. (1983), Cebenoyan et al. (1992), Cheng and Chan (1995) and Fuller and Glatzer (2003).

Table 8.6 reports CARs for UK acquirers engaged in cross-border acquisitions based on the type of target firms. Results in Table 8.6 show that UK acquiring firms that purchased foreign private firms earned positive returns in event windows $(-5, 5)$, $(-1, 1)$ and $(0, 1)$ days with the latter being significant at 1% level. On the other hand, acquirers of foreign public targets earned negative returns in all the event windows reported in Table 8.6. CAR differences show that acquirers of private targets outperformed consistently in all the event windows, and the differences are significant in event windows of $(-10, 10)$ and $(-1, 1)$ days. These results provide some support for Hypothesis 3, which stated that there should be a difference in performance between the acquirers of private targets and public targets. The findings of this study are consistent with various arguments that support the superior performance of acquisition of private targets such as the managerial motive argument (Draper and Paudyal, 2006), liquidity argument (Fuller et al., 2002), limited competition for private target, monitoring advantage and probability of deal completion stated by Chang (1998) and Fuller et al. (2002) and the possibility of a reduced level of hubris in the case of acquiring private targets (Conn et al., 2005). The findings are also in line with the earlier findings of Hansen

Table 8.6   Form of Target Firm

Event Window	CAR (%) Private Targets	Z-Statistic	CAR (%) Public Targets	Z-Statistic	Difference	Z-Statistic
CAR (−10, 10)	−0.8725	−0.4397	−1.0696	0.2731	0.1971	−1.9944**
CAR (−5, 5)	0.0214	0.7226	−1.1481	0.2604	1.1695	0.2473
CAR (−1, 1)	0.0156	1.3251	−1.4862	−2.6060***	1.5018	5.0619***
CAR (0, 1)	0.1816	2.6861***	−0.3937	0.9282	0.5753	0.4429

*p = .10. **p = .05. ***p = .01.

Table 8.7   Acquisition Strategy

Event Window	CAR (%) Related Acquisitions	Z-Statistic	CAR (%) Unrelated Acquisitions	Z-Statistic	Difference	Z-Statistic
CAR (−10, 10)	−1.0077	0.3748	−1.0202	−0.5927	0.0125	3.1302***
CAR (−5, 5)	0.2124	1.5137	−0.6381	−0.1677	0.8505	3.9220***
CAR (−1, 1)	0.0827	1.8638*	−0.5326	−1.2392	0.6153	3.7951***
CAR (0, 1)	0.2549	3.0581***	0.0157	1.5632	0.2392	1.4638

*p = .10. **p = .05. ***p = .01.

and Lott (1996), Chang (1998), Ang and Kohers (2001), Fuller et al. (2002) and Conn et al. (2005).

Table 8.7 reports the CARs for the UK acquiring firms engaged in CBM&A based on the acquisition strategy. It is evident from Table 8.7 that related acquisitions earn positive abnormal returns in the short-run and the returns are significant for the event windows (−1, 1) and (0, 1) days. Unrelated acquisitions produced statistically insignificant negative abnormal returns in all the event windows except the (0, 1) days event window. The difference in CARs for related and unrelated acquisitions show that related acquisitions outperformed unrelated acquisitions in all the event windows and the differences are statistically significant at 1% level in all event windows except event window of (0, 1) days where the difference is positive but statistically insignificant. These results strongly support the idea of performance difference between related and unrelated acquisitions reflected in Hypothesis 4, and are consistent with the notions that related acquisitions are superior to unrelated acquisitions because of the possibility of achieving economies of scale and scope and market power as suggested by Singh and Montgomery (1987). The results of this study regarding the performance of related and unrelated acquisitions are similar to the findings of Markides and Ittner (1994), Eun et al. (1996) and Gregory and McCorriston (2005) but are at variance with the findings of Datta and Puia (1995) and Pettway et al. (1993).

Table 8.8 reports CARs for the UK acquiring firms based on the geographic origin of the target firms. It is clear from Table 8.8 that UK acquirers earns statistically significant positive abnormal returns when they acquire North American targets in event windows (−1, 1) and (0, 1) days. However, returns for the acquirers of European targets are negative for all the event windows, although they are not statistically significant. Table 8.8 reports that differences in CARs for all the event windows are positive and are statistically significant. This clearly lends support for the idea that geographic origin of target firms impact on the returns

Table 8.8 Geographic Origin of Target Firms

Event Window	CAR (%) North American Targets	Z-Statistic	CAR (%) European Targets	Z-Statistic	Difference	Z-statistic
CAR (−10, 10)	−0.1332	1.5358	−0.9570	−0.1683	0.8237	4.9676***
CAR (−5, 5)	0.1302	1.5466	−0.0535	0.5568	0.1837	1.7301*
CAR (−1, 1)	0.3352	2.4177**	−0.8510	−1.3960	1.1862	4.4929***
CAR (0, 1)	0.6193	4.8784***	−0.3850	0.0126	1.0043	4.2622***

*$p = .10$. **$p = .05$. ***$p = .01$.

of acquiring firms as stated in Hypothesis 5. The results indicate that acquirers of North American targets outperformed those acquirers that purchased European targets. It has been argued that there is a difference between market for corporate control in North America (especially the US) and Europe (Corhay and Rad, 2000). More important, the US and European systems differ in terms of corporate governance systems reflected in the concentration of ownership, shareholders' rights and legal system (La Porta et al., 2000). Corhay and Rad (2000) pointed out that acquisitions of US targets may produce a better return compared to acquisitions of European targets because the European market for corporate control is more protected and less competitive. This might give rise to higher agency costs that may reduce the acquirers' gains from acquisition. The findings in this study support the idea that UK acquirers earn more return when they acquire North American targets compared to acquiring European targets. The findings here support the earlier findings of Kiymaz (2003), Corhay and Rad (2000) and Gregory and McCorriston (2005) and Moeller and Schlingemann (2005) but are at the variance with the findings of Fatemi and Furtado (1988) and Yook and McCabe (1996).

This study also finds some support for Hypothesis 6, which states that the return to UK acquiring firms engaged in CBM&A varies with the size of the deals. Table 8.9 shows that the returns to the UK acquirers engaged in smaller or medium-size deals are higher in all event windows than the return to the acquirers that made larger acquisition deals, although differences are not statistically significant except the window of (−10, 10) days, where the difference is significant at 1% level. The results reported in Table 8.9 lend some support to the managerialism hypothesis, which stressed that managerialism problems are more noticeable in cases of larger deals because of the possibility of enhanced reputation for management associated with larger deals. The results in Table 8.9 also stressed the fact that larger deals act as a deterrent for post acquisition integration of participating firms.

Table 8.9   Deal Size

Event Window	CAR (%) Smaller Acquisitions	Z-Statistic	CAR (%) Larger Acquisitions	Z-Statistic	Difference	Z-Statistic
CAR (–10, 10)	–0.5347	0.3013	–2.6329	–0.7199	2.0982	3.5654***
CAR (–5, 5)	0.1296	0.6769	–1.3768	0.8791	1.5064	–1.5663
CAR (–1, 1)	–0.0994	0.7576	–0.6516	–0.4339	0.5522	1.2684
CAR (0, 1)	0.1692	2.6032***	0.0354	2.0810**	0.1338	–0.9338

*$p = .10$. **$p = .05$. ***$p = .01$.

8.4.2   Cross-Sectional Analysis

Based on the insights drawn from the univariate analysis, this study has used a cross-sectional regression analysis to find out the combined effect of identified variables on the return of UK acquiring firms engaged in CBM&A. The dependent variable here is the return of UK acquiring firms and is represented by three-day CARs (–1 day to 1 day) surrounding the announcement date. The independent variables are payment method, form of the target firm, acquisition strategy, geographic origin of target firm and deal size. In the following, a brief description of the independent variables is given:

1. Payment method (*PAYMETH*): Although various methods of payment are used to acquire target firms, the prominent methods of payments are cash and non-cash consideration that include stock or a combination of stock and cash (UNCTAD, 2000). For regression analysis a value of 1 is assigned to the cash acquisitions and 0 for the non-cash acquisitions.
2. Form of target firm (*TARFOR*): Targets may be private, public, joint venture, subsidiary or even government owned. However, according to UNCTAD (2000), most frequent forms of target are either private or public. Therefore, this study has also analysed the private and public targets. A value of 1 is assigned when the target firm is private and 0 when it is public.
3. Acquisition strategy (*ACQSTRAT*): Acquisitions can be related or unrelated depending on the similarity between target and bidding firm. This study has identified acquisitions as related if the first two digits of primary SIC code of target and acquirer are same. If they are not the same then the acquisition is identified as unrelated acquisition. Independent variable *ACQSTRAT* takes the value 1 if the acquisition is related and 0 if the acquisition is unrelated.

4. Geographic origin of target firm (*TARNAT*): Most of the European countries are similar in terms of legal system and corporate governance system and collectively differ from North America, especially from the US (Gregory and McCorriston, 2005). Therefore, targets from Europe are grouped as European targets and targets from the US and Canada are grouped as North American targets. The reason behind grouping US and Canadian targets is their close similarities in terms of various economic indicators as presented in Moeller and Schlingmann (2005). North American targets are assigned a value of 1, and European targets are assigned a value of 0.

5. Deal value (*ACQVAL*): To find out the impact of deal size on the wealth effect of the acquiring firm, the dollar price of acquisitions are used. A negative sign of regression coefficient should imply the suitability of smaller acquisitions to enhance the shareholders' value of the acquiring firm.

Using these independent variables, the following regression equation has been used to measure the abnormal returns of UK acquiring firms:

$$CAR_{(-1,1)} = \alpha + \beta_1 \, PAYMETH + \beta_2 \, TARFOR + \beta_3 \, ACQSTRAT + \beta_4 \, TARNAT + \beta_5 \, ACQVAL + \varepsilon.$$

Table 8.10 reports the regression results. A closer look to models 1 to 5 indicates that incorporation of independent variables improves the explanatory power of the regression models. This is evident by the gradual increase of R^2 values and Durbin-Watson (D-W) values. The final regression model (model 5) shows that two of five independent variables are statistically significant. More specifically, target form and geographic origin of target firm have a statistically significant impact on the variation of returns of the UK acquiring firms. The overall regression result is significant based on the F-value which is statistically significant at 1% level. The positive sign of variable *TARFOR* indicates that UK acquirers earn statistically significant positive abnormal return when its targets are private firms. Similarly, a positive sign of the variable *TARNAT* indicates that UK acquirers earn statistically significant abnormal return when they acquire targets from North America. Consistent with the univariate analysis the study also finds that the short-run performance does not vary with the size of the acquisition deal. However, it is important to point out that the view that cash acquisitions and related acquisitions positively enhance the returns of UK acquirers as found in the univariate analysis was not supported. The finding that method of payment and acquisition relatedness has no influence on short-run performance is unsurprising in that the results may be explained by the differences in the event windows used in the multiple regression analysis as dependent variable compared with that used in the univariate analysis. Whereas the multiple regression utilized a shorter event window (−1, 1), the univariate analysis used a wider event window (−10, 10).

Table 8.10   Regression Results

	Regression 1	Regression 2	Regression 3	Regression 4	Regression 5
Constant	−0.353	−1.753	−2.338	−3.877	−3.428
	(−0.744)	(−2.086)**	(−2.482)**	(−3.186)***	(−2.779)***
A1	0.020	0.015	0.015	0.016	0.007
PAYMETH	(0.389)	(0.278)	(0.289)	(0.287)	(0.125)
A2		0.103	0.114	0.157	0.135
TARFOR		(1.96)**	(2.142)**	(2.736)***	(2.32)**
A3			0.073	0.073	0.078
ACQSTRAT			(1.367)	(1.302)	(1.403)
A4				0.127	0.118
TARNAT				(2.228)**	(2.082)**
A5					−0.109
ACQVAL					(−1.943)*
Adjusted R^2	−0.002	0.005	0.008	0.020	0.028
F-Value	0.152	1.95	1.93	2.65**	2.89***
D-W statistic	2.16	2.18	2.17	2.21	2.23

Notes: Dependent variable = CAR (−1, 1). D-W = Durbin-Watson. Figures in parentheses are *t*-values.
*p = .10. **p = .05. ***p = .01.

8.5   CONCLUSION

This chapter has examined the short-run stock price performance of 373 UK acquiring firms engaged in CBM&A between 1994 and 2003. Based on available literature on the performance of CBM&A, this study has hypothesized that the UK acquirers will earn positive abnormal returns in the short run, and their returns will depend on several transaction specific, firm specific and geographic characteristics such as payment method, form of the target firms, acquisition strategy, geographic origin of the targets and deal size. The results of this study are impressive and in line with several other earlier studies. For example, the study found that UK acquirers earned significant positive abnormal return on the announcement of cross-border acquisition decisions. However, the positive returns disappear as the event window increases. This is consistent with highly competitive market for corporate control such as the UK, where any abnormal gains will disappear quickly because of the competitive nature of the market. Although the abnormal returns for the whole sample becomes negative in the wider event windows, none of them is statistically significant, and this indicates that UK acquirers do not lose value by the announcement of acquisitions abroad. The results of the study also confirm that selected transaction-specific, firm-specific and geographic characteristics do affect the abnormal return of acquiring firms. For example the form of the target company, acquisition relatedness/strategy or deal size and geographic origin of the target firms have a statistically significant impact on the performance of acquiring firms as confirmed by both the univariate and the multivariate analysis. On the other hand, although the univariate analysis found some support regarding the impact of payment methods and acquisition strategies on the short-run performance of UK acquiring firms, the multivariate analysis could not provide support for them. The results in this study suggest that UK acquirers earn positive abnormal returns on the announcement of the acquisition of foreign firms. Given the assumption underlying the share-price-based studies that the investor is able to assess accurately the expected benefits of the takeover (Healy et al., 1997), the positive announcement period return represent investors' optimistic assessment of the acquiring firm's management decision to acquire the target. However, the optimism in assessment might not always be correct due to the information asymmetry between management and shareholders (Myers and Majluf, 1984). Therefore, it is the responsibility of the management to act and keep the confidence of the investors, which they have passed on to the management, by reacting positively at the announcement of the event. Management should start with a proper integration of the merging firms and after that should continue to use the pooled resources in a very productive way. If management can effectively and efficiently integrate the firms and deploy the acquired assets (both tangible and intangible) and capabilities to enhance production and productivity, then the initial value gain at the announcement of the event will be sustainable in future. Because mergers and acquisitions are significant event for any company and the effect of those events prevail for a relatively longer time, it is not enough to assess the short-run performance of the acquisition events to judge the overall success of those decisions. Rather, long-term performance should also be assessed to gain a complete picture of the success of the acquisitions.

NOTES

1. The classification of these sectors is taken from US SIC codes. The main two-digit SIC codes are 01–09 Agriculture, Forestry and Fishing; 10–14 Mining; 15–17 Construction; 20–39 Manufacturing; 40–49 Transportation, Communications, Electric, Gas, and Sanitary Services; 50–51 Wholesale Trade; 52–59 Retail Trade; 65 Real Estate; 70–89 Services; and 91–97 Public Administration.
2. The maximum size of event window is –12 to +12 months used by Conn and Connell (1990), and the minimum is –1 to 0 days used by, among others, Manzon et al. (1994) and Doukas (1995). But event windows of –20 to +20, –10 to +10, –5 to +5 and –1 to +1 are more common in studies examining the performance of CBM&A.
3. See http://en.wikipedia.org/wiki/FTSE_All-Share_Index.
4. For example, Powell and Yawson (2005) pointed out that the UK takeover market is more active than other comparable countries such as the US.

REFERENCES

Amihud, Y. and Lev, B. (1981). Risk Reduction as Managerial Motive for Conglomerate Mergers, *Bell Journal of Economics*, Vol. 12(2), pp. 823–837.

Andrade, G., Mitchell, M. and Stafford, E. (2001). New Evidence and Perspectives on Mergers, *Journal of Economic Perspectives*, Vol. 15(2), pp. 103–120.

Ang, J. and Kohers, N. (2001). The Takeover Market for Privately Held Companies: The US Experience, *Cambridge Journal of Economics*, Vol. 25, pp. 723–748.

Armitage, S. (1995). Event Study Methods and Evidence on their Performance, *Journal of Economic Surveys*, Vol. 8(4), pp. 25–52.

Asquith, P. and Kim, E.H. (1982). The Impact of Merger Bids on the Participating Firm's Security Holders, *Journal of Finance*, Vol. 37, pp. 1209–1228.

Asquith, P., Bruner, R.F. and Mullins, D.W. (1990). *Merger Returns and the Form of Financing*, Working Paper, MIT, Cambridge, MA.

Aw, M. and Chatterjee, R. (2004). The Performance of UK Firms Acquiring Large Cross-Border and Domestic Takeover Targets, *Applied Financial Economics*, Vol. 14, pp. 337–349.

Beaver, W.H. (1981). Econometric Properties of Alternative Security Return Methods, *Journal of Accounting Research*, Vol. 19, pp. 163–184.

Berger, P.G. and Ofek, E. (1995). Diversification's Effect on Firm Value, *Journal of Financial Economics*, Vol. 37, pp. 39–65.

Block, S. (2005). Are International Mergers Value Enhancing to Acquirer Shareholders? *Journal of Global Business*, Vol. 31(Spring), pp. 73–81.

Bowman, R.G. (1983). Understanding and Conducting Event Studies, *Journal of Business Finance & Accounting*, Vol. 10(4), pp. 561–584.

Brown, S.J. and Warner, J.B. (1980). Measuring Security Price Performance, *Journal of Financial Economics*, Vol. 8, pp. 205–258.

Cakici, N., Hessel, C. and Tandon, K. (1996). Foreign Acquisitions in the United States: Effect on Shareholder Wealth of Foreign Acquiring Firms, *Journal of Banking & Finance*, Vol. 20, pp. 307–329.

Campa, J.M. and Hernando, I. (2004). Shareholder Value Creation in European M&As, *European Financial Management*, Vol. 10(1), pp. 47–81.

Cebenoyan, A.S., Papaioannou, G.J. and Travlos, N.G. (1992). Foreign Takeover Activity in the US and Wealth Effects for Target Firm Shareholders, *Financial Management*, Vol. 21(3), pp. 58–68.

Chang, S. (1998). Takeovers of Privately Held Targets, Methods of Payment, and Bidder Returns, *Journal of Finance*, Vol. 53(2), pp. 773–784.

Chari, A., Ouimet, P. and Tesar, L.L. (2004). *Cross-Border Mergers and Acquisitions in Emerging Markets: The Stock Market Valuation of Corporate Control*, University of Michigan Working Paper

Chatterjee, R. and Kuenzi, A. (2001). *Mergers and Acquisitions: The Influence of Methods of Payments on Bidder's Share Price*, Research Papers in Management Studies, University of Cambridge.

Chatterjee, S. (1986). Types of Synergy and Economic Value: The Impact of Acquisition on Merging and Rival Firms, *Strategic Management Journal*, Vol. 7, pp. 119–139.

Cheng, L.T.W. and Chan, K.C. (1995). A Comparative Analysis of the Characteristics of International Takeovers, *Journal of Business Finance & Accounting*, Vol. 22(5), pp. 637–657.

Conn, C., Cosh, A., Guest, P.M. and Hughes, A. (2001). *Long-Run Share Performance of UK Firms Engaging in Cross-Border Acquisitions*, Working Paper 214, Centre for Business Research, University of Cambridge.

Conn, R.L. and Connell, F. (1990). International Mergers: Returns to US and British Firms, *Journal of Business Finance and Accounting*, Vol. 17(5), pp. 689–711.

Conn, R.L., Cosh, A., Guest, P.M. and Hughes, A. (2005). The Impact on UK Acquirers of Domestic, Cross-Border, Public and Private Acquisitions, *Journal of Business Finance & Accounting*, Vol. 32(5&6), pp. 815–870.

Corhay, A. and Rad, A.T. (2000). International Acquisitions and Shareholder Wealth: Evidence from the Netherlands, *International Review of Financial Analysis*, Vol. 9(2), pp. 163–174.

Danbolt, J. (2004). Target Company Cross-Border Effects in Acquisitions into the UK, *European Financial Management*, Vol. 10(1), pp. 83–108.

Datta, D.K. and Puia, G. (1995). Cross-Border Acquisitions: An Examination of the Influence of Relatedness and Cultural Fit on Shareholder Value Creation in US Acquiring Firms, *Management International Review*, Vol. 35(4), pp. 337–359.

Denis, D.J., Denis, D.K. and Yost, K. (2002). Global Diversification, Industrial Diversification and Firm Value, *Journal of Finance*, Vol. 57, pp. 1951–1979.

Dong, M., Hirshleifer, D., Richardson, S. and Teoh, S.H. (2005). Does Investor Misvaluation Drive the Takeover Market?, *Journal of Finance*, Vol. 61, pp. 725–762.

Doukas, J. (1995). Overinvestment, Tobin's q and Gains from Foreign Acquisitions, *Journal of Banking and Finance*, Vol. 19, pp. 1285–1303.

Doukas, J. and Travlos, N.G. (1988). The Effect of corporate Multinationalism on Shareholders' Wealth: Evidence from International Acquisitions, *Journal of Finance*, Vol. 43, pp. 1161–1175.

Draper, P. and Paudyal, K. (2006). Acquisitions: Private versus Public, *European Financial Management*, Vol. 12 (1), pp. 57–80.

Dunne, K.K. and Ndubizu, G.A. (1995). International Acquisitions Accounting Methods and Corporate Multinationalism: Evidence from Foreign Acquisitions, *Journal of International Business Studies*, Vol. 26, pp. 361–377.

Elgers, P. and Clark, J. (1980). Merger Types and Shareholder Returns: Additional Evidence, *Financial Management*, Vol. 9(2), pp. 66–72.

Eun, C.S., Kolodny, R. and Scheraga, C. (1996). Cross-Border Acquisitions and Shareholder Wealth: Tests of Synergy and Internalization Hypotheses, *Journal of Banking and Finance*, Vol. 20, pp. 1559–1582.

Fatemi, A.M. and Furtado, E.P.H. (1988). An Empirical Investigation of the Wealth Effects of Foreign Acquisitions, in S.J. Khoury and A. Ghosh (eds.), *Recent Developments in International Banking and Finance*, Vol. 2, Lexington, MA: Lexington Books, pp. 363–379.

Firth, M. (1980). Takeovers, Shareholder Returns and the Theory of the Firm, *Quarterly Journal of Economics*, Vol. 94, pp. 235–260.

Fishman, M.J. (1989). Preemptive Bidding and the Role of Medium of Exchange in Acquisition, *Journal of Finance*, Vol. 44, pp. 41–57.

Francoeur, C. (2005). *The Long-Run Performance of Cross-Border Mergers and Acquisitions: The Canadian Evidence*, HEC Montreal Working Paper.

Fuller, K. and Glatzer, M.B. (2003). Method-of-Payment Choice for International Targets, *Advances in Financial Economics*, Vol. 8, pp. 47–64.

Fuller, K., Netter, J. and Stegemoller, M. (2002). What Do Returns to Acquiring Firms Tell Us? Evidence from Firms that Make Many Acquisitions, *Journal of Finance*, Vol. 57, pp. 1763–1793.

Gaughan, P.A. (2002). *Mergers, Acquisition, and Corporate Restructuring*, New York: Wiley.

Gleason, K.C., Gregory, D.W. and Wiggins, R.A. (2002). Wealth Effects of US Acquisitions in the Pacific Rim, *Journal of Business & Economic Studies*, Vol. 8(2), pp. 28–47.

Goergen, M. and Renneboog, L. (2003). Value Creation in Large European Mergers and Acquisitions, *Advances in Mergers and Acquisitions*, Vol. 2, pp. 97–146.

Goergen, M. and Renneboog, L. (2004). Shareholder Wealth Effects of European Domestic and Cross-Border Takeover Bids, *European Financial Management*, Vol. 10(1), pp. 9–45.

Gregory, A. and McCorriston, S. (2005). Foreign Acquisitions by UK Limited Companies: Short- and Long-Run Performance, *Journal of Empirical Finance*, Vol. 12(1), pp. 99–125.

Halpern, P. (1983). Corporate Acquisition: A Theory of Special Cases? A Review of Event Studies Applied to Acquisition, *Journal of Finance*, Vol. 38(2), pp. 297–317.

Hansen, R.G. and Lott, J. (1996). Externalities and Corporate Objectives in a World with Diversified Shareholders/Consumer, *Journal of Financial and Quantitative Analysis*, Vol. 31, pp. 43–68.

Healy, P., Palepu, K. and Ruback, R. (1997). Which Takeovers Are Profitable? Strategic or Financial?, *Sloan Management Review*, Vol. 38(4), pp. 45–57.

Hisey, K.B. and Caves, R.E. (1985). Diversification and Choice of Country, *Journal of International Business Studies*, Vol. 16, pp. 51–65.

Hitt, M.A., Hoskisson, R.E., Ireland, R.D. and Harrison, J.S. (1991). Effects of Acquisitions on R&D Inputs and Outputs, *Academy of Management Journal*, Vol. 34, pp. 693–706.

Hubbard, R.G. and Palia, D. (1999). A Re-examination of the Conglomerate Merger Wave in the 1960s: A Internal Capital Markets View, *Journal of Finance*, Vol. 54, pp. 1131–1152.

Hughes, A., Mueller, D.C. and Singh, A. (1980). Hypotheses about Mergers, in D.C. Mueller (ed.), *The Determinants and Effects of Merger*, Cambridge, MA: Oelgeschlager, Gunn & Hain, pp. 27–66.

Ingham, H., Kran, I. and Lovestam, A. (1992). Mergers and Profitability: A Managerial Success Story?, *Journal of Management Studies*, Vol. 29(2), pp. 195–208.

Jensen, M.C. (1986). Agency Costs of Free Cash-Flow, Corporate Finance and Takeovers, *American Economic Review*, Vol. 76, pp. 323–329.

Kang, J-K. (1993). The International Market for Corporate Control: Mergers and Acquisitions of US Firms by Japanese Firms, *Journal of Financial Economics*, Vol. 34, pp. 345–371.

Kim, E.H. and McConnell, J.J. (1977). Corporate Mergers and the Co-Insurance of Corporate Debt, *Journal of Finance*, Vol. 32, pp. 349–365.

Kiymaz, H. (2003). Wealth Effect for US Acquirers from Foreign Direct Investments, *Journal of Business Strategies*, Vol. 20(1), pp. 7–21.

Kiymaz, H. and Mukherjee, T.K. (2000). The Impact of Country Diversification on Wealth Effects in Cross-Border Mergers, *The Financial Review*, Vol. 35(2), pp. 37–58.

Kroll, M., Simmons, S. and Wright, P. (1990). The Determinants of Chief Executive Officers Compensation Following Major Acquisitions, *Journal of Business Research*, Vol. 20(4), pp. 349–366.

La Porta, R., Lopez-de-Silanes, F., Schleifer, A. and Vishny, R. (2000). Investor Protection and Corporate Governance, *Journal of Financial Economics*, Vol. 58, pp. 3–27.

Leland, H.E. and Pyle, D.H. (1977). Informational Asymmetries, Financial Structure, and Financial Intermediation, *Journal of Finance*, Vol. 32, pp. 371–387.

Lewellen, W.G. (1971). A Pure Financial Rationale for a Conglomerate Merger, *Journal of Finance*, Vol. 26, pp. 521–537.

Lubatkin, M. (1987). Merger Strategies and Stockholder Value, *Strategic Management Journal*, Vol. 8(1), pp. 39–54.

Lubatkin, M. and O'Neill, H.M. (1987). Merger Strategies and Capital Market Risk, *Academy of Management Journal*, Vol. 30, pp. 665–684.

Manzon, G.B., Sharp, D.J. and Travlos, N.G. (1994). An Empirical Study of the Consequences of US Tax Rules for International Acquisitions by US Firms, *Journal of Finance*, Vol. 49, pp. 1893–1904.

Markides, C. and Ittner, C.D. (1994). Shareholders Benefit from Corporate International Diversification: Evidence from US International Acquisitions, *Journal of International Business Studies*, Vol. 25(2), pp. 343–366.

Markides, C. and Oyon, D. (1998). International Acquisitions: Do They Create Value for Shareholders, *European Management Journal*, Vol. 16(2), pp. 125–135.

Marris, R. (1964). *The Economic Theory of Managerial Capitalism*, Glencoe, IL: Free Press.

Mathur, I., Rangan, N., Chhachhi, I. and Sundaram, S. (1994). International Acquisitions in the United States: Evidence from Returns to Foreign Bidders, *Managerial and Decision Economics*, Vol. 15(2), pp. 107–118.

McWilliams, A. and Siegel, D. (1997). Event Studies in Management Research: Theoretical and Empirical Issues, *Academy of Management Journal*, Vol. 40(3), pp. 626–657.

Moeller, S.B and Schlingemann, F.P. (2005). Global Diversification and Bidder Gains: A Comparison between Cross-Border and Domestic Acquisitions, *Journal of Banking and Finance*, Vol. 29, pp. 533–564.

Morck, R. and Yeung, B. (1992). Internalization: An Event Study Test, *Journal of International Economics*, Vol. 33, pp. 41–56.

Morck, R., Shleifer, A. and Vishny, R.W. (1990). Do Managerial Objectives Drive Bad Acquisitions, *Journal of Finance*, Vol. 45(1), pp. 31–48.

Myers, S.C. and Majluf, N.S. (1984) Corporate Financing and Investment Decisions when Firms Have Information that Investors Do not Have, *Journal of Financial Economics*, Vol. 13 (2), pp. 187–221.

Peterson, D.R. and Peterson, P.P. (1991). The Medium Exchange in Merger and Acquisitions, *Journal of Banking & Finance*, Vol. 15, pp. 383–405.

Pettway, R.H., Sicherman, N.W. and Spiess, D.K. (1993). Japanese Foreign Direct Investment: Wealth Effects from Purchases and Sales of US Assets, *Financial Management*, Vol. 22(4), 82–95.

Powell, R. and Yawson, A. (2005). Industry Aspects of Takeovers and Divestitures: Evidence from the UK, *Journal of Banking & Finance*, Vol. 29(12), pp. 3015–3040.

Reed, R. and Luffman, G.A. (1986). Diversification: The Growing Confusion, *Strategic Management Journal*, Vol. 7(1), pp. 29–35.

Roll, R. (1986). The Hubris Hypothesis of Corporate Takeovers, *Journal of Business*, Vol. 59, pp. 197–216.

Schmidt, S. and Ruhli, E. (2002). Prior Strategy Process as a Key to Understanding Megamergers: The Novartis Case, *European Management Journal*, Vol. 20(3), pp. 223–234.

Servaes, H. (1991). Tobin's Q and Gains from Takeovers, *Journal of Finance*, Vol. 46(1), pp. 409–419.

Seth, A. (1990). Sources of Value Creation in Acquisitions: An Empirical Investigation, *Strategic Management Journal*, Vol. 11, pp. 431–446.

Seth, A., Song, K.P. and Pettit, R. (2000). Synergy, Managerialism or Hubris? An Empirical Examination of Motives for Foreign Acquisitions of US Firms, *Journal of International Business Studies*, Vol. 31(3), pp. 387–405.

Seth, A., Song, K.P. and Pettit, R. (2002). Value Creation and Destruction in Cross-Border Acquisitions: An Empirical Analysis of Foreign Acquisitions of US Firms, *Strategic Management Journal*, Vol. 23, pp. 921–940.

Shelton, L. (1988). Strategic Business Fits and Corporate Acquisition: Empirical Evidence, *Strategic Management Journal*, Vol. 9, pp. 278–288.

Shimizu, K., Hitt, M.A., Vaidyanath, D. and Pisano, V. (2004). Theoretical Foundations of Cross-Border Mergers and Acquisitions: A Review of Current Research and Recommendations for the Future, *Journal of International Management*, Vol. 10, pp. 307–353.

Shleifer, A. and Vishny, R.W. (1989). Management Entrenchment: The Case of Manager Specific Investments, *Journal of Financial Economics*, Vol. 25(1), pp. 123–139.

Shleifer, A. and Vishny, R.W. (1992). Asset Liquidity and Debt Capacity, *Journal of Finance*, Vol. 47, pp. 1343–1366.

Singh, H. and Montgomery, C.A. (1987). Corporate Acquisition Strategies and Economic Performance, *Strategic Management Journal*, Vol. 8, pp. 377–387.

Strong, N. (1992). Modelling Abnormal Returns: A Review Article, *Journal of Business Finance & Accounting*, Vol. 19(4), pp. 533–553.

Stulz, R.M. (1990). Managerial Discretion and Optimal Financial Policies, *Journal of Financial Economics*, Vol. 26, pp. 3–28.

Sudarsanam, S. (2003). *Creating Value from Mergers and Acquisitions: The Challenges*, London: Pearson Education Limited.

Trautwein, F. (1990). Merger motives and prescriptions, *Strategic Management Journal*, Vol. 11(4), pp. 283–295.

Travlos, N.G. (1987). Corporate takeover bids, method of payment and bidding firm stock returns, *Journal of Finance*, Vol. 42, pp. 943–963.

United Nations Conference for Trade and Development (UNCTAD) (2000). *World Investment Report 2000: Cross-Border Mergers and Acquisitions and Development*, New York and Geneva: United Nations.

Walker, M. (2000). Corporate Takeovers, Strategic Objectives and Acquiring Firm Shareholder Wealth, *Financial Management*, Vol. 20, pp. 53–66.

Wansley, J.W., Lane, W.R. and Yang, H.C. (1983). Shareholder Returns to USA Acquired Firms in Foreign and Domestic Acquisitions, *Journal of Business Finance & Accounting*, Vol. 10(4), pp. 647–656.

Yook, K.C. and McCabe, G.M. (1996). The Effect of International Acquisitions on Shareholders' Wealth, *The Mid-Atlantic Journal of Business*, Vol. 32(1), pp. 5–17.

Zaheer, S. (1995). Overcoming the Liability of Foreignness, *Academy of Management Journal*, Vol. 38, pp. 341–363.

9 A Study of the Changes in Operating Performance of UK Cross-Border Mergers and Acquisitions

9.1 INTRODUCTION

Mergers and acquisitions (M&A) have been considered as one of the most significant economic events for both individual firms and the economy as a whole. Weston et al. (2004) suggested that M&A create benefits for the economy by helping to move resources from lower value activities to higher value activities. At firm level, M&A may lead to improvement in competitiveness and may facilitate external growth in situations in which internal growth may be difficult and time-consuming. In this regard, Penrose (1959) pointed out that acquisitions relax the managerial constraints and allow higher rates of growth to be achieved. Other arguments put forward by scholars to explain why M&A take place include synergistic gain and market power (see Bradley et al., 1983; Lubatkin, 1983; Porter, 1987; Jensen, 1988; Seth, 1990; Chatterjee, 1992; Sudarsanam, 2003; Copeland et al., 2005). Based on these claims, much research has been done to find out the actual outcomes of M&A. These studies have examined M&A performance from the perspectives of two time horizons, namely short-run performance and long-run performance. Studies examining short-term performance have tended to use share-price information predominantly whereas both share-price information and accounting information have been used to evaluate the long-run performance of merging firms. However, it may be argued that performance evaluation using share-price information may not capture the full picture of merger event. Although share price is an important measure of wealth gain or maximization of shareholder wealth, Sudarsanam (2003) argues that share prices may be influenced by other factors such as market swings, fads and euphoria rather than the company's expected performance from acquisition strategy. Supporting this line of reasoning, Hirshleifer and Shumway (2003) argue share prices may even be influenced by expected weather condition on the trading day. Despite the various efforts by researchers to control these influences on the share price, there may be a possibility that share-price movements may not fully reflect the underlying performance of the company related to acquisition event (Healy et al., 1992). The stock price reaction to an acquisition can only represent the surprise component of the acquisition rather than the actual synergy effect of acquisition (Fuller et al., 2002). It is therefore not surprising that, a number of scholars have evaluated

M&As performance using operating performance measures (see Chatterjee and Meeks, 1996; Sharma and Ho, 2002; Tuch and O'Sullivan, 2007). While a number of studies have been carried out using accounting data to examine operating performance of domestic M&A, only a few studies examine operating performance of cross-border mergers and acquisitions (CBM&A) in the UK context. Prominent among those studies that has used accounting measures to examine long-run performance of CBM&A is that of Moeller and Schlingemann (2005), but it is important to note that the study is in the context of US cross-border acquisitions events. This is against the background that CBM&A activities have become increasingly an important phenomenon in the global market for corporate control. The United Nations Conference on Trade and Development (UNCTAD) database reveals that since 1987, the share of worldwide CBM&A to overall M&A activities is consistently more than 25%. The database also reveals that almost 80% of FDI flows during this period have been carried out through CBM&A. Considering the importance of worldwide CBM&A as a share of FDI flow and the dearth of research in respect of operating performance of CBM&A, this study attempts to fill this gap by using accounting-based measures to evaluate the performance of the UK acquiring firms. This is important because the data from UNCTAD suggest that the UK has been the top acquiring nation in the global market for corporate control for the last two decades. Despite this massive participation, UK has attracted relatively very little attention from the researchers. Almost all the studies that have addressed the long-run performance of UK acquiring firms have used share-price information to evaluate cross-border acquisition performance. The use of accounting information to evaluate the performance of UK acquiring firms engaged in CBM&A in order to find out the other part of the story is a logical step in advancing M&A. The purpose of this chapter is to examine the long-run performance of UK acquiring firms that made acquisitions between 1995 and 2007. Specifically, this study focuses on the following research questions:

1. What is the long-run operating performance of UK acquiring firms engaged in CBM&A?
2. What are the factors that determine the long-run operating performance of UK acquiring firms?

We pursue the preceding objectives by using accrual performance indicators and cash-flow performance measures. In addition, this study attempts to assess the impact of various firm-specific and transaction-specific characteristics of acquiring and target firms on the operating performance of acquiring firms.

The remainder of this chapter is structured as follows: The next section presents literature on operating performance of CBM&A and develops the hypotheses of the study. Section 9.3 describes the data and the methodology used in this study. Section 9.4 comprises the results and discussions and is followed in section 9.5 by a description of sensitivity tests. Cross-sectional analysis is in section 9.6 and the final section contains a brief conclusion about the findings of the study.

9.2   LITERATURE REVIEW AND HYPOTHESES

9.2.1   Post-Acquisition Operating Performance of Combined Firms

The use of accounting information has been a popular method for examining long-run performance of domestic M&As. Healy et al. (1992) and Sudarsanam (2003) suggest that the popularity of using operating performance in M&A stems from the fact that acquisition strategy is normally set out with the expectation of improving accounting indicators, and as such, evaluating acquisition performance based on operating performance improvements appears the logical way to do it. Although the volume of research using operating performance measures in domestic M&A is impressive, the results are not. Although a number of researchers have found post-acquisition operating performance to be positive, others have found negative wealth gain. For example, Healy et al. (1992) examined the 50 largest US takeovers between 1979 and mid-1984 by using pre-tax operating cash-flow returns on assets and reported a positive post-merger operating performance compared to their industry peers. The positive operating performance change after the M&A has also been supported by Rahman and Limmack (2004), Cosh et al. (1980) and Burt and Limmack (2003). Similarly, the studies such as Ingham et al. (1992), Switzer (1996), Manson et al. (2000), Linn and Switzer (2001), Heron and Lie (2002), Gugler et al. (2003), Ramaswamy and Waegelein (2003) and Powell and Stark (2005) have also rendered positive operating performance of merging firms.

On the other hand, using accounting based operating performance measures, Meeks (1977) examined the UK mergers and found that the post-merger profitability ranged between –5.3% and –7.3% over a seven-year period. Similarly, Singh (1971) examined 77 UK mergers consummated during the period from 1955 to 1960. The results indicated that the accounting profitability of merged firms reduced two years following the merger activities. More than 60% of the sample firms suffered losses during the merger year and the two years following the merger. The same results were arrived at by Utton (1974), Sharma and Ho (2002) and Ghosh (2001). Studies by Ravenscraft and Scherer (1989), Dickerson et al. (1997) and Cheng and Leung (2004) have also reported negative post-acquisition operating performance of merging firms. The conclusion to be drawn here is that the results are mixed in the context of domestic M&A.

9.2.2   CBM&A and Post-Acquisition Operating Performance

Unlike operating performance studies in domestic M&A, the number of studies that examined the operating performance of CBM&A is surprisingly very insignificant. The only notable study in this area has been conducted by Moeller and Schlingemann (2005). Using 36 cross-border transactions carried by US acquirers, the authors reported that the post-acquisition operating performance of combined firm is significantly negative compared to the combined pre-acquisition performance of the target and bidding firms. In the context of this study, we argue that the negative performance may be due high integrating and coordinating cost more than exceed the benefits of diversification involved in merging two firms located in different countries. Moreover, Roll (1986) suggests that managers of the bidding firms may suffer from hubris or they may overpay. As a result CBM&A may lead to higher costs and consequently lower profitability. This reasoning leads to our first hypothesis:

> *Hypothesis 1:* The UK acquiring firms engaged in CBM&A will experience a operating loss after acquisition.

9.2.3   Method of Payment and Operating Performance

One of the important financing decisions facing firms is the choice of method of financing an investment opportunity. Bos and Fetherston (1993) argue that the method or the choice of financing influences both the profitability and the riskiness of the firm and consequently affects the operating performance. For example, it may be argued that using cash to pay for acquisitions offer a number of advantages such as simplicity and preciseness. Cash has obvious value and is more likely to be preferred by vendors compared to equity, which has uncertain value, especially when markets are volatile. Cash provides other benefits such as the minimization of signalling effects arising from the notion of pecking order of capital structure (Myers, 1984; Myers and Majluf, 1984), benefit of debt (Peterson and Peterson, 1991), reduction of free cash flow (Jensen, 1986) and greater probability of replacing inefficient management with cash-financed acquisitions (Martin and McConnell, 1991). On the other hand, Ramaswamy and Waegelein (2003) pointed out that post-acquisition operating performance should be better for stock exchange acquisition rather than for cash acquisitions. They argue that the negative impact of cash acquisitions may stem from the increased interest burden arising from large debt obligation following cash payment for acquisitions. This interest burden may lead to a reduction in investments in R&D and other capital investments as management's attention is directed towards debt and interest payments. As a result, long-term sales revenue, profitability and overall performance may be seriously affected. Even where the acquiring firm has a huge cash reserve with which to pay for acquisitions this may still be very expensive in the context of cross-border acquisitions due to foreign exchange rate risk. In the light of the preceding discussion, we hypothesised that

> *Hypothesis 2:* Non-cash acquisitions by the UK acquiring firms in CBM&A will lead to better operating performance compared to cash acquisitions.

9.2.4   Form of Target Firms and Operating Performance

One of the limiting factors of post-acquisition operating performance is the overpayment by acquiring firms for the targets, and these overpayments impede the ability of the acquiring firms to make profitable investments in the post-acquisition periods, thereby holding back the post-acquisition operating performance of the combined firm. The managerialism hypothesis suggests that corporate managers are more interested to acquire large public targets in order to increase their reputation by extending their control on large pool of assets at the cost of the shareholders' benefit (Draper and Paudyal, 2006). The force of managerialism may lead to the payment of higher price for the large public targets and hinder the post-acquisition performance. However, in the case of private targets, manager's motivation arising from managerialism remain at a very lower stage, and therefore, they may be willing to pay less for such targets, leaving a considerable amount of money for further investment. The illiquid nature of private firm (Fuller et al., 2002) and limited competition for private targets (Chang, 1998) also work as the source of under payment for private targets. Acquisition of private targets also contributes to enhanced managerial performance in the post acquisition period. For example, Shleifer and Vishny (1986), Chang (1998) and Fuller et al. (2002) argued that private targets are closely held and that when acquired by stock transaction, they create outside blockholders in the post-merger firm. These outside blockholders can help to improve the post-acquisition performance of the firm because they serve as effective monitors of managerial activities of acquiring firm. In the light of these arguments, it is hypothesized that

> **Hypothesis 3:** *Acquisition of private targets by the UK acquiring firms in CBM&A will lead to better operating performance compared to acquisition of public targets.*

9.2.5 Acquisition Relatedness and Operating Performance

In the presence of imperfections and incomplete integration in the international capital markets, CBM&A serve a vital role for international diversification for the local firms (Harris and Ravenscraft, 1991; Bailey and Choi, 2003). International diversification through unrelated cross-border acquisitions offers the merging firms several advantages. Prominent among them are the benefits of co-insurance (Lewellen, 1971), reduction of risk (Hughes et al., 1980), reduction of firm's default risk and increasing the debt capacity (Halpern, 1983; Shleifer and Vishny, 1992) and creation of internal capital market (Stulz, 1990). Unrelated acquisitions may also create market power for the acquiring firm by increasing the absolute size and breadth of the firm (Singh and Montgomery, 1987). All these benefits may help the acquiring firm to enhance the post-acquisition operating performance. For example, the benefit of co-insurance helps to keep a balance in the post-acquisition cash flow or profitability of the combined firm due to a dissimilar correlation across different international markets. Enhanced debt capacity provides the acquiring firm the freedom to make profitable investments at lower cost and to enjoy the tax shield advantage in the post-acquisition period. Moreover, the internal capital market that a firm can create through unrelated acquisitions provides the combined firms the advantage of using low-cost funds for investment purpose without any adverse signalling effect. Based on these arguments, it is hypothesized that

> **Hypothesis 4:** *The post-acquisition operating performance of unrelated acquisitions would be better than the related acquisitions in the UK CBM&A.*

9.2.6   Deal Size and Operating Performance

Another important characteristic that might affect the post-acquisition operating performance is the deal size. There are several ways through which deal size can affect operating performance. First, Ingham et al. (1992) pointed out that small acquisitions are more beneficial because they are easier to integrate. Second, the extent of managerialism and hubris might be an increasing function of deal size (Seth et al., 2000). Third, large deals are more likely to be affected by signalling effect as those acquisitions are usually financed by exchange of stock rather than cash (UNCTAD, 2000, p. 113). However, from the perspective of Jensen's (1986) free cash-flow hypothesis, larger deals should help the acquiring firms to reduce the agency problem by reducing the free cash flows at the hands of acquiring firms' managers. The reduction of agency problem should contribute to the post acquisition performance by improving the quality of management capability and at the same time ensuring the discontinuation of value-decreasing investments that may arise from the availability of free cash flow at the hands of management. Large deals may also help the acquiring firm capture synergistic gains in post-acquisition years through the economies of scale and scope (Sudarsanam, 2003) and attainment of financial synergy (Myers and Majluf, 1984). Large deals may also contribute to the attainment of market power through which company can increase profitability through enhanced sales and control over the price of the product. Based on these arguments, it is hypothesised that

> **Hypothesis 5:** *The UK CBM&A post acquisition operating performance of large deals would be better than the post acquisition operating performance of smaller deals.*

9.3   DATA AND METHODOLOGY

9.3.1   Data Source

The initial sample information including date of acquisition, deal completion date, name of the acquirers, name and nationality of target firms, target and bidders' industry, form of target firm, method of payment and deal size were collected from Thomson One Banker Deal database. The information was further checked with the information provided by Acquisitions Monthly. Accounting information for the sample firms was collected from FAME database. Information on announcement of any significant event for each of the firms included in the initial sample frame was collected from Thomson One Banker company analysis.

9.3.2   Sample Selection

A total of 107 UK acquirers that engaged in acquisitions across the border were examined to find out the post-acquisition operating performance. In order to obtain comparable data for analysis, the following restrictions were imposed: (1) acquirers should be public limited companies and have initiated and completed acquisitions over the 1995–2007 period, (2) acquisitions in the financial sector are excluded from the sample because of the different nature of their operations and financial reporting system, (3) only the single acquiring firms are considered to ensure homogeneity in research outcome (see Asquith et al., 1983; Schipper and Thompson, 1983; Fuller et al., 2002) and (4) comparing operating performance for cross-border acquisitions using accounting data pose some problems due to differences in accounting standards, disclosure provision and reporting system among acquirer and target nations (e.g. Davis et al., 1991; Whittington, 2000; Bruner, 2002). For example, Mueller et al. (1997) identified four different accounting models: British–American, Continental, South American and mixed economy. This classification indicates that despite variations in accounting system, British and American accounting systems are closer to each other than with any other country. The similarity or closeness in British and American accounting systems has also been supported by other authors, including Zysman (1983), Nobes (1998) and Alexander et al. (2005). Due to empirical support regarding closeness in accounting system between the US and the UK, this study has only used UK acquisitions in the US to avoid any material comparison problems that may arise from differences in accounting and reporting systems. (5) The full set of tests used in this study also require accounting data be available for the sample of bidding and target companies and their respective controls for the period of up to six financial years. This period commences three years prior to the year in which the acquisition was initiated and, except for the target firms, extended to a period of three financial years following the end of the financial year in which the acquisition was completed. (6) For comparing the acquisition performance, this study used matched-control firms instead of industry averages. Therefore, only those acquiring firms for which there is a matched control firms are included in the sample. Control firms are selected based on the industry of the acquirer and the combined total assets of target and bidding firms as suggested by Sharma and Ho (2002). It is pertinent to point out that the selection of control firms in this study ensures that none of the firms was involved in acquisition activities within the test period. These restrictions produced a total of 107 bidding and target firms, representing 107 acquisitions and 107 control firms. The sample size of 107 acquisitions is comparable to similar types of prior studies on domestic M&As carried out by Sharma and Ho (2002), Healy et al. (1992) and Clark and Ofek (1994) for domestic M&As and Moeller and Schlingemann (2005) for international acquisitions.

9.3.4 Sample Statistics

Table 9.1 summarizes the salient characteristics of sample used in this study.

An examination of the final sample frame (panel A of Table 9.1) reveals that a majority of the acquisitions was consummated in the manufacturing (38%) and the service (24%) sectors.[1] Another important characteristic of the sample acquisition events is that most of the acquisitions were consummated during 1998 to 2000, with highest number of acquisitions occurring in 1999. Panel B of Table 9.1

Table 9.1 Sample Characteristics

Panel A: Year and Sector-Wise Distribution of Sample Acquisition Events

Year	No.	% in Total	Sector	No.	% in Total
1995	6	5.61	Agriculture, Forestry and Fishing	4	3.74
1996	2	1.87	Mining	5	4.67
1997	9	8.41	Construction	3	2.80
1998	14	13.08	Manufacturing	40	37.38
1999	22	20.56	Transport, Communication, Electric, Gas and Sanitary Services	9	8.48
2000	19	17.76	Wholesale Trade	11	10.28
2001	9	8.41	Retail Trade	6	5.61
2002	3	2.80	Real Estate	3	2.80
2003	2	1.87	Services	26	24.30
2004	3	2.80			
2005	8	7.48			
2006	2	1.87			
2007	8	7.48			
Total	*107*	*100*	*Total*	*107*	*100*

Panel B: Sample Characteristics of Acquisition Events

Description	Sample Characteristics	No. of Acquisitions	% in Total
Related vs Unrelated	Related	48	45
	Unrelated	59	55
Total		*107*	*100*
Form of Target	Private	65	60
	Public	42	40
Total		*107*	*100*
Payment Method	Cash	49	46
	Non-cash[1]	58	54
Total		*107*	*100*
Deal Size	Small and medium-size deals[2]	75	65
	Larger deals[3]	32	35
Total		*107*	*100*

[1] Non-cash payment methods predominantly include stock and a combination of cash and stock.

[2] Small and medium-size deals are deals that are valued at less than US$50 million.

[3] Larger deals are deals that are valued at more than US$50 million.

presents the characteristics of the sample acquisition events. The distribution of related and unrelated acquisitions is 45% and 55%, respectively. Private targets constitute almost 60%, with the rest being public firms. Of the 107 acquisitions, 58 were financed by non-cash considerations and the remaining by cash considerations. The table also shows that a majority of the deals (65%) has a deal value of less than US$50 million, with the remaining 35% deals valued at more than US$50 million.

9.3.5   Methodology

Following the argument put forward by Barber and Lyon (1996) who provide a comprehensive literature on the benefits of using matched control firms, this study has used performance of matched control firms as benchmark rather than industry average or median benchmark for comparison. Therefore, two-digit UK national SIC code has been used to find out matched control firms from the same industry of the acquiring firm. To ensure that the control firm is of the same size of the combined firm, the book value of total assets of the combined firm and the control firm on the year of acquisition is used. Firms closest to the combined firm in terms of total assets were selected as control firms.

9.3.6   Performance Measurement Variables

To measure the post-acquisition operating performance of combined firms, both the earnings-based measures and operating cash-flow-based measures are used in this study. Earning-based measures and operating cash-flow-based measurers have been used by various researchers to measure the operating performance to gain a comprehensive picture of M&A performance, this study used operating cash-flow-based performance measures in addition to earnings based measures. The use of both the earnings-based measure and the operating cash-flow-based measure is not rare as evidence by the studies by Ravenscraft and Scherer (1989) and Sharma and Ho (2002). Healy et al. (1992) define operating cash flow as sales minus cost of goods sold and selling and administrative costs plus depreciation and goodwill expenses. But it is evident from previous studies that goodwill treatment differs between the US and the UK. Weetman and Gray (1990) pointed out that the most dominant effect on earnings between the US and the UK is the differential treatment of goodwill. To avoid any measurement problem arising from the differences in goodwill treatment between the UK and the US, this study ignores the goodwill amortization expenses when operating cash flows are calculated. In addition, operating profit is used to calculate earnings-based performance measurement because it is helpful to avoid any policy differences with respect to depreciation, goodwill, interest, tax, extraordinary items and dividends between the UK and the US. The superiority of operating profit compared to other measures of profit has been supported by Burt and Limmack (2003). Table 9.2 summarizes how operating performance is measured.

Table 9.2   Earnings-Based and Operating Cash-Flow-Based Performance Measures

Measure of Performance	Definition of Measures Used
Operating Return on Sales	Operating profit is used as numerator and total amount of sales or turnover is as used as denominator. Operating profit is calculated as the difference between operating revenue and operating cost.
Operating Return on Total Assets	Operating profit as defined earlier divided by the amount of total assets.
Operating Cash Flow to Sales	Operating cash flows divided by the total amount of sales. Operating cash flows is pre-tax operating cash flow adjusted for depreciation and amortization expenditures.
Operating cash-flow to total assets	Here the numerator is operating cash flows, and the denominator is the book value of total assets. Operating performance is, therefore, operating cash flows deflated by the book value of total assets. Book values rather than market values were used partly to avoid the problems associated with market anticipation of the gains from acquisitions (Burt and Limmack, 2003). Moreover, Barber and Lyon (1996) demonstrate that using market values rather than book values adds little, if anything, to the measure of performance.

9.3.7   Comparison of Pre- and Post-Acquisition Performance

To examine the merger-induced changes in operating performance, this study used the following steps:

1. All the target firms' financial data are converted to UK currency using the yearly average exchange rate between US and UK currency for the respective years.
2. This study has calculated the control firm's adjusted pre-acquisition performance measurement values by subtracting the control firm's values from the combined firm's values for each of the three pre-acquisition years. To calculate combined firm values, this study has added the pre-acquisition cash flow and earnings data for the target and bidding firms to obtain yearly aggregate operating performance measures for the combined firms as suggested by Healy et al. (1992).
3. Post-acquisition control adjusted values are calculated by subtracting control firm's values from combined firm's values for each of the three post-acquisition years.
4. Finally, pre-acquisition control adjusted values are compared with post-acquisition control adjusted values to evaluate the merger-induced operating performance for the sample UK firms engaged in CBM&A.

9.4 RESULTS AND DISCUSSION

9.4.1 Univariate Analysis

This study uses mean control adjusted earnings and cash-flow-based measures to examine the operating performance of combined firms engaged in CBM&A in which acquiring firms are from UK.

9.4.2 Earnings-Based Measures

Table 9.3 reports the pre- and post-acquisition control adjusted mean earnings-based measures of the combined firms. As evident from Table 9.3, the control adjusted mean operating profit margins on sales are positive in all the three pre-acquisition years, indicating that combined firms perform better than do control firms in the pre-acquisition period. However, the post-acquisition results are exactly opposite of the pre-acquisition years. The results show that combined firms significantly underperformed in all the three post-acquisition years. The control adjusted mean operating profit margin on sales for three post-acquisition years is –3.22, which is statistically different from 0 at 5% level, indicating significant wealth loss in post acquisition years. A comparison of pre-acquisition and post-acquisition control adjusted mean operating profit margin measure also shows that combined firms significantly underperform after the acquisition. The poor performance of combined firms in post-acquisition period is also evident from the results of operating profit to total assets measure. Table 9.3 shows that control adjusted mean operating profit to total assets are negative and statistically different from 0 in all the three post-acquisition years. Comparison of pre- and post-acquisition years also reveals that the post-acquisition control adjusted mean performance measure is lower than the pre-acquisition mean performance and that the result is statistically significant at the 5% level.

Table 9.3 Control Adjusted Earnings-Based Operating Performance Measures

Year Relative to Acquisition	Operating Profit to Sales			Operating Profit to Total Assets		
	Control Adjusted Mean	% Positive	N	Control Adjusted Mean	% Positive	N
–3	0.2460	49	105	0.2297	56	106
–2	1.4088	55	106	1.3495	54	106
–1	0.2352	59	106	–1.9449	56	106
Mean for years –3 to –1	0.8617	51	107	–0.4329	49	107
1	–2.4450	43	105	–4.8052**	45	106
2	–3.7497*	39	106	–5.0905**	40	106
3	–3.1769*	43	106	–3.1147*	41	106
Mean for years 1 to 3	–3.2232**	47	107	–4.7080***	41	107
Pre–Post	4.0850***		107	4.2751**		107

*p = .10. **p = .05. ***p = .01.

The results based on earnings-based performance measures of operating performance of combined firms engaged in CBM&A strongly support the underperformance of combined firms compared to control firms that did not carry out acquisition activities during the test period. This result tends to provide a strong support for Hypothesis 1, indicating that the UK acquirers experience wealth loss after mergers CBM&A.

9.4.3 Cash-Flow-Based Measures

Table 9.4 reported the pre- and post-acquisition control adjusted mean cash-flow-based measures of the combined firms. As evident from the table, the control adjusted mean operating cash flow to sales are negative in the first two pre-acquisition years and are positive in the year immediately preceding the year of M&A. The mean for three pre-acquisition years is also negative. However, none of these is statistically different from 0. A comparison between pre- and post-acquisition performance in term of control adjusted mean operating cash flow to sales measure indicates the underperformance of combined firms in the post-acquisition period, but the result is not statistically significant. Post-acquisition operating performance of combined firms measured in terms of control adjusted mean cash flow to total assets also shows a deterioration of performance of combined firm in the post-acquisition period. The pre-acquisition performances are negative but statistically not different from 0 for all the three pre-acquisition years, including the combined mean for three pre-acquisition years. The post acquisition results are negative and statistically different from 0. The three-year post-acquisition control adjusted mean cash flow to total assets is also negative and statistically different from 0. The results render some support to the view that performance of the combined firms decline after the acquisition. Underperformance of combined firm is also evident from the comparison between pre- and

Table 9.4 Control Adjusted Cash-Flow-Based Operating Performance Measures

Year relative to acquisition	Cash Flow to Sales			Cash Flow to Total Assets		
	Control Adjusted Mean	% positive	N	Control Adjusted Mean	% positive	N
−3	−0.0884	48	106	−0.0239	55	106
−2	−0.1281	53	107	−0.0600	54	107
−1	0.0324	51	107	−0.0245	49	107
Mean for years −3 to −1	−0.0601	54	107	−0.0357	53	107
1	−0.1123	38	107	−0.0619**	44	107
2	0.0179	40	106	−0.0430*	49	107
3	0.0044	43	105	−0.0350	40	106
Mean for years 1 to 3	−0.0737	46	107	−0.0462***	43	107
Pre–Post	0.0136		107	0.0105		107

*$p = .10$. **$p = .05$. ***$p = .01$.

post-acquisition control adjusted mean cash flow to assets ratio, but the result is not statistically significant.

The results of this study on post-acquisition operating performance of the combined firms measured in terms of control adjusted mean cash flow to sales and cash flow to total assets suggest that the UK acquirers engaged in CBM&A experienced a wealth loss ranging between –3.2 and –4.7.

9.4.4　Cross-Sectional Analysis

This study has also used cross-sectional analytical technique suggested by Healy et al. (1992) to examine the post-acquisition operating performance of combined firms. To measure the merger-specific operating gain, Healy et al. used a regression model in which the dependent variable is the post-acquisition industry adjusted median cash flow of the combined firm, and the independent variable is the pre-acquisition industry adjusted median cash flow of the combined firms. The slope coefficient of this regression model measures the correlation between pre- and post-takeover cash-flow performance, and the intercept measures the average change in operating performance independent of pre-acquisition cash flow. Therefore, intercept is the merger-induced change in the operating performance which is not dependent on the pre-acquisition performance of the combined firms. The regression model used to examine the post-acquisition operating performance of sample combined firms:

$$Y_{zi} = \alpha + \beta X_{zi} + \varepsilon_{zi,}$$

where Y_{zi} is the mean post-acquisition control adjusted performance for company i and X_{zi} is the pre-acquisition control adjusted performance for the same company. The variable z represents each of the four operating performance measures used in this study. The variable β represents the correlation between pre-acquisition and post-acquisition control adjusted performance. A significant β indicates the effect of the pre-acquisition performance on post-acquisition performance. But if the value of β is 0, which indicates no influence of pre-acquisition performance on post-acquisition performance, then the intercept α should indicate the extent to which post-acquisition performance is dependent on the acquisition event.

The regression results reported in Table 9.5 indicate significant continuance of pre-acquisition performance into the post-acquisition periods. This is evident from statistically significant β values for all four performance measures used in this study. It is also clear from the results in Table 9.5 that the combined firms significantly under perform in the post-acquisition periods. The values for constant for all the four measures are negative, and three of them are statistically significant. This implies that operating performance of the combined firms, measured in terms of control adjusted mean operating profit to sales, operating profit to total assets and cash flow to total assets, deteriorates in post-acquisition periods. The regression results in Table 9.5 confirm the poor performance of combined firms in the post-acquisition period and are in line with findings of Ghosh (2001) and Sharma and Ho (2002) in the case of domestic M&A. The results in this study is also in line with the findings of Moeller and Schlingemann (2005), who examined post-acquisition operating performance of US CBM&A.

Table 9.5   Regression Results of Post-Acquisition Mean Measures on Pre-Acquisition Mean Measures

Ratio	Constant (α)	t-value	Beta (β)	t-value	R^2	F
Operating Profit to Sales	−3.742	−2.65***	0.517	4.633***	0.254	21.47***
Operating Profit to Total Assets	−4.559	−3.085***	0.328	2.65***	0.092	7.00***
Cash Flow to Sales	−0.038	−0.946	0.841	11.961***	0.703	143.07***
Cash Flow to Total Assets	−0.036	−2.184**	0.365	3.012***	0.119	9.07***

*$p = .10.$ **$p = .05.$ ***$p = .01.$

9.5   SENSITIVITY TESTS

To investigate the overall post-acquisition operating performance of combined firms, this study also examines the impact of several firm and transaction specific characteristics on post-acquisition operating performance. For example, the study examines the variation in post-acquisition operating performance based on payment methods used in the acquisition, forms of the target firms, relatedness between target and bidding firms and size of the acquisition deal. The main findings of these sensitivity tests are discussed in the following sub-sections.

9.5.1   Operating Performance and Payment Methods

Table 9.6 reports post-acquisition operating performance of combined firms based on variations in payment methods used in acquisition. Results reported in panels A and B of Table 9.6 show that non-cash acquisitions performed better in post-acquisition years when performance is measured in terms of earnings-based measures. The difference in performance between non-cash and cash acquisitions is not statistically significant when performance is measured in terms of control adjusted mean operating profit to sales. However, it is statistically significant when performance is measured in terms of control adjusted mean operating profit to total assets. This renders a moderate support for Hypothesis 2.

In the case of performance measured in terms of cash-flow based measures, the results reported in panels C and D in Table 9.6 shows that cash acquisitions performed marginally better than did non-cash acquisitions, but these results are not statistically significant. The insignificant results on the performance differences between cash and non-cash acquisitions measures in respect of cash-flow measures are consistent with the findings of Healy et al. (1992), Sharma and Ho (2002), Heron and Lie (2002), Ramaswamy and Waegelein (2003) and Powell and Stark (2005).

9.5.2   Operating Performance and the Form of the Target Firm

Table 9.7 reports post-acquisition operating performance of combined firms based on variation in forms of target firms.

Results in panels A and B of Table 9.7 show that the control adjusted mean earnings-based measures of combined firms that include private targets performed

Table 9.6 Operating Performance and Payment Methods

Panel A: Control Adjusted Operating Profit Margin

Year Relative to Acquisition	Non-Cash	N	Cash	N	Difference	t-Value
Year 1	−2.3703	58	−2.5252	49	0.155	0.039
Year 2	−1.4580	58	−6.1203	49	4.662	1.027
Year 3	−2.0733	58	−4.3593	49	2.286	0.633
Year 1 to Year 3	−2.3388	58	−4.1991	49	1.860	0.565

Panel B: Control Adjusted Operating Profit to Total Assets

Year Relative to Acquisition	Non-Cash	N	Cash	N	Difference	t-Value
Year 1	−3.3528	58	−6.3652	49	3.012	0.782
Year 2	−1.0800	58	−9.3776	49	8.298	1.71*
Year 3	−0.6348	58	−5.9619	49	5.327	1.46
Year 1 to Year 3	−2.2544	58	−8.0441	49	5.790	1.90*

Panel C: Control Adjusted Cash-flow to Sales

Year Relative to Acquisition	Non-Cash	N	Cash	N	Difference	t-Value
Year 1	−0.1827	58	−0.0347	49	−0.1481	−1.07
Year 2	0.0149	58	0.0211	49	−0.0062	−0.06
Year 3	0.0454	58	−0.0428	49	0.0882	0.90
Year 1 to Year 3	−0.1250	58	−0.0170	49	−0.1080	−0.76

Panel D: Control Adjusted Cash-flow to Total Assets

Year Relative to Acquisition	Non-Cash	N	Cash	N	Difference	t-Value
Year 1	−0.0879	58	−0.0331	49	−0.0548	−1.16
Year 2	−0.0313	58	−0.0558	49	0.0245	0.51
Year 3	−0.0432	58	−0.0257	49	−0.0175	−0.32
Year 1 to Year 3	−0.0542	58	−0.0374	49	−0.0168	−0.49

*$p = .10$.

better in all three post-acquisition years compared to combined firms that include public targets. The difference is statistically significant when performance is measured by control adjusted mean operating profit to total assets. However, the differences are not statistically significant when cash-flow-based operating performance measures (panels C and D) were used. In short, the results suggested that the approach using earnings-based measures provide support for the Hypothesis 3, whereas the cash-flow-based measures did not.

Table 9.7   Operating Performance and Form of Target Firm

Panel A: Control Adjusted Operating Profit Margin

Year Relative to Acquisition	Private	N	Public	N	Difference	t-Value
Year 1	−1.8955	64	−4.0936	41	2.198	0.48
Year 2	−2.9180	65	−6.4229	41	3.505	0.65
Year 3	−2.0158	65	−7.1962	40	5.180	1.21
Year 1 to Year 3	−2.4901	65	−5.4716	42	2.982	0.78

Panel B: Control Adjusted Operating Profit to Total Assets

Year Relative to Acquisition	Private	N	Public	N	Difference	t-Value
Year 1	−2.0295	63	−13.1321	42	11.103	2.64***
Year 2	−4.1978	65	−7.7687	42	3.571	0.66
Year 3	−1.4307	65	−8.9438	42	7.513	1.74*
Year 1 to Year 3	−3.0978	65	−10.8616	42	7.764	2.22**

Panel C: Control Adjusted Cash-flow to Sales

Year Relative to Acquisition	Private	N	Public	N	Difference	t-Value
Year 1	−0.0548	65	−0.2887	42	0.234	1.41
Year 2	0.0014	65	0.0721	42	−0.071	−0.58
Year 3	0.0030	65	0.0088	42	−0.006	−0.05
Year 1 to Year 3	−0.0164	65	−0.2495	42	0.233	1.38

Panel D: Control Adjusted Cash-flow to Total Assets

Year Relative to Acquisition	Private	N	Public	N	Difference	t-Value
Year 1	−0.0567	65	−0.0777	42	0.021	0.38
Year 2	−0.0388	65	−0.0557	42	0.017	0.34
Year 3	−0.0328	65	−0.0418	42	0.009	0.14
Year 1 to Year 3	−0.0422	65	−0.0584	42	0.0162	0.40

*p = .10. **p = .05. ***p = .01.

The results in the earning based measures are in line of the findings of Conn et al. (2005), who documented that acquisitions of private targets outperform the acquisitions of public targets in the case of UK CBM&A when using share-price information.

9.5.3   Operating Performance and Relatedness between Merging Firms

Table 9.8 reports post-acquisition operating performance of combined firms based on relatedness between target and bidding firms.

Table 9.8 Operating Performance According to Relatedness between Merging Firms

Panel A: Control Adjusted Operating Profit Margin

Year Relative to Acquisition	Unrelated	N	Related	N	Difference	t-Value
Year 1	−1.4263	59	−4.1429	47	2.717	0.66
Year 2	−3.2953	58	−4.3676	48	1.072	0.23
Year 3	−4.2025	58	−1.4986	48	−2.704	−0.73
Year 1 to Year 3	−3.1605	59	−3.3136	48	0.153	0.05

Panel B: Control Adjusted Operating Profit to Total Assets

Year Relative to Acquisition	Unrelated	N	Related	N	Difference	t-Value
Year 1	−3.2506	59	−7.0357	48	3.785	0.97
Year 2	−5.3237	59	−4.7640	48	−0.560	−0.12
Year 3	−3.4443	59	−2.6130	48	−0.831	−0.22
Year 1 to Year 3	−4.7644	59	−5.3562	48	0.592	0.19

Panel C: Control Adjusted Cash Flow to Sales

Year Relative to Acquisition	Unrelated	N	Related	N	Difference	t-Value
Year 1	−0.0356	59	−0.2228	48	0.187	1.29
Year 2	−0.0294	59	0.0889	48	−0.118	−1.13
Year 3	−0.0642	59	0.1165	48	−0.181	−1.84*
Year 1 to Year 3	−0.0430	59	−0.1178	48	0.075	0.50

Panel D: Control Adjusted Cash Flow to Total Assets

Year Relative to Acquisition	Unrelated	N	Related	N	Difference	t-Value
Year 1	−0.0358	59	−0.0994	48	0.064	1.33
Year 2	−0.0510	59	−0.0314	48	−0.020	−0.43
Year 3	−0.0501	59	−0.0139	48	−0.036	−0.65
Year 1 to Year 3	−0.0448	59	−0.0482	48	0.003	−0.10

*$p = .10$.

Results in panels A, B, C and D in Table 9.8 show the differences in post-acquisition operating performance, measured in terms of control adjusted mean earnings and cash-flow-based measures, of combined firms that include related target and bidding firms and the combined firms that include unrelated target and bidding firms. The results show no significant differences between the combined firms that include unrelated targets and bidders compared to the combined firms that include related targets and bidders in post-acquisition years. The overall results presented in all four panels of Table 9.8 do not provide support for Hypothesis 4. The findings are consistent with the findings of Sharma and Ho (2002), who found statistically insignificant superior performance of conglomerate mergers in the case of domestic acquisitions.

9.5.4   Operating Performance and the Size of the Acquisition Deal

Table 9.9 reports post-acquisition operating performance of combined firms based on size of the acquisition deals. Results in panels A, B, C and D of Table 9.9 indicate that the differences in post-acquisition operating performance using both control adjusted mean earnings-based and cash-flow-based measures for large deals and small deals were not statistically significant. We therefore reject Hypothesis 5.

Table 9.9   Operating Performance and Size of Acquisition Deal

Panel A: Control Adjusted Operating Profit Margin

Year Relative to Acquisition	Smaller Deal	N	Larger Deal	N	Difference	t-Value
Year 1	−1.5954	75	−4.7673	32	3.172	0.71
Year 2	−4.1486	75	−2.7641	32	−1.384	−0.27
Year 3	−3.4632	74	−2.4865	32	−0.977	−0.25
Year 1 to Year 3	−3.4685	75	−2.6373	32	−0.831	−0.23

Panel B: Control Adjusted Operating Profit to Total Assets

Year Relative to Acquisition	Smaller Deal	N	Larger Deal	N	Difference	t-Value
Year 1	−3.6590	75	−7.4347	32	3.776	0.90
Year 2	−5.8479	75	−3.3233	32	−2.525	−0.47
Year 3	−3.6371	75	−1.8547	32	−1.782	−0.52
Year 1 to Year 3	−5.0462	75	−4.9130	32	−0.133	−0.04

Panel C: Control Adjusted Cash Flow to Sales

Year Relative to Acquisition	Smaller Deal	N	Larger Deal	N	Difference	t-Value
Year 1	−0.1526	75	−0.0161	32	−0.137	−1.09
Year 2	−0.0535	75	0.1847	32	−0.238	−2.20**
Year 3	0.0150	75	−0.0193	32	0.034	0.32
Year 1 to Year 3	−0.1254	75	0.0498	32	−0.175	−1.30

Panel D: Control Adjusted Cash Flow to Total Assets

Year Relative to Acquisition	Smaller Deal	N	Larger Deal	N	Difference	t-Value
Year 1	−0.0470	75	−0.0972	32	0.050	0.97
Year 2	−0.0524	75	−0.0204	32	−0.032	−0.60
Year 3	−0.0313	75	−0.0445	32	0.013	0.26
Year 1 to Year 3	−0.0436	75	−0.0523	32	0.009	0.23

**$p = .05$.

9.6 CROSS-SECTIONAL ANALYSIS

In addition to the univariate analysis, we examined the impact of firm- and transaction-specific characteristics on post-acquisition operating performance. These characteristics include payment methods, forms of targets, relatedness of merging firms and deal size. The regression model is summarised as follows:

$$Y_{zi} = \alpha + \beta_1 X_1 + \beta_2 X_2 + \beta_3 X_3 + \beta_4 X_4 + \varepsilon_{zi},$$

where

Y_{zi} = mean post-acquisition control adjusted performance for company i;

z = selected post-acquisition control adjusted operating performance measure (one is mean earnings-based measure and the other one is mean cash-flow-based measure);

X_1 = payment method, where, 0 and 1 represent non-cash and cash acquisitions, respectively;

X_2 = form of targets, where 0 and 1 represent private and public targets, respectively;

X_3 = relatedness between target and bidding firms, where 0 and 1 represent unrelated and related acquisitions, respectively;

X_4 = deal size, where 0 and 1 represent smaller (less than US$50 million) and larger (more than US$50 million) deals, respectively;

β = slope coefficient for each of the independent variables;

α = constant of the regression model; and

ε_{zi} = unexplained variation, where mean is assumed to be 0.

Regression results are reported in Table 9.10. In the case of the earnings-based measure of performance, the regression procedure suggests that payment methods and forms of target firms have an impact on the post-acquisition operating performance of combined firms. The statistically significant negative coefficient for payment method indicates that non-cash acquisitions provide better returns to the combined firms. This supports the notion that cash acquisitions can be detrimental to post-acquisition operating performance because of the large interest burden associated with a cash payment financed by debt and the limiting role of debt on management freedom to make decisions. The statistically significant negative coefficient for the form of target firms indicates that acquisitions of private targets provide better returns to the combined firms and renders support for the arguments that acquisition of private targets involves lower payments because of low level of managerialism, illiquidity and lower competition for target firms and the benefit of better post-acquisition monitoring related with acquisition of private targets. The findings are consistent with the results reported by Healy et al. (1997), who reported that operating performance of non-cash acquisitions is better than that of cash acquisitions. In respect to the form of target firms, the findings of this study lend some support to the earlier research of Conn et al. (2005), who documented that acquisitions of private targets outperform acquisitions of public targets in the case of UK CBM&A.

Table 9.10   Regression Results of Operating Performance and Firm Characteristics

Variables	Earnings-Based Measure		Cash-Flow-Based Measure	
	Regression Values	*t*-Value	Regression Values	*t*-Value
Constant (α)	−0.056	−0.771	−0.125	−0.996
X_1 (Payment method)	−0.473	−3.215***	0.164	1.595*
X_2 (Form of targets)	−0.382	−2.742***	−0.378	−2.372***
X_3 (Relatedness)	0.115	0.878	0.035	0.257
X_4 (Deal size)	0.199	1.434	0.246	2.699***
R^2	0.159		0.172	
F	4.879***		3.782***	
D-W statistic	2.006		2.409	

D-W statistic = Durbin-Watson statistic.
*p = .10. ***p = .01.

However, deal size and firm relatedness did not have significant influence on CBM&A earnings. Regarding the cash-flow-based performance measure, payment methods, form of target firms and deal size appear to have a significant influence on the post-acquisition operating performance of combined firms. The negative sign of target form variable suggests that acquisitions of private targets generate more returns to the combined firms. In case of deal size, the positive sign of the coefficient indicate that large deals generate more return to the combined firms in the post-acquisition periods. This is consistent with the argument that large acquisitions may help avoid the problem of free cash flow, create synergistic gains and enhance market power (Jensen, 1986; Seth et al., 2000).

9.7   CONCLUSION

This study has examined the post-acquisition operating performance of combined firms engaged in CBM&A. The acquiring firms used in this study are UK public limited companies, and the target firms are both private and public companies that are from the US. A total of 107 acquiring firms and 107 targets were used to examine the operating performance by using matched control firms. Both earnings-based and cash-flow-based measures of performance were used to examine performance in which the means of those measures were used to compare performance over three pre-acquisition and three post-acquisition years. Although difficulties exist in comparing accounting data in case of international transactions because differences in accounting systems among the countries, the motivation of this study comes from recent evidences on narrowing down of accounting differences in international settings (e.g. Larson and Kenny, 1999) and a recent paper by Moeller and Schlingemann (2005), who examined operating performance of CBM&A using US data.

Using a multi-method approach, this study finds that the combined firms underperform in post-acquisition periods compared to the control firms used as benchmarks. The findings of negative performances of the combined firms in the post-acquisition period are consistent with earlier operating performance studies on domestic M&A and with similar studies on CBM&A. Despite the existence of various sources of synergy in M&A formation, the underperformance of combined firms in the post-acquisition period emphasizes the role of corporate managers in managing the acquisitions, especially the post-acquisition integration process as suggested by Haspeslagh and Jemison (1991). The study has also found that payment methods and the form of target firms have statistically significant impact on the variation on post-acquisition operating performance of combined firms. The study also finds that non-cash acquisitions and private targets perform better than do cash acquisitions and public targets, which supports the proposition that private firms are closely held and that stock acquisitions improve the monitoring of bidding firm management by the target shareholders as the exchange of stocks gives the target shareholders an access to participate in bidders' decision-making process (Fuller et al., 2002). The better performance of non-cash acquisitions also supports the argument of incentive creation as suggested by Chatterjee and Kuenzi (2001).

The regression result in this study confirms that post-acquisition performance of the combined firm is influenced by relative size of the deal. The study found that large deals perform better than the smaller and medium-size deals. This finding tends to support the proposition that large deals reduce the free cash-flow problem of the acquiring firm (Jensen, 1986). Moreover, the finding confirms that large deals are more likely to reap the benefits of economies of scale and scope as suggested by Sudarsanam (2003) and the financial synergy suggested by Myers and Majluf (1984).

It is pertinent to point out that the results in this study are consistent with several theoretical justifications available in prior M&As literature and are in line with previous findings of a number of studies in the area of both domestic and cross-border M&As, the results should be considered in light of the following limitation. Although there is evidence that international accounting differences are gradually narrowing and that the UK and the US are very close to each other in terms of accounting standards and financial disclosure, some differences in this area might still affect the results of this study.

NOTE

1. The classification of these sectors is taken from the US SIC codes. The main two-digit SIC codes are 01–09 Agriculture, Forestry and Fishing; 10–14 Mining; 15–17 Construction; 20–39 Manufacturing; 40–49 Transportation, Communications, Electric, Gas, and Sanitary Services; 50–51 Wholesale Trade; 52–59 Retail Trade; 65 Real Estate; 70–89 Services and 91–97 Public Administration.

REFERENCES

Alexander, D., Britton, A. and Jorissen, A. (2005). *International Financial Reporting and Analysis*, 2nd Edition, Hampshire, UK: Thomson.

Asquith, P., Bruner, F. and Mullins, J. (1983). The Gains to Bidding Firms from Merger, *Journal of Financial Economics*, Vol. 11(1), pp. 121–139.

Bailey, W. and Choi, J.J. (2003). International Market Linkage, *Journal of Economics & Business*, Vol. 55(5&6), pp. 399–404.

Barber, B.M. and Lyon, J.D. (1996). Detecting Abnormal Operating Performance: The Empirical Power and Specification of Test Statistics, *Journal of Financial Economics*, Vol. 41, pp. 359–399.

Bos, T. and Fetherston, J.A. (1993). Capital Structure Practices in the Pacific Rim, *Research in International Business and Finance*, Vol. 10, pp. 53–66.

Bradley, M., Desai, A, and Kim, E.H. (1983). The Rationale behind Inter-Firm Tender Offers, *Journal of Financial Economics*, Vol. 11, pp. 183–206.

Bruner, R.F. (2002). Does M&A Pay? A Survey of Evidence for the Decision Maker, *Journal of Applied Finance*, Vol. 12(Spring/Summer), pp. 48–68.

Burt, S. and Limmack, R. (2003). The Operating Performance of Companies Involved in Acquisitions in the UK Retailing Sector, 1977–1992, *Advances in Mergers and Acquisitions*, Vol. 2, pp. 147–176.

Chang, S. (1998). Takeovers of Privately Held Targets, Methods of Payment, and Bidder Returns, *Journal of Finance*, Vol. 53(2), pp. 773–784.

Chatterjee, R. and Kuenzi, A. (2001). *Mergers and Acquisitions: The Influence of Methods of Payments on Bidder's Share Price*, Research Papers in Management Studies, Cambridge: Cambridge University Press.

Chatterjee, R. and Meeks, G. (1996). The Financial Effects of Takeovers: Accounting Rates of Return and Accounting Regulation, *Journal of Business Finance & Accounting*, Vol. 23(5/6), pp. 851–868.

Chatterjee, S. (1992). Sources of Value in Takeovers: Synergy or Restructuring—Implications for Target and Bidder Firms, *Strategic Management Journal*, Vol. 13, pp. 267–286.

Cheng, L.T.W. and Leung, T.Y (2004). A Comparative Analysis of the Market-Based and Accounting-Based Performance of Diversifying and Non-Diversifying Acquisitions in Hong Kong, *International Business Review*, Vol. 13, pp. 763–789.

Clark, K. and Ofek, E. (1994). Mergers as a Means of Restructuring Distressed Firms: An Empirical Investigation, *Journal of Financial and Quantitative Analysis*, Vol. 29(4), pp. 541–565.

Conn, R.L., Cosh, A., Guest, P.M. and Hughes, A. (2005). The Impact on UK Acquirers of Domestic, Cross-Border, Public and Private Acquisitions, *Journal of Business Finance & Accounting*, Vol. 32(5&6), pp. 815–870.

Copeland, T.E., Weston, J.F. and Shastry, K. (2005). *Financial Theory and Corporate Policy*, 4th Edition, New York: Pearson Addison Wesley.

Cosh, A., Hughes, A. and Singh, A. (1980). The Causes and Effects of Takeovers in the United Kingdom: An Empirical Investigation for the Late 1960s at the Microeconomic Level, in D.C. Mueller (ed.) *The Determinants and Effects of Mergers*, Cambridge, MA: Oelgeschlager, Gunn and Hain, pp. 227–270.

Davis, E., Shore, G. and Thompson, D. (1991). Continental Mergers are Different, *Business Strategy Review*, Vol. 2(1), pp. 49–70.

Dickerson, A.P., Gibson, H.D. and Tsakalotos, E. (1997). The Impact of Acquisitions on Company Performance: Evidence from a Large Panel of UK Firms, *Oxford Economic Papers*, Vol. 49, pp. 344–361.

Draper, P. and Paudyal, K. (2006). Acquisitions: Private versus Public, *European Financial Management*, Vol. 12 (1), pp. 57–80.

Fuller, K., Netter, J. and Stegemoller, M. (2002). What Do Returns to Acquiring Firms Tell Us? Evidence from Firms that Make Many Acquisitions, *Journal of Finance*, Vol. 57, pp. 1763–1793.

Ghosh, A. (2001). Does Operating Performance Really Improve Following Corporate Acquisitions?, *Journal of Corporate Finance*, Vol. 7, pp. 151–178.

Gugler, K., Mueller, D.C., Yurtoglu, B.B. and Zulehner, C. (2003). The Effects of Merger: An International Comparison, *International Journal of Industrial Organization*, Vol. 21(5), pp. 625–653.

Halpern, P. (1983). Corporate Acquisitions: A Theory of Special Cases? A Review of Event Studies Applied to Acquisitions, *Journal of Finance*, Vol. 38(2), pp. 297–317.

Harris, R.S. and Ravenscraft, D.J. (1991). The Role of Acquisitions in Foreign Direct Investment: Evidence from the US Stock Market, *Journal of Finance*, Vol. 46(3), pp. 401–417.

Haspeslagh, P.C. and Jemison, D.B. (1991). *Managing Acquisitions: Creating Value through Corporate Renewal*, New York: Free Press.

Healy, P.M., Palepu, K.G. and Ruback, R.S. (1992). Does Corporate Performance Improve after Merger, *Journal of Financial Economics*, Vol. 31, pp. 135–175.

Healy, P., Palepu, K. and Ruback, R. (1997). Which Takeovers Are Profitable? Strategic or Financial?, *Sloan Management Review*, Vol. 38(4), pp. 45–57.

Heron, R. and Lie, E. (2002). Operating Performance and the Method of Payment in Takeovers, *Journal of Financial and Quantitative Analysis*, Vol. 37(1), pp. 137–155.

Hirshleifer, D. and Shumway, T. (2003). Good Day Sunshine: Stock Returns and the Weather, *Journal of Finance*, Vol. 58(3), pp. 1009–1032.

Hughes, A. Mueller, D.C. and Singh, A. (1980). Hypotheses about Merger, in D.C. Mueller (ed.), *The Determinants and Effects of Merger*, Cambridge, MA: Oelgeschlager, Gunn and Hain, pp. 27–66.

Ingham, H., Kran, I. and Lovestam, A. (1992). Mergers and Profitability: A Managerial Success Story?, *Journal of Management Studies*, Vol. 29(2), pp. 195–208.

Jensen, M.C. (1986). Agency Costs of Free Cash-Flow, Corporate Finance and Takeovers, *American Economic Review*, Vol. 76, pp. 323–329.

Jensen, M.C. (1988). Takeovers: Their Causes and Consequences, *Journal of Economic Perspectives*, Vol. 2(1), pp. 21–48.

Larson, R.K. and Kenny, S.Y. (1999). The Harmonization of International Accounting Standards: Progress in the 1990s, *Multinational Business Review*, Vol. 7(1), pp. 1–12.

Lewellen, W.G. (1971). A Pure Financial Rationale for a Conglomerate Merger, *Journal of Finance*, Vol. 26, pp. 521–537.

Linn, S.C. and Switzer, J.A. (2001). Are Cash Acquisitions Associated With Better Post Combination Operating Performance than Stock Acquisition?, *Journal of Banking & Finance*, Vol. 25, pp. 1113–1138.

Lubatkin, M. (1983). Mergers and the Performance of Acquiring Firm, *Academy of Management Review*, Vol. 8(2), pp. 218–225.

Manson, S., Powell, R., Stark, A.W. and Thomas, H.M. (2000). Identifying the Sources of Gains from Takeovers, *Accounting Forum*, Vol. 24(4), pp. 319–342.

Martin, K.J. and McConnell, J.J. (1991). Corporate Performance, Corporate Takeovers and Management Turnover, *Journal of Finance*, Vol. 46(2), pp. 671–687.

Meeks, G. (1977). *Disappointing Marriage: A Study of the Gains from Merger*, Cambridge: Cambridge University Press.

Moeller, S.B and Schlingemann, F.P. (2005). Global Diversification and Bidder Gains: A Comparison between Cross-Border and Domestic Acquisitions, *Journal of Banking and Finance*, Vol. 29, pp. 533–564.

Mueller, G.G., Gernon, H. and Meek, G. (1997). *Accounting: An International Perspective*, Chicago: Irwin.

Myers, S.C. (1984). The Capital Structure Puzzle, *Journal of Finance*, Vol. 39, pp. 575–592.

Myers, S.C. and Majluf, N.S. (1984). Corporate Financing and Investment Decisions when Firms Have Information that Investors Do not Have, *Journal of Financial Economics*, Vol. 13(2), pp. 187–221.

Nobes, C. (1998). Towards a General Model of the Reasons for International Differences in Financial Reporting, *ABACUS*, Vol. 34(2), pp. 162–187.

Penrose, E.T. (1959). *The Theory of the Growth of the Firm*, Oxford: Blackwell.

Peterson, D.R. and Peterson, P.P. (1991). The Medium Exchange in Merger and Acquisitions, *Journal of Banking and Finance*, Vol. 15, pp. 383–405.

Porter, M.E. (1987). From Competitive Advantage to Corporate Strategy, *Harvard Business Review*, Vol. 65(3), pp. 43–59.

Powell, R.G. and Stark, A.W. (2005). Does Operating Performance Increase Post-Takeover for UK Takeovers? A Comparison of Performance and Benchmarks, *Journal of Corporate Finance*, Vol. 11, pp. 293–317.

Rahman, R.A. and Limmack, R.J. (2004). Corporate Acquisitions and the Operating Performance of Malaysian Companies, *Journal of Business Finance & Accounting*, Vol. 31(3&4), pp. 359–400.

Ramaswamy, K.P. and Waegelein, J.F. (2003). Firm Financial Performance Following Mergers, *Review of Quantitative Finance and Accounting*, Vol. 20, pp. 115–126.

Ravenscraft, D.J. and Scherer, F.M. (1989). The Profitability of Mergers, *International Journal of Industrial Organization*, Vol. 7, pp. 101–116.

Roll, R. (1986). The Hubris Hypothesis of Corporate Takeovers, *Journal of Business*, Vol. 59, pp. 197–216.

Schipper, K. and Thompson, R. (1983). Evidence on the Capitalized Value of Merger Activity for Acquiring Firms, *Journal of Financial Economics*, Vol. 11, pp. 85–119.

Seth, A. (1990). Sources of Value Creation in Acquisitions: An Empirical Investigation, *Strategic Management Journal*, Vol. 11, pp. 431–446.

Seth, A., Song, K.P. and Pettit, R. (2000). Synergy, Managerialism or Hubris? An Empirical Examination of Motives for Foreign Acquisitions of US Firms, *Journal of International Business Studies*, Vol. 31(3), pp. 387–405.

Sharma, D.S. and Ho, J. (2002). The Impact of Acquisitions on Operating Performance: Some Australian Evidence, *Journal of Business Finance & Accounting*, Vol. 29(1&2), pp. 155–200.

Shleifer, A. and Vishny, R.W. (1986). Large Shareholders and Corporate Control, *Journal of Political Economy*, Vol. 94, pp. 461–488.

Shleifer, A. and Vishny, R.W. (1992). Asset Liquidity and Debt Capacity, *Journal of Finance*, Vol. 47, pp. 1343–1366.

Singh, A. (1971). *Takeovers: Their Relevance to the Stock market and the Theory of the Firm*, London: Cambridge University Press.

Singh, H. and Montgomery, C.A. (1987). Corporate Acquisition Strategies and Economic Performance, *Strategic Management Journal*, Vol. 8, pp. 377–387.

Stulz, R.M. (1990). Managerial Discretion and Optimal Financial Policies, *Journal of Financial Economics*, Vol. 26, pp. 3–28.

Sudarsanam, S. (2003). *Creating Value from Mergers and Acquisitions: The Challenges*, London: Pearson Education Limited.

Switzer, J.A. (1996). Evidence on Real Gains in Corporate Acquisitions, *Journal of Economics and Business*, Vol. 48, pp. 443–460.

Tuch, C. and O'Sullivan, N. (2007). The Impact of Acquisitions on Firm Performance: A Review of the Evidence, *International Journal of Management Reviews*, Vol. 9(2), pp. 141–170.

United Nations Conference on Trade and Development (UNCTAD) (2000). *World Investment Report 2000: Cross-Border Mergers and Acquisitions and Development*, New York and Geneva: United Nations.

Utton, M.A. (1974). On Measuring the Effects of Industrial Merger, *Scottish Journal of Political Economy*, Vol. 21(1), pp. 13–28.

Weetman, P. and Gray, S.J. (1990). International Financial Analysis and Comparative Corporate Performance: The Impact of UK versus US Accounting Principles on Earnings, *Journal of International Financial Management and Accounting*, Vol. 2(2&3), pp. 111–130.

Weston, J.F., Mitchell, M.L. and Mulherin, J.H. (2004). *Takeovers, Restructuring and Corporate Governance*, 4th Edition, Upper Saddle River, NJ: Pearson-Prentice Hall.

Whittington, M. (2000). Problems in Comparing Financial Performance Across International Boundaries: A Case Study Approach, *The International Journal of Accounting*, Vol. 35(3), pp. 399–413.

Zysman, J. (1983). Government, Markets and Growth: *Financial Systems and the Politics of Industrial Change*, Ithaca, NY: Cornell University Press.

10 Conclusion

10.1 INTRODUCTION

We conclude by highlighting briefly the important trends, drivers and performance of the UK CBM&A. First, over the past 30 years, CBM&A have become a popular means of worldwide flow of FDI. The growth of CBM&A activities in 1990s has been seen as the 'fifth merger wave' by scholars in this field. Most of the theories used to explain why FDI and domestic M&A take place including the eclectic paradigm, the internationalization theory, the resources-based view of firms, the industrial organization theory, synergy, the valuation theory and diversification are also applicable to CBM&A.

10.2 AN ANALYSIS OF TRENDS, PATTERNS AND DRIVERS OF UK CBM&A

Using the aggregate level data on FDI and CBM&A extracted from various official sources, we conclude the following:

1. *Global CBM&A:* The volume and number of global CBM&A has increased substantially during the period from 1991 to 2005. Second, the average deal value of CBM&A activities has increased significantly over the last 15 years, representing a massive competition in the global market for corporate control. Third, the CBM&A have been the most dominant mode of worldwide FDI flows, and this is evident by the fact that during the last 15 years, almost 60% of global FDI flows have been through CBM&A activities. Fourth, more and more countries, especially from the developing world, have participated in the global market for corporate control, which facilitates the pace of rapid globalization.

2. *Regional Trends in Global CBM&A:* The regional trends in global CBM&A show that developed countries dominated the global market for corporate control in terms of both cross-border purchase and sales. Among the developing countries, countries from Asia took the lead in cross-border purchase, and countries from Latin America and the Caribbean were ahead in cross-border sales.

3. *Sectoral Distribution of Global CBM&A:* The sectoral distribution of global CBM&A reveals that the service sector was the most active sector in CBM&A activities from 1996 to 2005, followed by the manufacturing and primary sectors. The most active industries in the cross-border purchase and sales for the 1991–2005 period include finance; transport, storage and communications; chemical and chemical products; electricity, gas and water; and business services.

4. *Trends in UK CBM&A:* Data on UK international M&A activities from 1991 to 2005 shows that during this 15-year period, the UK cross-border purchase and sales increased by about 11 times and 13 times, respectively. Considering the total flow of cross-border purchase and sales during the period from 1991 to 2005, the UK was the leading country in the case of cross-border purchase claiming 21.38% of global purchase and second in terms of cross-border sales claiming 15.09% of global sales.

5. *Industry Distribution of UK CBM&A:* From 1991 to 2005, the UK has been the most active in industries, such as, industrial, high technology, consumer product and services, media and entertainment and materials.

6. *Wave Pattern in UK CBM&A:* It was found from the analysis that UK CBM&A activities in 1990s were comparable with the merger wave pattern in the past. More specifically, the total value of CBM&A, in the case of both purchase and sales, was particularly high from 1998 to 2000 compared to other years from 1991 to 2005.

7. *Drivers of UK CBM&A:* We suggest that favourable acquisition laws, non-discriminatory treatment between national and international enterprises, long-term political, economic and regulatory stability along with a lower rate of tax and inflation, sophisticated world-class capital market, uncontrolled exchange regime, labour productivity and wage condition, overall investment climate and technological change, international competition, deregulation and privatization in various industrial sectors might have contributed to an increased level of CBM&A activities in the UK.

10.3   MACROECONOMIC INFLUENCE OF CBM&A IN THE UK

Regarding the macroeconomic determinants of CBM&A activities in the UK over the 1988–2005 period, we found that several macroeconomic variables significantly influence the inward UK CBM&A, including the level of GDP, interest rates, share prices and inflation and the money supply. The results of this study are consistent with earlier findings and have a significant bearing on managerial decision making. The statistically significant relationship between CBM&A inflows and outflows with selected macroeconomic variables suggests that managers should consider the changes in macroeconomic variables when making acquisition decisions in order to make the right timing decisions for acquisitions to avoid being a follower of competitors. Carow et al. (2004) pointed out that acquirers who make acquisition decisions early earn a better return than acquirers who make acquisition decisions later. Therefore, managers can make the acquisition decision in response to the movements of macroeconomic factors to ensure an early decision so that they can remain ahead of their competitors to ensure better acquisition induced return.

10.4   MOTIVES OF CBM&A IN THE UK

A number of researchers have attempted to identify and evaluate the motivations of domestic M&A both theoretically and empirically. Using the survey responses from the top-level managers for evaluating M&A motives, our exploratory factor analysis using varimax rotation produced eight underlying factors that explain 74.41% of the observed variance in the sample. The eight factors may be summarized as operational synergy, financial synergy, managerial synergy, internalization, location, market power, managerialism and other motives. The study finds that the relative importance of the motives varies most with the size of the acquirer, to a moderate extent with the cash flow of the acquirer, large acquirer with multiple acquisition experience and sector of acquirer and to a modest extent with acquirer's intangible assets. These findings provide some support for the operating and managerial hypothesis of M&A, Jensen's (1986) free cash-flow hypothesis, the internalization hypothesis of FDI and the OLI Paradigm, the industrial organization hypothesis and the oligopolistic reaction hypothesis of FDI. The results also render support for the strategic acquisition hypothesis of CBM&A and the location hypothesis of FDI.

10.5   MANAGING THE POST-ACQUISITION INTEGRATION SYSTEM

We find that management accounting system integration goes through four-staged phases, namely

- pre-integration,
- integration planning,
- implementation options and
- review and evaluation.

The study also finds that all the acquirers (regardless of the size industry and the implementation strategy to be used) follow the similar activities outlined in the first two stages of MAS integration framework, that is pre-integration and integration planning. However, at the implementation phase, the activities to be performed are contingent on the implementation option adopted. Companies adopting immediate absorption tend to undertake minimal changes, whereas companies adopting gradual integration tend to perform a number of activities ranging from coordination, standardization of documents and consolidation. In addition, we find that large acquirers are more likely to immediately absorb the MAS of the relatively smaller acquired system. This is not surprising given that integrating a relatively small firm tends to be easier. However, when the acquired system is unrelated, the acquirer is more likely to retain the MAS and allow it to operate independently.

Notwithstanding the common activities we documented and that are normally performed by all management accountants, it is pertinent also to point out that we also find that each acquisition tends to be unique and different with many contextually divergent issues influencing the integration approach to be adopted or used. Another important conclusion to be drawn from this study is the importance of communication. We identified communication as a major tool for reducing the uncertainty among the people involved. Gathering important information about the target MAS is a key to stabilising volatile situations and reduce the dysfunctional effects likely to undermine the integration process.

10.6 SHORT-RUN PERFORMANCE OF CBM&A OF UK ACQUIRING FIRMS

Regarding the short-run share-price performance of the UK acquirers, we found that UK acquirers earned significant positive abnormal return on the announcement of cross-border acquisition decisions. However, the positive returns disappear as the event window increases. Although the abnormal returns for the whole sample becomes negative in the wider event windows, none of them are statistically significant and this indicates that UK acquirers do not lose value by the announcement of acquisitions abroad. The results of the study also confirm that selected transaction specific, firm specific and geographic characteristics do affect the abnormal return of acquiring firms. For example, form of the target company, deal size and geographic origin of the target firms have a statistically significant impact on the performance of acquiring firms as confirmed by both univariate and multivariate analysis. On the other hand, although the univariate analysis found some support regarding the impact of payment methods and acquisition strategies on the short-run performance of UK acquiring firms, the multivariate analysis could not provide support for them. The univariate analysis in this study has found that short-run performance of cash acquisitions is better than non-cash acquisition is. However, the statistical insignificance of the payment method variable may be an outcome of the neutralizing effect of the cash bid in the case of CBM&A as pointed out by Conn et al. (2005). Moreover, the insignificance of the acquisition strategy variable in explaining short-run bidder return, as found in multivariate regression in this study may be due to the ineffectiveness of related acquisitions in the case of CBM&A due to the increased level of cultural difference between target and bidder firms from two countries (Datta and Puia, 1995).

10.7 OPERATING PERFORMANCE AFTER MERGER IN UK CBM&A

Using univariate and multivariate analytical tools, this study has found that combined firms underperform in post acquisition periods compared to the control firms used as benchmarks. The results of underperformance are more robust when earnings-based performance measures are used. The findings of negative performance of the combined firms in the post-acquisition period are consistent with earlier operating performance studies on domestic mergers and acquisitions and with similar studies on CBM&A. This study has also found that payment methods and form of target firms have a statistically significant impact on the variation of post-acquisition operating performance of combined firms. The better post-acquisition performance of non-cash acquisitions and of acquisitions of private targets support the proposition that private firms are closely held and that stock acquisitions improves the monitoring of the bidding firms' management by the target shareholders as the exchange of stocks gives the target shareholders access to participate in the bidders' decision-making process. The regression results in this study confirms that post-acquisition performance of the combined firm is influenced by relative size of the deal. The study also found that larger deals perform better than the smaller and medium-size deals. This finding tends to support the proposition that larger deals reduce the free cash-flow problem of the acquiring firm. Moreover, the finding confirms that larger deals are more likely to produce the benefits of economies of scale and scope and financial synergy.

10.8 IMPLICATIONS OF THE STUDY

The results of this study have several normative implications for those who are interested in the acquisition process and activities. Prominent implications include, first, that managers should consider macroeconomic determinants at the time of making international acquisition decisions. The large explanatory power of the models used in the study suggests that managers should think carefully about the acquisition decision and in particular pay attention to changes in macroeconomic variables to ensure a pioneering position rather than becoming a follower of the competitors. Second, traditionally the motives and success of M&A events were judged in terms of financial gain. However, it was found in this study that strategic reasons also heavily influence the acquisition decision. Motives, such as speed of entering the foreign market, attaining market power and market share, sharing of intangible assets, matching complementary assets and reducing dominance of competitors, are found to be significant as motives along with traditional operational and financial synergistic motives. This renders support for the observation made by Grinblatt and Titman (2002) that acquisitions in the 1990s are strategic in nature. The findings that non-financial strategic motives are significant, implying that CBM&A success should not only be judged with respect to financial gain rather sufficient consideration regarding long-term strategic gains should also be given proper attention. Third, the results in this study suggest that UK acquirers earn positive abnormal returns on the announcement of acquisition of foreign firms. Given the assumption underlying the share-price-based studies that individual investor is able to assess accurately the expected benefits of the takeover (Healy et al., 1997), the positive announcement period return represents investors' optimistic assessment of the acquiring firm's management decision to acquire the target. However, the optimism in assessment might not always be correct due to information asymmetry between management and shareholders (Myers and Majluf, 1984). Therefore, it is the responsibility of the management to act and keep the confidence of the investors by ensuring proper integration of the merging firms and, afterwards, by continuing to use the pooled resources in a more productive way. Fourth, the findings of negative performance of the combined firms in the post acquisition period emphasises the role of corporate managers in managing the acquisitions, especially the post-acquisition integration process. Haspeslagh and Jemison (1991) suggested that value creation in the post acquisition period was mostly dependent on proper integration of the merging firms. The negative post-acquisition performance of UK CBM&A may point to the fact that managers of those firms could not integrate the merging firms properly. Therefore, special care should be taken by the UK acquisition managers to ensure proper integration of the target and acquiring firms immediately after the acquisition event. Fifth, this study has found that several firm and acquisition related characteristics do affect the short-run and long-run performance of the acquiring firm and the combined firm. Therefore, care should be taken at the time of making the acquisition decision, particularly with respect of the payment methods, the deal size, the form of target and the geographic origin of the target firm.

REFERENCES

Carow, K., Heron, R. and Saxton, T. (2004). Do Early Birds Get the Return? An Empirical Investigation of Early-Mover Advantages in Acquisitions, *Strategic Management Journal*, Vol. 25, pp. 563–585.

Conn, R.L., Cosh, A., Guest, P.M. and Hughes, A. (2005). The Impact on UK Acquirers of Domestic, Cross-Border, Public and Private Acquisitions, *Journal of Business Finance and Accounting*, Vol. 32(5/6), pp. 815–870.

Datta, D.K. and Puia, G. (1995). Cross-Border Acquisitions: An Examination of the Influence of Relatedness and Cultural Fit on Shareholder Value Creation in US Acquiring Firms, *Management International Review*, Vol. 35(4), pp. 337–359.

Grinblatt, M. and Titman, S. (2002). *Financial Markets and Corporate Strategy*, 2nd Edition, Boston, MA: McGraw-Hill Irwin.

Haspeslagh, P.C. and Jemison, D.B. (1991). *Managing Acquisitions: Creating Value through Corporate Renewal*, New York: The Free Press.

Healy, P., Palepu, K. and Ruback, R. (1997). Which Takeovers Are Profitable? Strategic or Financial? *Sloan Management Review*, Vol. 38(4), pp. 45–57.

Jensen, M.C. (1986). Agency Costs of Free Cash-flow, Corporate Finance and Takeovers, *American Economic Review*, Vol. 76, pp. 323–329.

Myers, S.C. and Majluf, N.S. (1984). Corporate Financing and Investment Decisions When Firms Have Information That Investors Do Not Have, *Journal of Financial Economics*, Vol. 13(2), pp. 187–221.

Index

For Product Safety Concerns and Information please contact our EU
representative GPSR@taylorandfrancis.com Taylor & Francis Verlag GmbH,
Kaufingerstraße 24, 80331 München, Germany

Printed and bound by CPI Group (UK) Ltd, Croydon, CR0 4YY
08/05/2025
01864370-0013